Women, Unions and the Labour Market

New Perspectives

*To
my dearest Student
of all time
— Maria Peluso
In friendship
Joya
Nov 16 . 92*

Women, Unions and the Labour Market

New Perspectives

JOYA SEN

Mosaic Books

Copley Publishing Group

Copublished by Mosaic Books, India and
Copley Publishing Group, USA.

Mosaic Books
29 Sunder Nagar Market
New Delhi 110 003, India

Copley Publishing Group
138 Great Road, Acton
Massachusetts 01720, USA

ISBN 81-85399-23-9 (Mosaic Books)
ISBN 0-87411-562-0 (Copley Publishing Group)

PRINTED IN INDIA

Published jointly by Mosaic Books and Copley Publishing
Group. Typeset at Bookshelf, 29 Sunder Nagar Market, New
Delhi 110 003 and printed at Rajkamal Electric Press, G.T.
Karnal Road Industrial Area, New Delhi.

To
My highest teacher
SWAMI SHYAM
who guided me to
the realization that

All Life Is One

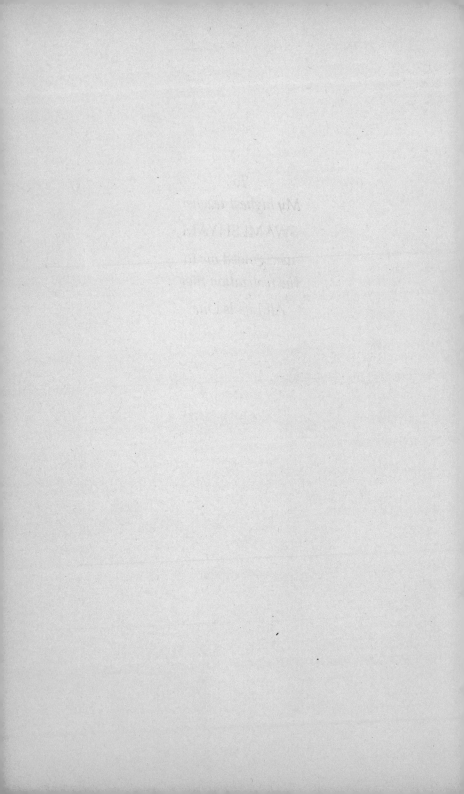

Contents

Foreword

There has been in Canada, as elsewhere, a tendency to forget, overlook and set aside, any understanding or recognition of the part played by women in the founding and shaping of this country. This approach to the writing of Canadian history in almost every dimension, was made possible by the insistence that the terms man and mankind subsume woman and womankind, and that the telling of the stories of Canadian men would automatically describe the lives of Canadian women.

This interpretation of history has been rethought in the past quarter century, primarily as a result of the entry of significant numbers of women into many scholarly disciplines, intellectual pursuits and professional occupations. The re-examination of the details of our history, both recent and more distant has revealed the broad involvement of women in every sphere of our collective Canadian lives.

Dr Joya Sen has been an active participant in this rediscovery. And in this book, *Women, Unions and the Labour Market—New Perspectives*, she has brought together her professional interests in women in the industrial workplaces, her understanding of organizational structure and function and her appreciation that feminist epistemology and methodology can illuminate the corners of our minds. She has produced a work which will interest scholar and layperson alike.

As an Introduction, Chapter 1 sets out the context of the investigation to follow concerning the entry of women into the workplaces of Britain, the USA and Canada, and their unionization during the past century. Sen's analyses of the relevant scholarly literature reveals a dearth of pertinent study. This is particularly so in the case of the multi-discipline of industrial relations. With data garnered from Reports from Statistics Canada, Sen sketches the numerical and temporal dimensions of the matter to demonstrate that the entry of Canadian women into the workforce in significant numbers is a relatively recent phenomenon, and that three-quarters of these women are located in "the service, finance, trade and public administration industries."

Unionization of Canadian women has not kept pace with their labour market participation. And it is this discrepancy which is the subject of her queries, as she seeks to place their unionization "in the total societal context of Canadian society."

Sen takes us through the relevant literature which focuses on data collection with respect to market force participation, market localization, wages and women's participation in the labour movement as it emerged in Canada over the last century. She examines the several theories put forward to explain the limited unionization of women, and finds these to be wanting. Her own quest leads her to examine the structural and ideological barriers to the organization of women in their several workplaces; the structural elements of the Canadian socioeconomic system which delimit opportunities for labouring women and the evolving patterns of socialization of women and men which continue to focus on women's reproductive role in society, the educational system put in place to ensure the propagation of this socially constructed imperative, the legislative systems created to enforce this imperative and the resulting financial dependence of women on men and their coupled oppression/suppression in the workplace.

Chapter 2, Women in the Canadian Economy, traces the movement of Canadian women into the labour force from the 19th century beginnings of Canadian capitalism to its modern post World War II phase. Its paints a very new economic picture, in which a majority of women (and a majority of these married) are now active participants in the labour market. The entry of women into the workforce now exceeds that of men, by a factor of 10. The available data from Statistics Canada are analysed for parameters which are significant for women's lives, including four age groupings, marital status, educational status, parental status and labour market location and participation rate.

Chapter 2 proceeds with a brief historical analysis of Canadian unions and the involvement of women as members and organizers. Sen proposes that the hierarchical structure and primary internationalization of Canadian unions continue to place barriers in the path of women as workers and with respect to their organization into unions. Nonetheless, the unionization of women almost doubled during 1962–88, with the major activity concentrated in Ontario and Québec, the most populous industrialized provinces. The most successful unions are those in the service sector, especially in government, where the largest and most concentrated groups of women are employed. The problems of the ghettoization of women in the labour force and their exclusion from male enclaves is explored.

Chapter 3 begins a theoretical analysis of the role of Patriarchy and Sex-role Ideology on working women in Canada, and their organization into unions. It weaves in feminist analyses with the earliest wave of feminism beginning in the 19th century. This is an important chapter which brings to bear relevant knowledge from the disciplines of philosophy, biology, anthropology, sociology, economics and political science on the establishment of "patriarchy as a sexual system of power in which men possess superior power and privileges ... (in) the male hierarchical ordering of society. Patriarchal culture ... is a universal mechanism auto-structured and auto-regulated, rooted in biology and independent of history and economy, preserved through marriage and the family. In this system, sex as personal also becomes political, and women are the victims of oppression because of the sexual politics of men." Sen traces the history of patriarchy from its beginnings, and emphasizes the communal sexual division of labour in our earliest societies, the subsequent overthrow of women's mother-right, and the evolution of class suppression of women by men, down to our own times.

Chapter 4 presents a historical analysis of Barriers to Women's Participation in the Labour Market and their Unionization. It traces the evolution of capitalism in Great

Britain, the USA and Canada from the late 17th century, and the associated mobilization of labour from the early artisan guilds which, until very recently, formed the basic patriarchal and hierarchical unit in the organization of industrial workers. Women have been excluded from the mutating powerful male-dominated industrial guilds which have emerged with the transformations of capitalism. As a result they were, and continue to be segregated into labour markets identified as economically marginal, and as a pool of cheap, unskilled labour. The exclusion of women from the industrial workplace has been aggravated by the rise of the male professions, especially those based on rapidly-emerging science and technology, especially since World War II.

Chapter 5 examines the problems posed by Monopoly Capital in the Post World War II era. It explores the changing philosophical, theoretical, economic and pragmatic facets of capitalism in Canada and elsewhere, and its reorganization of pools of working men and women as a reserve army of labour, so created by their replacement by the increasing use of technology. Women find themselves increasingly a part of this labour reserve, and within the secondary labour market with limited mobility, relatively low pay and most frequently, in segregated and ghettoized segments of the economy. As such women are subject to wage discrimination, job discrimination, employee discrimination, and employer discrimination.

The Canadian data show that since World War II, women are increasingly employed largely in the clerical sector, the service sector, as low-ranking professionals (eg. nurses, physio-therapists) and in commerce. The service sector, primarily in government domains, has become the prime industrial ghetto for women. "The discrimination against working women is clearly evident by their segregation into low-paying occupations, and within each occupation, women earn less than men ... At each level of education, the female percentage of the labour force has increased and the male percentage decreased". The outcome is that "in order to participate in a labour market, a woman must have a given educational qualification required by an employer regardless of whether or not the job itself requires it."

Sen analyses the impact of educational trends for women, their marital and familial status on their participation in the labour force, and in the union movement through membership and leadership. Women continue to face barriers to their full, equal and equitable participation due to the long and tenacious traditions of patriarchy, sex stereotyping and sex segregation in all workplaces and labour markets.

In Chapter 6 Dr Sen proceeds to Testing the Hypothesis, in which she carries out A Statistical Analysis of Labour Market and Institutional Barriers. The six hypotheses, initially set out in Chapter 1, represent six postulates concerning the above-mentioned barriers still confronting women in all workplaces in Canada and elsewhere. The study builds upon the comprehensive "ideological, historical and theoretical" analyses contained in preceding chapters, and which point to the significant impact "of structural factors as the major barriers to womens' unionization."

As one approach to such an analysis, Sen chose to gather "first-hand information from workers, union members and union executives on their perception of the barriers to the unionization of women." The study set out here was directed to union executives as presented in the most recent *Directory of Labour Organizations, Canada*. This includes listings of executive membership of Canadian unions affiliated with one of the national or international labour congress bodies, and "of those not affiliated but subject to collective bargaining legislation."

The main implement of the study was a questionnaire, answered and returned by 453 participants, female and male. Of the six hypotheses tested two were disproved, two were confirmed and two were partially confirmed by the study. Perhaps the most important outcome is the finding that "all the hypotheses find consistently more support from women executives than from men executives." This means that in all hypothesized variables ... women union executives show deeper and greater perception of the barriers to unionization of women workers, than men executives do."

Dr Joya Sen has done a great service to all students of the development of industrial capitalism in Canada and elsewhere, with an interweaving anthropological, social, cultural, economic and industrial management theory and practice. The specific focus on women, labour and unionization examined within a feminist perspective is particularly welcome. Together with analyses of primary and secondary data, this comprehensive study of women in the Canadian workplace is particularly timely. A summing-up is found in Chapter 7.

One can only look forward to the further studies and analyses by Dr Sen as Canada, and our "global village" enter a new phase of transformation of the economy and industrial capitalism. The current de-industrialization of the Canadian workplace, the trends toward future re-industrialization in a highly technology-oriented mode will continue to impact upon, and be shaped by working women everywhere. It is crucial that these events are well and truly recorded.

Vice-Rector, Academic   DR ROSE SHEININ
Concordia University
Montréal, Québec
Canada

May 18, 1992

Preface

Women's work and wages—the explosive areas of the economics of discrimination and inequality—is now a major social concern. Despite this, till a few years ago, discussion on the subject was largely confined to non-academic publications and polemical writings thrown up by the feminist movement. Today, the significance of the issue is recognized across many conventional boundaries of academic disciplines and the urgent need for serious studies and research in the area is keenly felt, not only as a matter of theoretical interest but also as a guide to action aimed at changing the current deplorable overall picture of women's place in the labour market.

This book, an outcome of four years of extensive theoretical and empirical research, therefore attempts to look exhaustively at women's work from the historical, empirical, economic, sociological, anthropological and contemporary global (geopolitical) perspective.

On the basis of the extensive and multidisciplinary historical and empirical data presented, I have sought to account for the persisting barriers faced by women in obtaining employment outside the pale of ghettoized "women's jobs", in getting equal pay for equal work, and in entering and gaining status/leadership in labour unions.

In my penultimate chapter I put forward the constructs of a new theory which I call the "Barriers Theory of Unionization of Women", on the basis of the testing of six hypotheses through a survey of the experience of a sample of some 1400 union executives (male and female) of Canadian trade unions.

I close this volume with some suggestions concerning areas in which further research could yield significant and useful results.

ACKNOWLEDGEMENTS

My first debt is to the late Professor Syed Hameed who inspired and guided me throughout my academic career, urging me on when things got difficult. I cannot adequately express my gratitude to Professor Wahidul Haque for guiding me through the intricacies of research with rigour and persistence; to late Professor Madan Handa who always supported and deeply appreciated my intellectual and active pursuits. My dear friend, Dr Zohra Husaini, I must thank for her constant support and help through many years of friendship, personal and intellectual. To my long time friend and academic guide Professor George W. Bancroft for being there always, encouraging and supporting me, my deep appreciation. My thanks to Dr. Praful Sanghvi for connecting me to one of the finest editors—Samuel Israel. I would also like to express my deep appreciation to Samuel Israel for his editorial advice and other assistance, rendered always with great warmth and understanding.

Without the generous support of my department at Concordia University, Montreal, and especially of Professor Rose Sheinin, who granted me a two-year sabbatical, this work would never have been completed. For this and for Professor Sheinin's kind foreword, I am most grateful.

I would like to thank my colleagues, especially Professors Mohammad Jamal, V.V. Baba and Bakr Ibrahim for their assistance. I must also acknowledge the friendship and personal guidance of Professor J.P. Das and Gita Das.

Themistocles Politof, through his affectionate and neverfailing support, has contributed more than I can express to my fulfilment, both professional and personal. I cannot thank him enough.

Department of Management   JOYA SEN
Faculty of Commerce and Administration
Concordia University
Montreal, Canada

Chapter 1
Introduction

THE FACTORS affecting unionization of women or lack of it have not been systematically treated in the literature on industrial relations. Lack of union tradition, employer opposition and fragmentation of the work-force have often been cited, but a deeper analysis should include labour market and institutional barriers which, in addition to the factors just mentioned, should cover also education, legislation, family socialization and union discrimination.

There are certain characteristics of women workers in the labour market which are distinct from their institutional attributes. For theoretical and analytical purposes, it is essential to examine them separately, although at times they appear to be interdependent. For instance, education is both a labour market and institutional phenomenon which affects women's entry and long-term attachment to the labour force; on the other hand, it determines the pattern of family socialization as well as the propensity to join unions. The thrust of this study is to place unionization in the total societal context rather than treat it as a marginal or peripheral event in the overall plurality of the Canadian society.

According to the 1981 census there are more women than men in Canada (12,274,890 women compared to 12,068,258 men). However, their entry into the labour force as a large and relatively permanent work-force is of recent origin (approximately 25 years). Apparently, because of the level of their education and skill in relation to job market requirements, they are concentrated in the service, finance, trade and public administration industries where they constitute 78.4 percent of total female employment. But there are more fundamental structural factors responsible for this concentration which must be identified through a historical-theoretical analysis as part of an investigation of the problem of women's unionization.

In recent years, women's membership in unions has increased enormously, from 16 percent in 1962 to 30 percent by 1976. Nine hundred thousand women belong to unions. The increase in numbers has been accompanied by increased visibility and militancy. Women unionists have been at the forefront of struggles for the right to organize, the right to strike, for equal pay, for maternity and parental leave, and around issues relating to technological change. They have also pushed unionists to make political alliances with women's movements on issues from which unions have traditionally shied away.

While the union movement is central as an arena for women's struggle for equality, feminist research in this area remains "underdeveloped"; especially, the history of women in the Canadian trade union movement is woefully incomplete, while little material is available on their contemporary situation. Since Jean Scott published her pioneering study (1892)[*] of Toronto women workers in 1891, there have been very few academic studies of women in the Canadian trade union movement. In the last few years, Sangster (1981) points out, studies on working women focused on two major areas. The first consisted of statistical studies of their numbers, wages, places of work, etc.; the second discussed how and where the female labour market is concentrated within the capitalist economy, and why (Connelly, 1978; Armstrong and Armstrong, 1978).

According to MacLeod (1974:325), women's participation in the labour movement was hindered by their double oppression and their "perceived and actual status as second class workers", encouraged by female socialization. Some essays also emphasize the oppressive effects of patriarchal ideology. According to Roberts (1976:53), many writers blame "feminine psychology" for women's failure to organize, ignoring their resistance as working class women. Roberts' *Honest Womanhood* re-examines women's involvement in the labour movement in Toronto from 1880 to 1914, utilizing again the Marxist

---

[*] References in parentheses are expanded in the Bibliography at the end of this book.

framework which stresses structural barriers to women's organization. He points out that their participation in unskilled jobs, their interrupted work history, and geographical separation from fellow workers are responsible for their failure to organize. This work served as a pathbreaker, especially in stressing women's active role in the history of the labour movement in the so-called Progressive Era (1890–1920).

Rosenthal (1979:37), like Roberts, lays emphasis on the role of women in the labour movement, attacking the myth of their unorganizability, giving examples of women organizing within and outside trade unions. She notes enormous difficulties like economic marginality and male unionist prejudice as well as feminist psychology of women's role of domesticity and maternity which became a barrier to large-scale organizing efforts. The prevalent ideology shaped women's expectations that they would marry and escape the paid work-force, an expectation "reinforced by celebration of love and marriage for women in the mass media" (:54). Strong Boag (1974:158) pointed out that while the culture of femininity may not have been "crippling" to the organization of working class women, it was distinctly different from the dominant culture of masculinity and one needs to understand the dynamics of its interaction with dominant masculine ideology.

Academic debate in Canada, as shown by Sangster (1981:3), was focused on the Progressive Era (1890–1920), and not much material is available on periods before and after. There is very little information available for the Depression years. Studies by MacLeod (1974) and Dumas (1975) bring out the role of working women in protesting against wage cuts and underemployment in the 1930's and also the limit of their protest because of the overwhelming economic crisis and indifference of male trade unionists to women's long-term economic needs. These also refer to women's efforts to maintain their families through part-time work and to organize resistance to unemployment. In addition to their participation in the trade unions, women have often organized as essential support groups in labour struggles, as auxiliaries to unions and labour councils, etc. The role of women as participants in the organization of industrial unions in Canada is also important.

Sangster (1981:4) points out that in the 1930's and 1940's, the organization of working women was supported by the socialist and communist groups, as is noted by Abella (1973) and Penner (1976), who, however, do not bring out the specific role of leftist women. In fact, except for some biographical sketches of female leaders like Annie Buller and Madeleine Parent, there is no research material on women leaders in the Canadian labour movement.

The number of women trade unionists has doubled in recent years, with growing numbers in service and clerical occupations, and contemporary trends and attitudes of women in Canadian trade unions are described in works by Julie White (1980) and Patricia Marchak (1973). White concludes that, although women's rapid growth to unionization is promising, they continue to be clustered in unskilled, low-paid occupations and under-represented in union leadership positions. Marchak's research findings show that female white collar workers are greatly interested in unionization though they perceive that they would receive less benefit from unions than male unionists. Their lower membership is mainly due to the prejudiced attitudes of male unionists rather than their own apathy. It is worth noting that a study for the Royal Commission on the Status of Women on male attitudes towards women workers came to a similar conclusion (1974).

Thus, though there is historical evidence of women's organizability and militancy, Canadian women workers have been unionized less than male workers. This contradiction needs to be explained. What are the structural and ideological barriers to women's organization, both within and outside trade unions? Often, questions are themselves so posed that the responsibility for "failure" to unionize is placed on women themselves. But we need to analyse the structural components of the socio-economic system which has designated a subordinate role for women within the labour movement as well as in the larger society. Hence, an analysis of the labour market and other institutional barriers to women's unionization becomes imperative. This means that women's wage labour should be analysed in relation to their family and their socialization process, their reproductive role in the society, and in relation to the systems of education and legislation, and how each of these has perpetuated the dependence and oppression of women, thus forming an interlocking system of barriers to women's organization. Also, it is often suggested (Sangster, 1981) that an understanding of Marxist and feminist theories, as well as those of academics and present-day activists, is essential for grasping the nature of the special exploitation of women workers within monopoly capitalism.

Barriers to Unionization

The labour market and socio-psychological factors which explain why, despite the increasing rate of unionization, women workers are less unionized than men fall under four broad categories:

(a) Nature of women's occupations
(b) Societal attitudes and sex role ideology
(c) Protective legislation
(d) Nature of the collective bargaining process

The literature on unionization of women documents the fact that the accelerated growth in their unionization is largely attributable to the organizational efforts of national unions and government employee organizations such as the Canadian Union of Public Employees, Public Service Alliance of Canada, Ontario Public Service Employees Union, Quebec Teachers' Corporation and the Alberta Union of Provincial Employees. International unions, on the other hand, have unionized women to a much lesser extent. This increased unionization is, as White (1980) notes, a response to the increased participation of women in the labour force, and is also partly a response to industrial changes. As is evident from Table 1.1, the percentage

Table 1.1: **MAJOR TRENDS IN LABOUR FORCE PARTICIPATION OF WOMEN, CANADA, 1901–76**

Year	Female Labour Force in Thousands	Women as percent of Labour Force	Married Women as percent of Labour Force	Clerical Workers as percent of Female Labour Force	Pers. Service Workers as percent of Female Labour Force
1901	238	13.3		5.3	42.0
1911	365	13.4		9.4	37.1
1921	489	15.5		18.7	25.8
1931	665	17.0	10.0	17.7	33.8
1941	834	18.5	12.7	18.3	34.2
1951	1,164	22.0	30.0	27.5	21.0
1961	1,764	27.3	49.8	28.6	22.1
1971	2,831	33.3	56.7	32.7	22.3
1976	3,859	37.4	59.6	35.8	16.7

SOURCE: Julie White, *Women in Unions,* The Canadian Advisory Council on the Status of Women, Ottawa, 1980, p. 38

distribution of women in the labour force has increased from 13.3 in 1901 to 37.4 in 1976. An analogous increase has taken place in the number of unionized women, though, as was pointed out earlier, it is not proportionate to the growth of their numbers in the labour force. The reasons for the difference are discussed below.

(a) *Nature of Women's Occupations*

Some researchers (O'Neill, 1969; Wertheimer and Nelson, 1975) argue that low unionization among women can be traced to the nature of their jobs and low work commitment. Prior to World War I, gainful employment was restricted only to single women or poor wives. Middle-class women were used only as a reserve labour force (Connelly, 1978) with a sporadic, part-time work history, varying with changes in their life-cycle or economic situation. None of these women were likely to show work commitment or concern for long-term improvement of working conditions. Hence they had no incentive to join and work for unions. But over the last two decades the situation is changing and many women no longer view their jobs as temporary; they are becoming career oriented and are now more likely to benefit from unionization. Nevertheless low unionization still persists among them, a fact often attributed to the segregated nature of women's occupations.

Labour Canada (1977) states that sectors with the highest proportion of female workers are (i) service, (ii) finance, (iii) insurance, and (iv) real estate (See Table 1.2). Here women are clustered in menial and clerical positions with low job control and low mobility potential. Industries with the highest proportion of white collar women workers generally have the *lowest* rate of unionization among women employees. Conversely, industries with a high degree of unionization are those which have small numbers of women workers, e.g., public administration, which has the lowest proportion of women (6 percent), has the highest rate of female unionization.

Historically, unions have organized blue collar production jobs in construction, transportation and manufacturing. These industries remain highly unionized today but only 20.8 percent of all women workers are employed in them compared with 48.5 percent of men. Unions have not been able to unionize the white collar segment of the labour force where 62 percent of the women employees work in white collar positions. The reason, Marchak (1973) points out, is that clerical workers are easily replaceable and therefore have a weak bargaining position. White collar workers often reject unionism because of its association with manual work, uniformity, destruction of the merit system and alienation from the employers (Mills, 1951; Strauss, 1954). So, despite many organizing drives, efforts on the part of blue collar industrial and craft unions to organize white collar workers have not succeeded. Consequently, the majority of white collar women workers do not belong to unions.

White (1980) notes that one problem in unionizing women workers relates to "job fragmentation", i.e., small groups of women workers scattered in establishments across a city or

Table 1.2: **FEMALE PARTICIPATION AND UNION MEMBERSHIP BY INDUSTRIAL DISTRIBUTION, CANADA, 1976**

Industry	Females as percent of all workers	Females as percent of female workers	Percent of females unionized
Community, business, personal service	59.0	43.4	30.1[b]
Finance, insurance, real estate	57.5	8.1	2.2
Trade	39.9	18.7	7.4
Public administration	32.0	6.2	63.3
Manufacturing	25.6	14.1	36.2
Transportation, communication and other utilities	19.3	4.6	45.6
Agriculture[a]	24.3	3.3	1.1

a.   The figures here vary from the pattern; of 24,000 women only 270 are unionized, representing 1.1 percent; similarly, the men too are poorly organized as of 82,000 male employees only 2,734 are organized, representing only 3.3 percent of all male employees. This suggests that other reasons exist to explain not only a very low degree of female unionization but also a low degree of unionization in industry as a whole.

b.   This statistic, on the surface, may appear high; however, of all unionized women 42.6 percent form a majority in their uion. These unions include the Quebec Teachers Corporation, Service Amalgamated Clothing & Textile Workers, Hospital Employees Union, Service Employees International Union, Alberta Association of Registered Nurses, Ontario Public Service Employees Union, Registered Nurses Association of B.C., etc. These unions, predominantly female, are all service-oriented and generally white collar. It is these unions that account for the comparatively high figure of 30 percent. Thus the writers feel that the argument holds true, that where there is a large percentage of female workers, unionization, particularly in male-dominated organizations, is low (*Corporations and Labour Unions Returns Act*, Part II, 1976, p. 49).

SOURCE: Baker and Robeson, "Trade Union Reaction to Women Workers" in the *Canadian Journal of Sociology*, Vol. 6, No. 1, 1981, p. 26.

province rather than concentrated in large centralized units. Examples are employment in bank branches, restaurants and stores. In manufacturing industry, for example, only 20 percent of women employees work in establishments with over 500 workers as compared with 35 percent of all employed men (Statistics Canada, 1976). Due to the limited resources, efforts at unionization are directed more at larger establishments where more workers can be unionized more quickly than at numerous small workplaces. For this reason also, women are less unionized than men.

(b) *Societal Attitudes and Sex-role Ideology*

White (1980) points out that, with respect to the role of women, Canadian unions have not shaped societal attitudes and mores but have mirrored traditional norms. Like other social institutions, unions have operated within the prevailing ideology emphasizing women's primary role within the family. The general belief that women should not work outside the home has been documented by many writers. The primary role of women is presumed to be that of consumers and homemakers, not legitimate workers. This domestic stereotype is further reinforced by the widespread assumption among men that, even if women join the labour force, they have different abilities or at least socialization different to that of men and, therefore, should be segregated into different, i.e., unskilled, jobs and lower pay scales. Many unions accepted this ideology. Townson (1975) cites examples of Canadian collective agreements which have recently been negotiated with separate pay scales for men and women.

McFarland (1979) studied 59 collective agreements in New Brunswick to determine their orientation to women's issues such as equal pay, maternity leave, non-sexist language in contracts, etc. She discovered that most collective agreements did not show any awareness of women's issues and five contracts actively discriminated against women.

Many writers point out that, in the early history of the trade union movement, women faced open discrimination and lack of support to their cause (O'Neill, 1969; Auchmuty, 1975). Without going into detail, this lack of support can be shown by pointing to the fact that female trade unionists were forced to form separate organizations to organize women and fight for women's union membership. In 1874, for example, the Women's Protective and Provident League was established to assist working women. Even now, trade union women, aligned with the feminists, continue to organize their own groups and provide political socialization to women workers. Organized Working Women (OWW) in Ontario perceives that the union movement has done little for women workers, and is attempting to lobby with the organized labour movement to take up the cause of working women. The Coalition of Women's Labor in America, formed in 1974, is committed to encouraging unions to organize working women and to strengthen their participation, especially at decision making levels. The very existence of these organizations is an indication that, often, women believe that they cannot further their cause within the established union movement if it is allowed to continue on the sexist basis. Hence a change has to be wrought in the very ideology of the unions.

(c) *Protective Legislation*

Earlier protective legislation for women was advocated by the unions. It was designed to ameliorate harsh working conditions and shorten long hours and night work for women, but it was based on sexist arguments, viz., that "women's constitutions were weaker and [their] morals in danger" (Baker and Robeson, 1981). The result of such legislation was that women were successfully excluded from higher-paid jobs. In some cases, protective legislation promoted discrimination, in most cases it was simply ineffective. Those women who worked in private homes and stores were not covered by it. Despite the continued opposition by women activists, most North American unions still advocate similar protective legislation (Cook, 1968).

Unions have been highly ambivalent in their attitudes and actions towards working women, torn between their ideology on the domesticity of women and their role of defending workers' interests against employers. While in specific instances the union movement was able to move beyond the limits of prevailing ideology and support women's rights as workers, on the whole this ambivalence has persisted.

Landsbury (1972) argues that unions supported protective legislation for women in order to retain higher-paying positions for men and exclude women from skilled jobs and higher wages. In Canada, for example, in the early twentieth century, craft unions blocked female entrance into these unions for similar reasons (Klein and Roberts, 1974). One particular reason for this exclusion was that women were perceived as a threat to men's jobs. There is ample evidence from historical literature that women were used as cheap labour by employers. MacLeod (1974) shows how employers in the garment industry in Toronto fired men during the Depression and hired women at one-half of the wages of men. The male workers reacted by attempting to exclude women from unions and from the labour force.

(d) *Nature of Collective Bargaining Process*

Since unions usually bargain for those issues which receive majority support, they have not responded enthusiastically to women workers' demands because many of their concerns do not receive active support from male union members. Geoffroy and Sainte-Marie (1971) found that while about three-fourths of Canadian male workers agreed that women's demands such as maternity leave with pay and retaining seniority position should be granted, less than one-third were willing to go on strike for them. Thus the collective bargaining process is disadvantageous for women because, as workers and as unionists, they form a small powerless group, a minority in the unions within a minority in the labour force, occupying a very small percentage of the executive positions of the unions.

Women have faced discrimination in every institution. But what distinguishes the trade union movement from other institutions is that it seems now to be beginning to respond to women's issues. Throughout its history, the union movement has stated its commitment to the welfare of working people in general and to its own membership in particular. As women in Canada now form 41 percent of the work-force and 30 percent of the union membership, the welfare of working women becomes an unavoidable component of workers' interests. Hence trade unions now have the potential to translate women's aspirations into action, help improve their working conditions and get involved with larger societal issues.

The literature on trade unions and women has not, so far, concerned itself with the impact of education on the labour force participation and unionization of women. To date, no research has been conducted on the relevance of education to the question under investigation, namely, women's aspirations for and achievement of leadership positions in union executive boards. This question acquires crucial importance now that (i) more women than men are joining the trade union movement—a fact which will very soon bring women's issues into the foreground—and (ii) trade unions are beginning to respond to women's issues. For example, as more married women join the labour force, more maternity clauses and child care facilities will be needed. As more middle-class women go in for "careers" instead of "jobs", the issue of equal work and equal pay becomes more important. Hence women need to increase their membership in the unions and also in the leadership roles so that their bargaining position becomes strong and "women's issues" gain priority in collective bargaining.

Theories of the Trade Union Movement

Forming collectivities of working people for the purpose of raising wages and improving working conditions was historically a new social experiment for which scholars attempted to find laws and explanations. There are several theories but only four significant ones are selected for comment here because they offer economic, psychological, social and political causalities as conceptually independent variables.

John R. Commons (1924) studied the shoemakers of America in a historical perspective and found that it was the economic phenomenon of market expansion which explained the formation of unions. As market A, which was originally self-sufficient and segregated, became linked with market B, exchange of goods began to take place. If market A produced shoes cheaper than market B and began to undersell them in that market, master-craftsmen in market B had to reduce production costs, including wages. Journeymen and craftsmen who originally had no conflict began to experience the menaces of the market in their relationship. Journeymen began to recognize their interests separately from master-craftsmen, producing a genesis of a collectivity of journeymen. At each stage of market expansion, there was added incentive for the collectivity to grow because the competitive menaces of the market grew correspondingly and the workers, in order to protect their job territory, organized themselves in larger groups. Waterways, highways, railways and other channels of transporting goods and services worked as incentives for forming local, regional, national and international unions. Commons' theory explains not only the genesis and growth of unions but also posits a social purpose for them. He agrees with Marx to the extent that scarcity is the basic problem in the society which leads to conflict. However, unlike Marx, Commons believes that conflict is reconcilable through unions making pragmatic and job-centred demands.

Although Commons built the Wisconsin school of thought on the economic parameters of unionism, his colleague Selig Perlman (1958) made a departure and postulated psychological explanatory variables for unionization of workers. According to Perlman, workers have a job-consciousness: they are afraid of losing jobs and are therefore continuously trying to protect them. In his view, management is cost-conscious and therefore constantly tries to reduce the unit wage cost, which comes into direct conflict with workers who want to protect and enhance job interests.

Behind his simple psychological explanation for the motive to join unions, Perlman had a grand scheme for explaining the ideological stand of the American worker. He identified three criteria for declaring that American workers were job-conscious and were not interested in overthrowing the government or taking over management. These criteria are: (i) trade union maturity, (ii) the resilience of capitalism, and (iii) the role of intellectuals.

If we compare Russia, the USA and Britain at the time of the Russian revolution, we find that trade union maturity and the resilience of capitalism were missing in Russia, but there was a significant influence of intellectuals on the trade unions. This, by the Perlman criteria, provided a perfect setting for a revolution. The USA was on the other end of the continuum with Britain somewhere in between. Thus, Perlman's theory of job consciousness has a societal component in which trade union maturity plays a dominant role in determining whether or not a society becomes revolutionary.

Frank Tannenbaum (1958) adopted a sociological approach to the phenomenon of unionization. According to him, workers in rural communities have no need for unionization as they live in a socially related nexus. As industrialization begins to take place, workers move from rural areas to factory dominated urban centres. In the changed social context, workers miss their social relatedness and begin to look for a new industrial identity. Workers are motivated to join unions in order to establish a new sense of social belonging.

Marx offers a political insight into the behaviour of industrial workers as he works through his labour theory of value—the theory of exploitation. Under capitalism, the worker performs surplus labour for which he is not paid. He is paid for the necessary labour in order to be able to reproduce his labour power. The unpaid labour produces surplus value which the capitalist appropriates for himself and other elements of the bourgeoisie. The worker is thus exploited through this part of his labour.

Like Perlman's theory, which had a societal component, the Marxian conceptualization makes labour an integral part of social change. Dialectical materialism advances society through the stages of thesis, antithesis and synthesis. In an existing order, such as a feudal society (thesis), there develops its own internal class struggle between tenants and landlord. This class struggle (antithesis) transforms the society into a capitalist order which is a new synthesis. As the new synthesis becomes an existing order (thesis), it develops its own internal class struggle (antithesis) between the working and capitalist classes. This is where the exploited, oppressed and unemployed army of workers rise in revolt against the existing state power in order to establish a dictatorship of the proletariat. The sole purpose of workers joining unions at this stage is to politically overthrow the government.

All the four theories examined in this section treat workers as though they were all male, whereas the labour market and the institutional characteristics of women workers are distinct and unique in many ways. Theories of unionization attempted to predict the behaviour pattern of workers on the assumption of a profile which was male, blue collar, and probably, in the US context, a recent immigrant from Europe who found the American economic opportunities overwhelming. But over the years, as the structure of the work-force has changed with an unprecedented increase in the participation of women, the latter have brought to it a changed skill pattern and a different outlook towards work and unionization. These traditional theories of unionization have ceased to be in tune with the new realities of the labour market.

John R. Commons' theory is no longer applicable to female banking clerks despite their desire to control their job territory. Commons never visualized the influx of the female into the labour force and, therefore, could not foresee that expansion of markets would not explain the phenomenon of women's unionization.

Selig Perlman's theory fails to explain why a significant portion of the work-force consisting of women is not unionized. How women perceive their jobs and what barriers they face in the way of unionization is not Perlman's concern. His concept of trade union maturity has an ideological connotation but nowhere is it mentioned that in the formulation of this ideology women have any part to play.

Frank Tannenbaum in his theory of social relatedness did not take into consideration the role of women in the labour force or even in the family context. Is the degree of need for social relatedness identical in men and women workers? Tannenbaum's theory lumped them together and assumed that they joined unions when they found themselves lacking a sense of social belonging in an alienated industrial, urban centre.

Marxian theory, with all its multi-dimensionality and comprehensiveness, made no distinction between the conditions that motivate men and women. Does the family socialization process condition women to the same degree of political commitment as men? If it does not, then the theory is remiss in expecting women to join unions for political purposes.

A basic question that invariably arises while making generalized statements is: To what extent does a theory suffer from impaired validity because the target group is assumed to be homogeneous? Obviously, the greater the non-homogeneity of the target group, the greater is the impaired validity of the theory. For this reason, all the four unisex theories examined above have limited validity. Industrial and occupational shifts in the structure of the economy have created job hierarchies in which women have come to be concentrated in semi-skilled or unskilled, low-paid jobs. Their incentive to join unions is not a volitional act any more; it is predicated by the labour-market barriers they face.

A Separate Theory of Female Unionization?

The massive female entry into the labour force during the past two and a half decades is a major event in the history of capitalism. Their problems are distinct from those of the bluecollar prototype workers who have different occupations, different drives and different outlooks towards the work environment. It is the contention of this study that women form a unique group in the labour force and therefore a separate and specific theory of unionization pertaining to them is warranted.

Treating unionization of women as a dependent variable, it is necessary to find relevant causal independent variables. These variables have to explain why in recent years the rate of female unionization has been faster than that of men and why women, despite this fast growth, are still less unionized than men.

This should not be misinterpreted as implying that a separate theory of female unionization is called for because of the biological differences between the sexes. It is the contention of this study that, given the right circumstances, women can be as pro-union and militant as men.

Historically, the evolution of the family as well as the marketplace brought in a division of labour which was not conducive to women's equal role in the society compared to that of men. What we see today is the legacy of a history in which women have a stereotype image which is further bolstered by labour-market and institutional barriers.

The process of unionization has never been easy, either for men or women. However, the barriers faced by women are distinct and much more inhibitive than they are for men. Historical developments and social attitudes have provided women with restricted opportunities which are manifest in every walk of life, including their desire to improve working conditions through unions.

Constructs of a Theory of Unionization of Women

In developing the constructs of a theory of unionization of women, the following three factors need to be considered carefully:

(1) Unionization and the technological structure of the society

(2) The changing role and status of women in the society

(3) Variables affecting unionization of women

Unionization and the Technological Structure of the Society

Rostow (1967) looked at the evolution of societies in a historical perspective by identifying five stages, namely, traditional, pre-take-off, take-off, drive-to-maturity, and mass-consumption societies. In these stages of technological development, unionization is not directly affected, but it is possible that changing market conditions or business cycles encourage social legislation conducive to unionization. On the other hand, if we view the evolution of societies in terms of feudal, capitalist and socialist stages, the role of unionism is markedly different in each stage.

In the feudal stage, where the factory system is not developed, there is no logic of collectivity. With the advent of the capitalist system, unions begin to acquire practical meaning to the workers. What is important to note is that the role of women in the production process changed from the early stages of capitalism to the present-day mode of monopoly capital. Their entry into the labour market in large numbers, their longer period of attachment with the labour force, and their concentration in certain low-paid occupations are the present-day phenomena which distinguish their situation from that of the men workers. Unionization at this stage of technological development has different meanings for men and women workers; their perceptions are coloured by their respective experiences and by their status in the society. The cost of technology and its ability to alter skill requirements in the labour market not only inhibit unionization in general but also squeeze women out of high technology jobs. This tends to create a dual labour market where women, concentrated in low-skill and low-paid occupations, fall outside the orbit of the union influence.

While technology in a capitalist society tends to inhibit unionization, it does not necessarily have the same impact in a socialist economy. Even social-democratic countries like Sweden are examples of countries where governments seek union cooperation in a centralized collective bargaining system. And since the socialist mode of production does not necessarily create dual labour markets, women are not generally syphoned off to low-paid occupations and thus unionization remains within their reach.

It may be emphasized here that the constructs of a theory of female unionization which are being explored here are limited to capitalist societies. The market and institutional processes, largely determined by technology, create special circumstances in a capitalist society which place barriers in the unionization prospects for women.

The Changing Role and Status of Women in the Society

While technology affects both unionization and the position of women in the labour market, education has its impact on societal norms and the status of women in domestic as well as market-oriented production. To some, perhaps small, extent, education is changing the family socialization process and men are no longer looked upon as symbols of authority, either at home or in the workplace. The strict division of labour which kept women home-bound has drastically weakened, freeing them for paid labour in the market.

Through various feminist movements and the increasing education received by women, there is a rising awareness of women's rights. Feminist movements have raised the level of consciousness in the society on issues such as equal pay for equal work. In the Canadian society, we find that women with higher levels of education or para-professional training are not only in better-paid jobs but are also unionized. The case of teachers and nurses is in point. In contrast, bank clerks, with lower education, are not only ill-paid but also vastly hand-icapped in their efforts to unionize. This issue has been totally neglected in the industrial relations literature, especially by those searching for causes of success and failure in the unionization of women.

The point has often been made in industrial relations litera-ture that a female secretary working close to the boss iden-tifies with management and, therefore, does not feel attracted to unions. This is no longer true as a general statement. With the increased influx of women into the labour force, there is a concentration of women in certain occupations which takes away the management identification women earlier had. One would argue that this growing impersonality will act as an incentive for unionization. There are also other changes in the labour market; for example, women now have a greater commitment to the labour force compared to that which inspired the "two-hump" theory of female labour force par-ticipation which prevailed until very recently. More and more, women are having fewer children, using day care facilities, and showing evidence of long-term continuous attachment with the labour force.

Within the family unit there are gradual changes in the division of labour between husband and wife. Women with growing economic independence are beginning to assert them-selves in domestic decisions. This allows for an imperceptible change in the female psyche which tends to spill over to the work environment outside the home.

It may not be out of order here to suggest that, while the role and status of women in the Canadian society have improved as a result of the macro impact of higher levels of schooling on the socialization process, women are still handicapped in not having acquired specific education and training required in the labour market. It is also necessary to stress that the value structure of a society changes according to the needs of the underlying economic structure; perception and attitudes may show superficial changes due to higher levels of education among women but they remain very deeply rooted in the economic base.

Variables Affecting Unionization of Women

In the industrial relations literature, there is no theory on the unionization of women. Motives and attitudes attributed to men have been considered equally applicable to women. It is the contention of this study that such is not the case: that women workers constitute a separate identifiable and unique group. Their characteristics and their environment are so vastly different from those of men that a separate theory explaining why they join or do not join unions is called for.

A generalized theoretical statement may here be put forward which will be empirically tested in this study:

> Unionization of women in a capitalist society is inversely related to the institutional and labour-market barriers that women face.

This relationship is not simply associational but also causal, which means that unionization of women is a dependent variable and the barriers are independent variables. The following diagram indicates this:

INDEPENDENT VARIABLES

```
Labour Market Barriers
(1) Sexual Division of Labour
(2) Segregated Labour Market
(3) Labour Market Discrimination
    (Last Hired, First Fired)
```
                                              DEPENDENT VARIABLE
```
                                              Unionization of
                                              Women
```
```
Institutional Barriers
(1) Family Socialization
(2) Lack of Pro-Union Legislation
(3) Union Discrimination
```

Taking institutional considerations first, women in Canada unionized rapidly in the past two decades primarily because of permissive legislation in the public sector. Theoretically, lack of pro-union legislation has been included as an independent variable. None of the earlier theories of unionization considered the impact of legislation. Furthermore, relatively lower unionization among women compared to that among men is on account of special barriers that women encounter. With regard to the predictive aspect of the theory, it indicates, for example, that, as women acquire higher levels of education and skill and the society also experiences wider awareness and a liberalizing change in the value structure, the barriers to unionization will decrease.

But beneath the surface of these institutional factors lie submerged the fundamental structural factories. Wasn't permissive legislation in the public sector inescapable, but a legal expression of the inevitability of the organization of workers coming together *en masse* in a public monopoly? Wasn't higher education another way of defining the labour force itself in the public sector markets—hospitals, schools and government offices? Was it education or the very nature—monopolistic—of these industries that was responsible for unionization? Our theory should serve to address these questions, as we propose to in subsequent chapters.

A logical deduction from the statements made above is that the removal of all the labour-market and institutional barriers will result in total unionization of women. That deduction is correct but, in practice, highly improbable as in a capitalist society there are certain fundamentals which are unalterable. Freedom in the marketplace and freedom in the institutional processes within a pragmatic framework of plurality make the barriers a subject for social action. As education, formal and informal, i.e., conscientization (Freire, 1970), makes women aware of the forces of change and pressure group action in the society, the barriers will tend to decrease. Growth of technology, dictated by the needs of capital, on the other hand, has the potential of increasing labour-market barriers by restructuring the work force, requiring specific training and skill and making management conscious of utilizing human resources more profitably.

"Barriers Theory"

In a historical perspective, Canadian organized labour is a minority within a nation which subscribes to the norms and logic of individualism. Property and management rights are fully entrenched in the socio-political fabric of the society. Unionization as a collective effort goes against the established norms of the production system as the former attempts to democratize management and restrict its prerogatives. In this context, it is not at all surprising that today 73 percent of Canadian working women are not unionized. They have faced innumerable labour-market and institutional barriers which this study purports to identify and analyse. To this end, we formulate a series of six hypotheses that emerge from a study of the literature and reflection towards a "barriers theory" of unionization.

If we observe the industrial and occupational breakdown of unionization, we find a high proportion of women in clerical and white collar employment which is grossly unorganized. Shister (1953) and Kornhauser (1961) found a correlation between high concentration of women in certain occupations and low unionization.

Classical economists viewed the labour market in terms of "non-competing groups" which existed because of skill and educational differentials. In the present-day context, women constitute a non-competing group by virtue of their hitherto unproven attachment to the labour market, their image of being transitory workers and, consequently, their indifference toward unions (Shister, 1953). This explanation by itself is not complete as a number of other factors are equally important in explaining lower unionization among women. Could low level of unionization itself be one of them?

HYPOTHESIS 1: *Union executives perceive that Education is a key factor in unionization of women.*

Sex Segregation

Very little research has been done to examine women and their special problems in the workplace; most literature in industrial relations and industrial sociology is "unisex" (Brown, 1976). Almost all theoretical and empirical work starts with the assumption that male workers in any industry or occupation constitute the norm. This has to be seriously questioned as the increasing number of women in the work-force are gravitating to occupations with low pay, low skill and uncertain tenure. Treating the male worker as a norm, many researchers and policy-makers tend to ignore the inequality between the sexes at the workplace. Consequently, unisex bias in the literature makes it difficult to explain why women find it difficult to join unions. The barriers that women face in joining them are often erroneously attributed to biological factors.

At this point it is important to distinguish between labour-market segmentation and sex segregation as two distinct labour-market barriers as they seemingly merge into one another. The former signifies that women constitute a distinct labour market of their own which has peculiar characteristics not conducive to unionization. In the case of women, the homogeneity of the labour market breaks down and, as far as comparisons in wages and working conditions are concerned, men and women operate in orbits which are not comparable. As a result, the factors which are conducive to unionization of men are not operative in the case of women. Sex segregation, on the other hand, has a reference to feminine attitudes which, looking at the Canadian scene, range from militancy in the public administration sector to passivity in the finance and trade sector. Undoubtedly, much of this attitude formation has to do with their bargaining power in the two sectors, besides other institutional factors which will be discussed later.

HYPOTHESIS 2: *Women workers being clustered in low-paid, semi-skilled or unskilled occupations have very little bargaining power, which contributes to their low unionization.*

Job Fragmentation

Another feature of the work situation of Canadian women working in a cross section of industries and occupations is that their jobs are usually in small establishments. The sense of solidarity and strength which automatically takes root in a large collectivity is often missing in places where women work like small bank branches, restaurants or in households as domestics. It is established in the industrial relations literature that most workers join unions as a result of peer group pressure; where workers are employed in small numbers, such pressure is non-existent (see Seidman, 1951). Women working in small establishments thus have very little sense of solidarity and therefore an idea of collectivity like unionization has very little chance of taking root.

HYPOTHESIS 3: *Job fragmentation in the case of women unionizing is a very strong deterrent second only to employer opposition.*

Institutional Barriers

It is the objective of this study to go beyond labour market barriers and examine in depth the institutional barriers which inhibit women from joining unions. In terms of their significance and relevance, four basic institutional barriers are identified, namely education, law, family socialization, and unionization itself.

Family Socialization

Despite great strides made by the feminist movement in breaking down the female stereotype, the Canadian society has not completely shaken off its patriarchal nature. Family socialization, social roles and ideology tend to make women submissive even in their interaction with management. When it comes to unionization, they often consider other alternatives such as quitting or postponing the issue. The act of signing a union card is likely to be viewed as an act of insubordination against management. However, one significant factor encouraging women to join unions is a family background in which one of the members has been a unionist. Family socialization thus plays an important role in formulating women's attitudes towards unions.

HYPOTHESIS 4: *Where there is a family member or friend who is a trade unionist, a woman in that household would be less reluctant to join a union.*

Law

The Public Service Staff Relations Act and other provincial government legislations have made it possible for a large number of government employees to join unions. A substantial proportion of these employees is women. Legislation has always been a significant factor in legitimizing unions and encouraging workers to join them. So far, there is no history of special legislation facilitating unionization of women, although, considering that the vast majority of women are still unorganized, there seems to be a legislative gap which warrants serious consideration.

HYPOTHESIS 5: *If special legislation is passed to encourage women to form their separate bargaining units, unionization of women will be greatly facilitated.*

Trade Union Discrimination

Historically, the labour movement came into existence primarily to protect and enhance the job interests of male craft workers. It tried to exclude women from the work-force for fear that their entry would undercut union wages. Consequently, male-dominated trade unions, in order to protect their own job territories, reduced work opportunities for women. At the same time, union leaders, in their organizing campaigns, have avoided female job ghettos where they would perforce have to face questions concerning inequality and discrimination vis-a-vis female employees. In recent years, there have been in Canada some efforts at the federation level to establish a White-Collar Organizing Committee which has, at best, met with limited success.

HYPOTHESIS 6: *The attitude of male union members towards women joining unions is either negative or indifferent; in bargaining for specific female issues, there is reluctance or opposition from male union members.*

The formulation of these hypotheses, based on our preliminary perception of the problem of unionization has to be followed by a conceptualization of the problem. It is at this second stage that we notice that unionization is rooted in labour-market participation. Participation is theoretically and temporally prior to unionization. An objective understanding of the labour-market barriers to women's unionization will therefore necessitate a theoretical and historical analysis of women's labour-market participation as capitalism unfolded since its inception in Canada in the late nineteenth century. In the same epistemological vein, the study of participation needs to be accompanied by a study of the sex-role ideology and the way it laid down the contours of child socialization and, more generally, of the place of family in the societal context. Since feminist writers lay the explanatory burden of women's oppression and exploitation on "patriarchy"—radicals fully and Marxists partly—we need to dissect this very phenomenon by tracing its origin in prehistory and pursuing its development throughout the career of capitalism.

The evolution of the barriers to women's unionization will be observed in this historical perspective; the six hypotheses will be weighed and judged throughout the course of development of monopoly capitalism. The insight gained from this historical-theoretical analysis will then be further tested against contemporary data. For this purpose, opinion and experience data from a sample of union executives have been collected. The hypotheses will be tested by statistical methods with the help of this sample. The historical and sample survey results will then be consolidated.

Chapter 2
Women in the Canadian Economy

WITH THE DEVELOPMENT of capitalism in Canada in the last quarter of the nineteenth century, women began to be drawn into the labour market. The pattern was that young girls would join the labour market and stay there until their marriage, on which they would return to the household to raise a family. This pattern continued until about the end of World War II. As Table 2A[1] shows, from 1931 onwards, the percentage of females in the Canadian labour force rose secularly. Having reached the peak of 31.4 percent in 1945, this percentage slumped to 23.2 percent and remained slightly above 22 percent until 1953. With the year 1953, there began another phase of secular growth in the percentage of females in the labour force reaching the ever highest figure of 41.1 percent in 1982.

Table 2B brings out the most significant structural change in the labour market, i.e., the rise of married women as the "new proletariat". From the 80.6 percent share of the female labour force in 1931, the unmarried women in 1981 constituted only 29.8 percent of the female labour force. On the contrary, married women increased their share from 10.2 percent in 1931 to 60.0 percent in 1981. This pattern of reversal of trend has to be probed in fundamental terms as we shall try to do in later chapters.

Meanwhile, we present some basic historical data on women's labour market participation and unionization in Canada. This quantitative picture gives a preliminary perception of the "women's question" as a background for ideological, historical and theoretical reflection on this question in Chapters 3–5.

At first sight, it may seem odd that sex and age-specific comparisons should be the point of departure of a study which proposes to analyse the specific problems related to participation and unionization that women face in the labour market. However, we are dealing with women in the labour market and the hypotheses stated in Chapter 1 imply that women face unequal treatment vis-a-vis male workers in this market and that male workers are to a great extent responsible for this discriminatory situation. Male–female comparative data should therefore be the starting point of our enquiry. Age-specific comparative data on participation and unemployment of male and female workers, especially concerning young adults, will also serve as a forerunner for our analysis in Chapter 5 of women as a reserve army of labour in the so-called Secondary Labour Market.

The data were collected and studied in annual time-series form. Unfortunately, the historical series are not uniform. Since they are of varying lengths it seems impossible to fill the gaps. However, in the interest of concise presentation, in some cases, data for only a selected series of significant years is here presented since it is felt that they provide enough insight into changes to support our analysis.

A. Composition of Canadian Labour Force

Table 2.1 gives Canadian labour force by sex and age for the period 1953–90. It shows that women's labour-market participation increased from 1,191,000 in 1953 to 10,542,000 in 1990—an increase of 785.1 percent over the 37 year period or an average annual growth rate of 21.2 percent. Distinct patterns emerged for the four age groups: youth (14–24 years), prime married life (25–44 years), the empty nest period (45–64 years), and adult (25 years and over).

Women in the age group 25–44 are more likely to be married with children at home. Their labour force participation increased from 487,000 in 1953 to 4,463,000 in 1990, an 816 percent increase in the 37 year period, implying an average annual growth rate of 22.0 percent.

The category of women in the age group 45–64 represents those who have finished their principal domestic duty of bearing and rearing children. They have an "empty nest" at home and hence are free to seek a job outside. Their participation increased from 214,000 in 1953 to 2,613,000 in 1990. This represents a growth of 1,121 percent in 37 years or an average annual growth rate of 30.3 percent.

Adult women, as a whole, increased their participation from 721,000 to 8,707,000—a total growth of 1108 percent or an average annual growth rate of 29.91 percent.

As to men's labour-market participation, the overall change is from 4,206,000 in 1953 to 10,030,000 in 1990 registering a total growth of 138.5 percent or an average annual growth rate of 3.7 percent. Males in all age groups achieved growth.

This dramatic entry of women, especially of married women, into the labour market is one of the watersheds in the history of capitalism throughout the Western world. Women constitute the "new proletariat" in the monopoly stage of capitalism. We shall pursue this theme in Chapter 5. Meanwhile, let us look at women's participation in more recent years, i.e., in the decade of the 1970's.

Reference to Table 2.2 will show that the number of labour force participants of both sexes increased from 8,395,000 in 1970 to 11,207,000 in 1979. Male participation registered a 22 percent increase from 5,571,000 in 1970 to 6,799,000 in 1979; female participation increased from 2,824,000 to 4,408,000 in the same period—an increase of 56 percent. Thus, male participation grew at an average annual rate of 2.2 percent while the corresponding figure for women was 5.6 percent. This fact roused considerable academic interest and research was undertaken on the socio-economic factors which led to increased work-force involvement of Canadian women.

Young women's participation increased from 940,000 in 1970 to 1,379,000 in 1979, a growth of 46.7 percent over the decade. In comparison, young men's participation grew from 1,190,000 in 1970 to 1,646,000 in 1979, a growth of 38.3 percent. A preliminary explanation for this growth rate differential is two-fold: (a) young men spend a longer time at school than young women and (b) women now marry later and thus stay longer at the labour market than they used to. Turning to adult women, their participation increased from 1,883,000 in 1970 to

Table 2.1: **LABOUR FORCE BY SEX AND AGE, CANADA, 1953–90 (selected years)**

	Total*	14–24 years	25 years and over	45 years and over	25–54 years	55 years and over	14–19 years	20–24 years	25–44 years	45–64 years	65 years and over
					BOTH SEXES (in thousands)						
1953	5,397	1,275	4,122	1,634	3,357	765	545	730	2,488	1,420	215
1954	5,493	1,278	4,215	1,667	3,446	769	551	727	2,549	1,454	213
1955	5,610	1,278	4,332	1,714	3,550	782	548	729	2,618	1,501	213
1960	6,411	1,404	5,007	2,055	4,104	903	627	777	2,951	1,826	230
1965	7,141	1,674	5,468	2,361	4,438	1,030	738	935	3,107	2,139	222
1970	8,374	2,147	6,227	2,668	5,074	1,153	861	1,286	3,558	2,462	206
1975	10,015	1,766	7,249	2,863	6,059	1,189	1,148	1,618	4,386	2,682	181
1980	18,139	4,574[a]	13,565	6,691	2,431	4,260	2,275[a]	2,299	6,874	4,524	2,107
1985	19,470	4,205[a]	15,265	7,281	2,508	4,774	1,905[a]	2,299	7,984	4,811	2,470
1990	20,572	3,732[a]	16,840	8,013	2,832	6,181	1,801[a]	1,931	8,826	5,164	2,849
					MEN (in thousands)						
1953	4,206	806	3,401	1,400	2,725	676	332	473	2,001	1,205	195
1954	4,263	802	3,461	1,416	2,789	672	330	472	2,045	1,224	191
1955	4,341	802	3,539	1,444	2,860	679	327	475	2,095	1,254	190
1960	4,754	857	3,897	1,620	3,162	735	359	498	2,277	1,428	192
1965	5,065	998	4,067	1,853	3,273	794	420	578	2,314	1,576	177
1970	5,684	1,253	4,431	1,910	3,572	860	492	760	2,521	1,748	163
1975	6,499	1,599	4,900	2,000	4,034	866	658	940	2,900	1,863	137
1980	8,891	2,316[a]	6,575	3,149	1,212	1,937	1,159[a]	1,157	3,426	2,206	943

1985	9,515	2,130[a]	7,385	3,422	2,359	1,063	974[a]	1,157	3,962	2,359	1,063
1990	10,030	1,897[a]	8,133	3,769	1,411	2,358	922[a]	975	4,363	2,551	1,218

WOMEN (in thousands)

1953	1,191	470	721	234	632	89	213	257	487	214	20
1954	1,231	477	754	251	657	97	221	255	503	230	21
1955	1,269	476	793	270	689	104	222	254	523	247	23
1960	1,657	547	1,110	435	942	168	268	279	674	398	37
1965	2,076	675	1,401	608	1,165	235	318	357	793	563	45
1970	2,690	894	1,796	758	1,502	294	369	526	1,038	715	43
1975	3,515	1,167	2,348	863	2,025	323	489	677	2,485	819	44
1980	9,248	2,258[a]	6,990	3,542	1,219	2,323	1,116[a]	1,142	3,448	2,318	1,224
1989	9,955	2,075[a]	7,881	3,859	1,256	2,503	932[a]	1,143	4,022	2,452	1,407
1990	10,542	1,835[a]	8,707	4,244	1,421	2,823	880[a]	955	4,463	2,613	1,631

* All the columns will not add up to the Total because of overlapping age categories.

[a] For the years 1980, 1985 and 1990, the age group is 15–24 years.

NOTE: For Definitions, information on sampling error, and other explanatory material, see notes at the end of the publication mentioned below.

SOURCE: Statistics Canada, *The Labour Force*, Catalogue 71-001, December issues, 1975, 1990.

3,029,000 in 1979, implying a decennial growth of 60.9 percent. Adult male participation rose from 4,381,000 to 5,153,000, a growth of a meagre 17.6 percent over the decade.

Thus, from Table 2.2 we see that the seventies saw an annual growth rate of 5.6 percent for female and 2.2 percent for male participation in the labour force. The corresponding growth rates for young women, young men, adult women and adult men were 4.7, 3.8, 6.1 and 1.8 percent respectively. The phenomenal growth rate of adult women's participation, as will be shown in Chapters 4 and 5, was due to the fact that, while prior to the 1930's women generally left the labour market on marriage, after World War II, married women continued to participate in it, and in ever-increasing numbers. This phenomenon, as also the high rate of growth in youth participation, both male and female, will be seen to have been caused by structural shifts in the Canadian economy in favour of the (labour-intensive) tertiary section (service, sales, commerce and finance), long considered the domain of women. The sluggish rate of growth of participation by adult males will be seen to be due to capital-intensive technological change in the monopoly sector where the production jobs—"men's jobs"—lie.

In terms of increasing participation, adult women are still the most dynamic with a growth rate as high as 6.1 percent, though this is significantly lower than the phenomenal 9.8 percent experienced earlier. However, this high growth rate does not tell the whole story. What percentage of the adult labour force accrues to adult women? Tables 2C and 2D show the percentage of females in the total labour force of each of several age groups for the period 1953–81 with the exception of 1978. Adult women's share of adult labour force (25 years and over) secularly increased from 17.5 percent in 1953 to 38.8 percent. The corresponding share of young women (14–24 years) increased from 36.9 percent in 1953 to 42.0 percent in 1975. The share of young women (15–24 years) increased from 45.0 percent in 1976 to 45.9 percent in 1981. This comparison shows that young women captured about 46 percent of the

Table 2.2: LABOUR FORCE CANADA, 15 YEARS AND OVER POPULATION BY AGE AND SEX 1970–79 ANNUAL AVERAGES FOR SELECTED YEARS

	1970	1972	1974	1976	1978	1979
BOTH SEXES (in thousands)						
15 and over	8395	8897	9639	10206	10882	11207
15–24	2130	2322	2618	2742	2916	3025
15–19	851	963	1113	1145	1200	1259
20–24	1279	1359	1485	1597	1715	1766
25 and over	6265	6576	7022	7464	7966	8182
MEN (in thousands)						
15 and over	5571	5707	6163	6369	6650	6799
15–24	1190	1290	1450	1498	1591	1646
15–19	460	521	613	614	651	678
20–24	730	769	837	884	941	968
25 and over	4381	4507	4713	4871	5059	5153
WOMEN (in thousands)						
15 and over	2824	3101	3477	3837	4232	4408
15–24	940	1032	1168	1244	1324	1379
15–19	391	442	520	531	550	581
20–24	549	590	648	712	775	798
25 and over	1883	2068	2308	2593	2908	3029

SOURCE: Compiled from Historical Labour Force Statistics, Actual Data, Seasonal Factors Seasonally Adjusted Data Cat. #71–201, Annual. Statistics Canada, pp. 24, 25, 26, 29, 30, 31, 34, 35, 36.

youth labour force in 1981 whereas adult women constituted about 39 percent of the adult labour force. Although adult women are behind young women by about 7 percentage points in their respective age-specific labour force share, the significantly higher participation growth rate (if maintained) of the former will more than offset this in a short while.

Table 2.3 reveals further aspects of the position of women in the labour market. Apart from their highest growth rate in participation, adult women dominate the female portion of the labour market. On the other hand, while the adult share of the male labour force fell, the young males' share increased. Given the adult women's higher participation growth rate and significantly higher base in the female labour force than those of young women, the former are the dominant group in the female work-force. In contrast, young men are assuming growing importance in the male portion of the labour market.

B. Labour-market Participation Rates

The labour-market participation rate of a given population group is defined as the percentage of the number of persons in that group that participate in the labour market. This is not to be confused with the participation growth rate of the last section (the percentage rate of change per annum in the number of persons in the given population group that participate in the labour market).

From Table 2.4 we see that the adult (25 years and over) participation rates show a rising pattern, increasing from 52.7 percent in 1953 to 59.8 percent in 1975, for all persons in this age category. This steady increase, however, covers a significant variation which is disclosed when these data are analysed by sex breakdown. From this table it is evident that the participation rates for adult males (25 years and over) had a declining trend; it decreased from 86.7 percent in 1953 to 83.0 percent in 1975, whereas these rates increased sharply and continuously for adult females from 18.5 percent in 1953 to 37.8 percent in 1975, i.e., slightly more than doubling over this

Table 2.3: PERCENTAGE DISTRIBUTION OF YOUTH AND ADULT LABOUR FORCE BY SEX, CANADA, 1970–79,* ANNUAL AVERAGE

	1971	1972	1973	1974	1975	1976	1977	1978	1979
BOTH SEXES									
15–24	25.4	26.9	26.8	27.2	27.1	26.7	26.9	26.8	16.9
25 and over	74.6	73.1	73.2	72.8	72.9	73.3	73.1	73.2	73.1
MEN									
15–24	21.4	21.8	22.9	23.5	23.6	23.5	23.8	23.9	24.2
25 and over	78.6	78.2	77.1	76.5	76.4	76.5	76.2	76.1	75.7
WOMEN									
15–24	33.3	33.5	33.4	33.5	33.1	32.4	31.9	31.9	31.3
15 and over	66.6	66.5	66.6	66.5	66.9	67.6	68.1	68.7	68.7

* For reference, see Source in Table 2.2.

Table 2.4: PARTICIPATION RATES (%) BY SEX AND AGE, CANADA, 1953–75 (SELECTED YEARS)

	Total	14–24 years	25 years and over	45 years and over	25–54 years	55 years and over	14–19 years	20–24 years	25–44 years	45–64 years	65 years and over
BOTH SEXES											
1953	53.1	54.5	52.7	44.6	59.7	34.8	42.4	69.3	59.8	55.6	19.4
1955	52.9	53.0	52.9	44.7	60.2	34.1	40.7	68.5	60.2	56.3	18.2
1960	54.2	50.3	55.4	47.4	63.1	35.6	37.7	68.9	62.7	60.2	17.7
1965	54.4	48.1	56.7	48.7	64.2	36.3	34.5	69.8	64.7	62.4	15.6
1970	55.8	49.9	58.1	48.6	67.9	35.6	34.6	71.0	68.0	62.9	13.1
1975	58.8	56.4	59.8	46.8	71.7	32.5	41.7	75.2	73.1	62.0	10.0
MEN											
1953	82.9	70.0	86.7	74.7	97.1	60.5	51.7	92.9	97.6	91.8	34.8
1955	82.1	67.4	86.3	73.9	97.0	58.7	48.6	92.2	97.6	91.7	32.3
1960	80.7	61.9	86.5	74.4	97.4	59.3	42.8	91.2	97.8	92.6	30.3
1965	77.9	57.2	85.5	73.4	97.1	57.2	38.7	87.6	97.6	91.8	16.3
1970	76.4	57.3	84.3	72.1	96.3	55.7	38.6	83.2	96.7	90.6	22.7
1975	77.7	63.7	83.0	68.8	95.9	51.0	46.6	85.5	96.8	87.9	17.4
WOMEN											
1953	23.4	39.6	18.5	13.1	22.4	8.2	33.2	47.2	23.1	17.2	3.6
1955	23.9	38.9	19.4	14.3	23.4	9.2	32.9	45.3	23.8	19.0	3.9
1960	17.9	39.0	24.5	20.2	28.9	13.2	32.6	47.9	28.3	26.7	5.6

1965	31.3	39.0	28.6	24.7	33.9	16.2	30.2	52.6	32.6	32.9	6.0
1970	35.5	42.3	32.9	26.7	39.9	17.3	30.4	58.5	39.6	36.0	5.0
1975	40.9	48.7	37.8	26.9	47.7	16.4	36.5	64.4	49.4	37.2	4.4

NOTE: Definitions, information on sampling error, and other explanatory material, are given at the end of the publication mentioned below.

SOURCE: Statistics Canada, *The Labour Force*, Catalogue 71–001, December 1975.

period. Hence, much of the increase, as already indicated, in the overall participation rates of adults during this period is accounted for by the increasing female participation in the labour force. For the youth category (14–24 years), the male percentage has fallen from 70.0 in 1953 to 63.7 in 1975 whereas the corresponding female figure has risen from 39.6 to 48.7. These two tendencies almost offset each other so that the figure for both sexes in this age category has risen slightly from 54.5 to 56.4. This happened through two phases: a secular decline of youth participation rates, dipping to 47.6 percent in 1964, followed by a secular rise, except for the year 1970 when it fell slightly below the trend to 49.9 percent. The participation rate of women aged 25–44 years increased from 23.1 to 49.4 percent and the rate for the age group 45–64 increased from 17.2 to 37.2 percent. This again shows the increasing involvement of married women in the labour market.

Table 2.5 extends the data of Table 2.4 through the period 1976–89 with the exception of (a) 1978, for which comparable data (annual averages) are not available, and (b) the figures for men. It shows that the adult female participation rate secularly rose from 40.9 percent in 1976 to 56.4 percent in 1989. The total adult rate figure also maintained a rising trend from 60.5 percent in 1976 to 66.1 percent in 1989. In the youth category, the female rate rose from 56.9 percent in 1976 to 64.1 percent. The total youth rate rose from 62.6 percent in 1976 to 65.8 percent in 1989.

Table 2.6 gives seasonally adjusted population figures for Canada for the period 1970–79. Table 2.7, obtained by dividing the figures in Table 2.2 by the corresponding figures in Table 2.6, gives seasonally adjusted participation data for 1970–79 and as such the figures for the overlapping years 1970–75 in Tables 2.4 and 2.5 differ somewhat. In any case, the data on participation rates presented in Table 2.7 reveal the pattern described below.

In the case of male labour force participants only, it is evident from Table 2.7 that little change has occurred in the participation rates of overall working age male population of 15 years

Table 2.5: FEMALE LABOUR FORCE PARTICIPATION RATE BY AGE FOR CANADA BY YEARS, 1976–89 (Selected years)

Age	1976		1979		1981		1986		1989	
	Total	Female	Total	Female	Total	Female	Total	Female	Total	Female
15–24 years	62.6	56.9	66.2	61.0	67.9	63.2	64.4	62.3	65.8	64.1
25 years and over	60.5	40.9	62.3	44.9	63.6	47.9	64.7	52.6	66.1	56.4
45 years and over	46.5	29.0	46.7	30.4	46.3	31.0	63.6[a]	48.0[a]	65.5[a]	52.6[a]
25–54 years	73.5	52.1	76.4	57.8	78.8	62.7	83.2[b]	73.1[b]	85.4[b]	77.7[b]
55 years and over	31.4	17.5	31.5	18.5	30.5	18.2	27.4	17.1	26.3	17.2
15–19 years	49.9	47.0	54.1	50.8	55.7	53.1	49.4	48.5	54.7	53.8
20–24 years	76.2	67.3	78.9	71.3	79.7	73.0	77.0	73.8	76.2	73.5
25–44 years	74.7	53.7	77.9	60.0	80.3	65.1	83.2	72.6	85.4	77.7
45–64 years	62.9	41.1	64.0	43.7	64.5	45.2	63.6	48.0	65.5	52.6
65 years and over	9.3	4.1	9.0	4.2	8.6	4.4	7.3	3.5	6.8	3.5
Total	61.1	45.0	63.3	48.9	64.7	51.6	64.6	54.5	66.0	57.8

[a] Relates to age group 45–64 years only.
[b] Relates to age group 25–44 years only.
SOURCE: Statistics Canada, *The Labour Force*, Cat. 71–00, December issues, 1976, 1977, 1979, 1980, 1981, 1986, 1989.

Table 2.6: POPULATION CANADA, YOUTH AND ADULTS BY AGE AND SEX, 1970–79, ANNUAL AVERAGE* (UNADJUSTED SERIES) IN THOUSANDS

	1970	1971	1972	1973	1974	1975	1976	1977	1978	1979
BOTH SEXES										
15–24	3806	3927	3996	4080	4190	4297	4394	4470	4530	4567
15–19	2018	2084	2134	2178	2220	2258	2299	2320	2333	2327
20–24	1788	1843	1862	1902	1970	2039	2095	2150	2197	2239
25 and over	10722	10946	11190	11446	11734	12026	12311	12586	12852	13124
MEN										
15–24	1905	1965	2004	2047	2103	2157	2266	2248	2283	2305
15–19	1022	1056	1082	1103	1125	1145	1168	1180	1187	1185
20–24	883	909	922	944	979	1012	1038	1068	1096	1120
25 and over	5257	5364	5475	5595	5731	5857	6003	6129	6249	6370
WOMEN										
15–24	1901	1962	1992	2033	1087	2141	2188	2222	2247	2262
15–19	996	1028	1052	1057	1095	1113	1131	1140	1146	1143
20–24	905	934	939	958	992	1028	1057	1082	1101	1119
25 and over	5465	5582	5715	5851	6003	6156	6308	6457	6603	6754

15 AND OVER

Both Sexes	14528	14872	15186	15526	15924	16323	16706	17057	17381	17691
Men	7162	7329	7479	7642	7834	8026	8209	8378	8531	8676
Women	7366	7543	7707	7884	8090	8297	8496	8679	8850	9016

*Compiled from *Historical Labour Force Statistics, Actual Data, Seasonal Factors Seasonally Adjusted Data*, Cat. #71–201, Annual, Statistics Canada, pp. 194, 197, 198, 200, 201, 202.

Table 2.7: PARTICIPATION RATES BY AGE AND SEX, CANADA, 1970–79 (SELECTED YEARS), ANNUAL AVERAGES

	1970	1972	1974	1976	1978	1979	*Increase* %
BOTH SEXES							
15 and over	57.9	58.1	59.7	61.1	62.6	63.3	5.4
15–24	56.0	58.1	62.5	62.4	64.4	66.2	10.2
15–19	42.2	45.1	51.0	49.8	51.5	54.1	11.9
20–24	71.6	73.0	75.4	76.2	78.1	78.9	7.3
25 and over	58.3	58.6	59.5	60.6	62.0	62.3	4.0
MEN							
15 and over	78.3	77.3	78.2	78.4	77.9	78.4	0.1
15–24	62.5	64.4	68.9	67.9	69.7	71.4	8.9
15–19	45.0	48.2	54.5	52.6	54.8	57.2	12.2
20–24	82.7	83.4	85.5	85.1	85.8	86.4	3.7
25 and over	83.3	82.3	82.2	91.1	81.0	80.9	-2.4
WOMEN							
15 and over	38.3	40.2	43.0	45.2	47.8	48.9	10.6
15–24	49.5	51.8	56.0	56.8	58.9	61.0	11.5
15–19	39.3	42.0	47.5	47.0	48.0	50.8	11.5
20–24	60.7	62.8	65.4	67.4	70.3	72.3	11.6
25 and over	34.5	36.2	38.5	41.1	44.0	44.9	10.4

SOURCE: Joya Sen, *Unemployment of Youth: the Importance of Education for Their Adjustment in the Canadian Labour Market,* Toronto: OISE, 1983, p. 52.

and over. Their participation rates have remained constant at about 78 percent. Hence the increase in the overall participation rates of the Both Sexes category has to be accounted for by other age and sex categories. Table 2.7 shows that these rates have increased steadily for young males (15–24 years) by 8.9 percent over the period 1970 to 1979, but have declined for the male adult working population (25 years and over) by 2.4 percent during this period. It is obvious then that much of the increase in total participation rates is attributable to an increasing participation of young males of 15 to 24 years and females of all age groups.

The story of female labour force participation rates in Canada is an astounding one of ever-increasing participation of all age categories of women during the past decade. As seen from Table 2.7, in the 15 years and over age bracket, female participation rate increased by 10.6 percent as compared with the 11.5 percent increase in the rate for females of 15 to 24 years, and the 10.4 percent increase in the rate for adult females of 25 years and over. A further breakdown of the female youth category into 15 to 19 years and 20 to 24 years shows rates of increase of 11.5 and 11.6 percent, respectively.

A comparison of male participation rates with those of the females reveals that, over the 1970's, the female participation rate for all working age females (15 years and over) has increased by 10.6 percent, whereas it has increased by only 0.1 percent for the males in the same age category. It declined by 2.4 percent for adult males (25 years and over) but increased by 10.4 percent for adult females.

In sum, except for adult males, all groups have substantially increased their labour-market participation rates in the seventies. Women and youth of both sexes have become significant members of the labour market though, as we shall see in Chapters 4 and 5, as marginal workers in secondary market segments with lower wage and inferior working conditions than those of adult men.

As to the participation rates themselves, there are significant differences between those for men and women. In the case of men, a comparison of three age categories, viz., the total working, age male population, male youths and adult males, shows that the highest participation rate was found for each year among the adults of 25 years and over. But dividing the youth category into 15 to 19 and 20 to 24 years age groups, it is the latter that shows the higher participation rate for each year and also a participation rate higher than that of the total working-age male population. In fact, beginning from 1971, the participation rate of male young adults exceeded that of adult males each year and, beginning from 1970, young adult male participation was on a secularly increasing path while that of adult males was more or less on a declining track, resulting in the difference between the two groups. In 1979, the participation rate of young adult males 20–24 years of age was 86.4 percent compared to 80.9 percent for adult males aged 25 years and over. The participation rate of the male teenagers, on the other hand, was the lowest amongst all age categories, in each year.

These statistics clearly establish that, even among the male workers, it is the young adults who showed the highest participation rate as compared with male adults on the one hand and male teenagers on the other. In the context of the present study, it can be argued that male youth in the 20–24 year age bracket are more likely to have received higher education, joined the labour market and found work than male youths in the lower age category of 15–19 years. Since a lower level of education does not constitute an encouragement factor for joining the labour force, and since the young in the lower age category are anxious to complete their education, it is not surprising that the lowest participation is found among this age category. What is both surprising and distressing, as will be shown in the next section, is that, despite their participation rate being the lowest, the teenagers experienced the highest unemployment rate for the entire period under study. From this it can be argued that both the high participation rates of the 20 to 24 years age bracket and lowest participation rates of the teenager are, in different ways, consequences of their education or lack of it.

The foregoing discussion has shown that the male participation rate ranks in ascending order as: teenagers (15–19), adults (25—), young adults (20–24).

The comparative participation rates of women of different age categories presented in Table 2.7 reveal a pattern similar to that of men. From 1970 to 1979, for each year, the young adult females of 20 to 24 years show the highest participation rate among all female age categories. But unlike adult males, the participation rates of adult females of 25 years and over are far lower than those of young females. In fact, the lowest participation rate is found each year in the 25 years and over age bracket. In 1970, whereas the participation rate of young adult females was 60.7 percent, that of the adult females was 34.5 percent; in 1979, it was 72.3 and 44.9 percent, respectively. This is a significant difference and is found to be consistent with the general phenomenon of the "twin phase pattern" of female labour force participation which sociological research has found to be prevalent among North American women. Many research studies assert that, in general, two high peaks are found in the work cycle of North American women, before 25 and after 45 years (Connelly, 1978; White, 1980). During the middle years of their life-cycle which are more likely to be devoted to the raising of children and care of the family, women's work-force participation rate declines sharply. The highest participation rate is found among young women of 20 to 25 who are still free from family responsibilities; the second highest among older women of 45 and over who face what is known as the "empty nest" stage of their life-cycle, when the children have grown up and left home. These women, despite many difficulties in re-entering the world of work at a mature age, rejoin the work-force and swell the numbers in that age bracket. The participation pattern of young Canadian females partly supports this sociological explanation of women's twin-phase participation pattern. This, however, should be viewed in the perspective of the previous section where we found that the percentage of young women in the female labour force was significantly lower than that of adult women and that the latter's rate of growth of participation was much higher.

Within the female youth category, the difference in the participation rate between young adult females (20–24) and female teenagers (15–19) is very high. The rates of young adult females range from 60 to 71 percent in 1970 and 1979 respectively, as compared with the rates of teenage females which are found at 39 and 50 percent for these two years, respectively. The difference between the participation rates of female teenagers and adult females is positive but much lower than the young-adult–teenager differential. In ascending order, the female participation rates rank as: adults, teenagers, young adults.

It would be relevant at this stage to consider the process of women's increasing work-force participation and identify the economic, social and cultural context in which it has taken place. The general picture, covering all categories of women, is this: In addition to the fact that there have been shifts in the occupational and industrial structure of Canada from heavy male-oriented occupations to more white collar and service-oriented occupations, in which women have found a foothold, there has been a definite change in the perception of the female role in society and in family. The perception and self-perception of women's role has changed as a result of changes in social and cultural norms concerning sexual equality, equality of educational opportunity, small families, etc. Women are no longer viewed in purely nurturant roles as they used to be; they have now also gained some respect in their instrumental, productive role which enhances their power in the family and society. Consequently, they can, to a large extent, effectively exercise the choice of joining or not joining the work-force. These issues will be elaborated on in later chapters.

As to the increasing participation of women of different age categories, we can say that the participation of adult women (25–44), who would presumably be married, has increased both because of their economic needs as well as the more flexible job opportunities now open to them, like part-time or temporary employment. The increase in the participation rate of women in the 20–24 year age bracket reflects their economic needs and their attitude towards making a career by utilizing their education, training and other skills.

From 1970 onwards, the participation rate of female teenagers, though lower than that of the 20–24 age bracket, rose significantly, indicating larger numbers of drop-outs from school. This increase in the labour force participation rate of this age category is a serious commentary on the "holding power" of schools and the female teenager's perception of the relevance of available education as preparation for the future. In fact, this conclusion holds for all teenage workers, both male and female. We can then conclude that the increasing participation rates of all teenage youth can, in part, be interpreted as reflecting the inability of educational institutions to attract and hold them in schools.

We have given above an intertemporal picture of women's participation in the labour market in comparison with that of men. We have seen that women's participation is increasing and have suggested economic needs and career opportunities accessible via education as plausible causes of this increasing participation. In economic terms, this suggestion, of course, involves the demand for a supply of women's labour power. We shall have to wait until Chapter 5 to consider these economic issues in some detail. Meanwhile, let us probe another question. Women have expressed their desire to work through intertemporally increasing both participation and participation rates. How successful have they been in this regard? As a quantification of this success, we now take up the question of female unemployment. Zero unemployment will mean 100 percent success, i.e., whoever participates is also employed. What is the nature of the departure from this ideal? We investigate this below.

C. Unemployment

We have seen above that the women's labour market participation rate has been secularly increasing for all age groups since 1933. For adult men, this rate has been on a declining trend since 1953; young men's participation rate was on a descending path from 1953 to 1969 but from 1969 it has been secularly rising. How do these rates translate into actual economic gains? We now consider this question in terms of unemployment of these sex-age categories in order to make a preliminary economic assessment.

In Table 2.8, we observe a lower unemployment rate of adult women compared to that of adult men for each year in the period 1953–69. The adult male unemployment rate was two to three times higher than that of adult female unemployment which was spectacularly low, varying between 1.1 and 2.5 percent, a range of 1.4. In contrast, the adult male unemployment rate varied between 2.8 and 7.2 percent. For the period 1953–74, Chart 1 ranks the age-sex groups in ascending order of unemployment as: adult female, adult male, young female and young male. This implies that the burden of unemployment fell least on the adult females and most on young males.

Are these tendencies consistent with our earlier participation profile? Both the participation rate and the participation growth rate of adult women have been rising. This may be considered to be a reflection of the low unemployment rate of adult women. Low unemployment may be viewed as being an "encouragement factor" to labour force participation. Observing a low unemployment rate, a worker may feel that her/his chance of being employed is good. So she/he stays on in the market. For adult men, a high unemployment rate may be seen as a disincentive to participation resulting in the observed low participation growth rate and declining participation rate. By the same argument, the participation and unemployment rate differentials between young males and females may be rationalized.

Table **2.8:** UNEMPLOYMENT RATES BY MAIN AGE AND SEX
CATEGORIES, CANADA, 1953–69

Year	All Ages	14–24	25 years & over		
	Total	Total	Total	Men	Women
1953	3.0	4.5	2.5	2.8	1.1
1954	4.6	6.9	2.8	4.3	1.7
1955	4.4	6.7	3.7	4.1	1.9
1956	3.4	5.2	2.9	3.2	1.4
1957	4.6	7.3	3.9	4.4	1.6
1958	7.0	11.0	5.9	6.7	2.5
1959	6.0	9.4	5.0	5.8	1.9
1960	7.0	11.0	5.8	6.8	2.3
1961	7.1	10.9	6.1	7.2	2.5
1962	5.9	9.4	4.9	5.8	2.2
1963	5.5	9.3	4.5	5.2	2.1
1964	4.7	7.9	3.7	4.3	2.0
1965	3.9	6.5	3.1	3.6	1.7
1966	3.6	6.0	2.8	3.3	1.8
1967	4.1	6.8	3.2	3.7	1.9
1968	4.8	8.2	3.7	4.3	2.1
1969	4.7	7.9	3.6	4.0	2.4

SOURCE: Compiled from table 32 of the *The Labour Force Monthly*, January
1975. Statistics Canada Cat. #71–001, p. 59.

This is of course a typical Marshallian kind of explanation
with "other things remaining the same". But other things do
not remain the same. So far as working women are concerned,
they have a "double day of labour"—domestic work in addition to paid work. A married woman may have some free time
left after deducting the time needed for domestic work. She
may want to spend this extra time in paid work. Howsoever
low the wages be, she may desperately want to have the extra
money. Indeed, she may not care about the pecuniary benefit
at all—she may just want to run away from domestic drudgery
and "meet people" in the workplace. With such a psyche, she
stays on in the market—participates, regardless of the rate of
unemployment. In such a case, both a high participation rate
and a high participation growth rate may coexist with a high

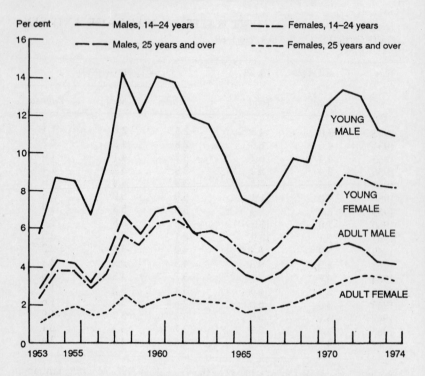

CHART 1: Unemployment Rate, Two Age Groups, by Sex, Canada, 1953–74

SOURCE: Based on data from Statistics Canada.

NOTE: From *People and Jobs: A Study of the Canadian Labour Market* (Ottawa: Economic Council of Canada, 1976), p. 75.

SOURCE: Joya Sen, *Unemployment of Youth*, op. cit., chart 6, p. 50.

unemployment rate. Women's participation, the supply of female labour power, will be considered further in Chapter 5.

The "paradox" of the last paragraph will be appreciated if we look at Table 2.9, an extension of the data in Table 2.8 over 1970–79, with two additional factors: a more elaborate age-breakdown and, more importantly, the data in Table 2.9 are seasonally adjusted whereas those in Table 2.8 are unadjusted. In any case, this table gives the sex-age unemployment rates for each year in the ascending order: adult male, adult female, young female and young male. Compared to the position seen in Table 2.8, in Table 2.9 adult male and adult female now trade places, with the rest of the ordering remaining intact. Unemployment rates are now much higher for both adult males and adult females than seen in Table 2.8; within the adult category, the female unemployment rate is much higher than the male one. Yet, in terms of participation growth rates, men lag far behind women. In spite of high and increasing unemployment rates, the undaunted adult women vigorously participate in the labour market. They need, and hope to get, the money!

Comparative figures for increase in unemployment of youth and adults for both sexes together, within the male category and within the female category, show different patterns. Whereas the adult unemployment rate increased by 1.8 percent that of the youth increased by 3 percent, which is more than one and a half times the adult unemployment rate.

In the two sub-categories of male youth, viz. the 15 to 19 and 20 to 24 year age brackets, we find a greater increase in the unemployment rate among young adults of 20–24 years whose unemployment rate increase is 2.3 percent as compared with the male teenagers' unemployment rate increase at 1.3 percent. Hence it seems that over the years 1970 to 1979, increasingly large numbers of young adult males, 20 to 24 years old, moved into the category of the unemployed, which did not happen to the same extent in the case of male teenagers. However, it needs to be stressed here that although the increase in the unemployment rates of young adults is high, teenage males

Table 2.9: UNEMPLOYMENT RATES BY AGE AND SEX, CANADA, 1970–79, ANNUAL AVERAGES

	1970	1971	1972	1973	1974	1975	1976	1977	1978	1979	Increase	Range
BOTH SEXES												
15 and over	5.7	6.2	6.2	5.5	5.3	6.9	7.1	8.1	8.4	7.5	1.8	3.2
15–24	10.0	11.1	10.9	9.6	9.3	12.0	12.7	14.4	14.5	13.0	3.0	4.8
15–19	13.9	15.1	14.0	12.0	11.6	11.6	14.9	17.5	17.9	16.1	3.8	6.3
20–24	7.5	8.4	8.7	7.8	7.6	9.9	10.5	12.2	12.2	10.8	3.3	4.7
25 and over	4.2	4.5	4.6	4.1	3.9	5.0	5.1	5.8	6.1	5.4	1.2	2.2
25–54	4.1	4.5	4.6	4.1	3.9	5.1	5.3	6.0	6.3	5.7	1.6	2.4
MEN												
15 and over	5.6	6.0	5.8	4.9	4.8	6.2	6.3	7.3	7.6	6.6	2.0	2.8
15–24	11.2	12.0	11.9	10.9	9.6	12.5	13.3	14.9	15.1	13.3	2.1	5.5
15–19	15.1	16.3	15.3	12.6	12.1	15.4	16.3	18.1	18.5	15.4	1.3	6.4
20–24	8.8	9.3	9.6	8.2	7.7	10.5	11.1	12.6	12.7	11.1	2.3	5.0
25 and over	4.1	4.3	4.1	3.4	3.3	4.3	4.2	4.9	5.2	4.5	0.3	1.9
25–54	3.9	4.2	4.0	3.3	3.2	4.3	4.3	5.0	5.3	4.6	0.7	2.1
WOMEN												
15 and over	5.8	6.6	7.0	6.7	6.4	8.1	8.4	9.4	9.6	8.8	3.0	3.8
15–24	8.6	9.8	9.6	9.2	8.9	11.4	12.1	13.8	13.9	12.7	4.1	5.3
15–19	12.1	13.6	12.4	11.7	10.9	14.4	15.1	16.7	17.2	15.8	3.7	5.5
20–24	5.8	7.1	7.4	7.3	7.4	9.1	9.8	11.7	11.5	10.4	4.6	5.9
25 and over	4.4	5.0	5.7	5.4	5.1	6.5	6.6	7.4	7.7	7.0	2.6	3.3
25–54	4.5	5.3	5.9	5.6	5.3	6.8	7.0	7.8	8.1	7.4	2.9	3.6

SOURCE: Joya Sen, Ibid., Table 14, p. 65.

show significantly higher rates than young adult males each
year.

An examination of female unemployment rates as
presented in Table 2.9 reveals that these rates increased for
all the categories of female labour force participants during
the past decade, but to varying degrees. The highest increase is found among the category of female youth of 15 to
24 years, for whom the rate increased by 4.1 percent as
compared with an overall increase of 3 percent in the unemployment rates of females aged 15 years and over, and
an increase of 2.6 percent in those of adult women of 25
years and over. Here again, we see the emergence of a
pattern of rising unemployment among young women
similar to the one earlier seen among young men.

Breakdown of the female youth category into teenagers and
young adults also reveals the same pattern of unemployment
increase as was found for the young males sub-categories
during the period under investigation. The unemployment
rate increase was 3.7 percent for teenage females and 4.6
percent for young adult females. But again we should note that
the female teenage unemployment rate, like the teenage male
unemployment rate, is higher every year than that of young
adult females, though the latter shows a higher increase over
the 10-year period. This fact of increasing unemployment
among the young adult females and males is a reflection on
the absorptive capacity of the Canadian economy and on the
adequacy of Canadian education institutions for equipping
young men and women with skills relevant to the needs of this
economy.

On the basis of the statistical evidence presented above, we
can state our findings thus: Over the seventies, as far as unemployment is concerned, women have been 2 to 9 times
worse off than men. Age-wise, the highest increase in the rate
of unemployment was among the youth category, 15 to 24
years (and in both of its sub-categories: teenagers and young
adults). The same conclusion holds even after the analysis of
the data by sex breakdown with one difference: the unemploy-

ment rate increase in the case of young adult females is not only the highest compared to all other female age categories, but is also the highest among all sex-age categories. Hence we conclude that it is young women of 20 to 24 years who have been facing increasing unemployment over the years, more than any other age bracket. We also conclude that the unemployment rate for adult women is more unstable than that for adult men, as seen from the range of unemployment given in Table 2.9.

To interpret the tendencies in unemployment rates given in Tables 2.8 and 2.9, we show in Table 2.10 the arithmetic mean $\bar{x}$, standard deviation, s, and coefficient of variation, C, for the adult male and female unemployment rates for the periods 1953–69 and 1970–79 separately.

We must interpret these figures in the perspective of post World War II developments in monopoly capitalism which will be presented in Chapter 5. Let us here simply point out that under monopoly capitalism adult male workers are concentrated in monopoly sector jobs—the production jobs; women and other marginal workers—youth, immigrants, etc.—are drawn into two adjuncts of the monopoly sector, namely, the public sector and the competitive sector. The competitive sector consists of some manufacturing but mostly service, retail trade and financial intermediaries. The monopoly sector tries to stabilize (a) product demand through planned market creation, and (b) employment via an internal (intra-firm) labour market.

Table 2.10: MEAN, STANDARD DEVIATION AND COEFFICIENT OF VARIATION FOR ADULT MALE AND FEMALE UNEMPLOYMENT RATES, 1953–69, 1970–79

	1953–69			1970–79		
	$\bar{x}$	s	C	$\bar{x}$	s	C
Adult Male	4.7	1.3	28	4.2	.54	13
Adult Female	1.9	1.4	74	6.1	.98	16

We can now look at Table 2.10 in the light of this theoretical perspective. Our comparison between the periods 1953–69 and 1970–79 will be somewhat inaccurate because data for the latter period are deseasonalized. First of all, post-war developments created an extraordinary expansion of the tertiary sector (service, trade, finance, etc.) and the public sector. Women's low average unemployment rate, 1.9 percent in the fifties and sixties, reflects this expansion which was fuelled by cheap female labour. The substantially higher figure, 6.1 percent, in the seventies reflects the crisis in the capitalist economy which began in the late sixties and continues until today. The higher average female unemployment rate of 6.1 percent reflects the slack in the demand for goods and services in the non-monopoly sectors. In the competitive women's ghettos, women easily pulled out of and pushed back into the "reserve army of labour". On the contrary, adult male unemployment rates for the two periods hardly differ from one another. This reflects the fact of comparative stability of the monopoly sector where most adult men worked.

Looking at the standard deviations and coefficients of variation, we see from Table 2.10 that they are lower for adult males than for adult females. This is yet another manifestation of the phenomenon of the stability of the monopoly sector and instability of the competitive sector. In fact, the figures for adult males show that the monopoly sector had stabilized even more in the seventies, the crisis period, than in the fifties and sixties, the heydays of the growth of monopoly capitalism. Not only did the average male unemployment rate fall somewhat in the seventies but also the standard deviation and coefficient of variation. There were less vagaries in adult male unemployment levels in the seventies as the low range of unemployment of 1.9 percent in Table 2.9 shows. In contrast, the adult female unemployment rate had a range of 3.3 percent.

A few words on lower unemployment rates of female youth than those of male youth are in order here. As mentioned earlier, in the age of monopoly capitalism, most women get channelled into low salaried, low prestige, sex-specific dead-end occupations in the tertiary sector—service, retail trade, banking and finance, for which not much training is required. Most young Canadian women can find a niche in such occupations (particularly if they have no family responsibilities and therefore are not too concerned about pay scales) with relatively greater ease than young men who may find that vacancies require more training or educational qualifications than they possess. If this be the case, then it is not surprising that young male unemployment rates are higher than young female unemployment rates.

Women's labour-market participation has thus been thwarted through various inequities. Male workers have organized unions for improving working conditions for all workers, in principle. Yet, as we shall see in Chapter 4, both employers and male workers have been responsible for various forms of discrimination against women. These discriminatory acts include the ambivalence of male unionists towards fighting for specific feminine issues through existing unions and their reluctance to organize women workers in general. While postponing discussion of these substantive issues until Chapter 4, we now present a brief outline of the structure of Canadian unions and the extent of women's presence in them.

D. Unions

A little over one-quarter of female workers in Canada are unionized. In contrast to the 43 percent of male workers that were unionized in 1976, only 27 percent of women workers belonged to unions. The situation has improved somewhat recently as will be seen in what follows.

Before presenting statistical data on unionization, it will be necessary to give a brief account of the structure of the trade union movement in Canada. This is because the history of the trade union movement itself reflects the barriers women faced in unionizing. Specifically, the areas in which these unions themselves were organized and their special features as well as structures posed barriers to the unionization of working women. Hence, a brief account of this history is necessary for an understanding of the present situation.

In Canada, there are three kinds of unions: international, national and government employees' associations. The first category is based in the United States; the latter two are indigenous Canadian institutions. At the grassroots level, a unionized worker belongs to a local union which is a part of a Canadian or an international union. The Canadian and international unions are affiliated to central labour bodies which bring unions together for concerted action on common issues.

Local Unions

The local union is the basic unit of labour organization in Canada. It is formed by a majority of workers belonging to a particular plant, office or locality in order to bargain with the employer on wages and working conditions in concert rather than in isolation. Generally speaking, a legal procedure is followed for a local to be "certified" by the provincial Labour Relations Board. This body and the ministry of labour in each province administer labour relations legislation. Certain workers are either excluded from unionization or are subject to different laws from other workers. Workers who are eligible to join a union constitute the so-called "bargaining unit". A certified (local) union can force the employer to "bargain in good faith" so as to arrive at a collective agreement. Usually the Labour Relations Board holds an official hearing when a bargaining unit applies for certification. Once a decision is made to join a union, those workers who wish to join sign cards and pay a small fee to become members. In most provinces, a certain percentage of workers must join the union before an application for certification may be made to the Labour Relations Board or the labour commissioner-general. A collective agreement (or contract) between the union and employer, once negotiated and signed, is legally binding on both sides.

A local may be formed as the result of an organizing drive by a larger union or by the concerned workers directly who then decide to affiliate to a particular union.

Canadian Unions

Canadian Unions are entirely based in Canada. In 1978, one and three-quarter million workers, 52.6 percent of all unionized workers in Canada, belonged to Canadian unions; the rest, one and one-half million, belonged to international unions.[2] The majority of members of Canadian unions work in the public sector—government employees, teachers, hospital workers, etc. Since many female workers are in this sector, it is not surprising that, according to Julie White[3], 65.5 percent of unionized women belong to Canadian unions.

Each Canadian union holds a membership convention annually or biennially. Locals submit resolutions to be discussed at these conventions and send their elected delegates to take part in the deliberations. Canadian union policy decisions are made and the elections of national officials of the union are held at these conventions.

The Canadian union headquarters receives a proportion of members' dues with which a number of activities and administrative expenses are financed. These include: research, legal advice, organizing-negotiating staff, publications, education programmes, strike fund, and national-regional office expenses. Some unions are provincial only, for example, the Alberta Union of Provincial Employees (AUPE). Some are national with provincial, and sometimes district, offices and organizations; for example, the Canadian Union of Provincial Employees (CUPE). Any local union may call upon larger unions for services to help deal with problems like certification, negotiation, grievance, strike pay, etc.

International Unions

International Unions are those unions which are based in the United States and have a predominantly American membership, Canadian membership accounting for less than 10 percent.[4] In the North American labour movement, the early unions, that is those founded in the 19th century, were craft unions organized by the American Federation of Labor (AFL). For well over a century the Canadian craft unions were largely affiliated to this body and by 1911 almost 90 percent of them had this affiliation.[5] These unions were of a "horizontal" character, organized as they were not by workplace but on the basis of the trade. Building trades and painting are prime examples of craft unions. In building, for instance, 20 different unions separately represent carpenters, electricians, sheet metal workers and so forth.

With industrialization, a new kind of union, industrial unions as opposed to trade (craft) unions, arose on the American scene, most of which were organized in the 1930's and 1940's. Industrial unions were organized "vertically" at the workplace, emphasizing numbers—skilled and unskilled, relying on numerical strength and not on skill. These were organized in such areas as steel, mining and refining, automobiles, retail and wholesale trade, rubber, clothing, meat packing and textiles. With industrialization and mechanization, skill took second place to the machine. Most of the workers had to be unskilled by the logic of the situation. Consequently, they could not join the craft unions. Industrial unions organized by the Congress of Industrial Organizations (CIO) were the answer. As most of Canadian industry is of the branch-plant type, with headquarters in the United States, logically again the Canadian locals of the industrial unions were organized by the CIO and were affiliated to it until its merger with the AFL in 1955.

As noted earlier, 90 percent of Canadian unionists belonged to the International Unions in 1911. The figure fell to 47.4 percent in 1978. This happened mainly due to the spectacular growth of Canadian unions in the public sector.

Central Labour Bodies

National and International Unions affiliate to central labour bodies for concerted action on common issues, strengthened by pooling their resources together. Table 2.11 shows membership of these bodies. It is to be noted that the Canadian Labour Congress (CLC) is the largest central body with 58.6 percent of union membership. A good 17.9 percent of national unions are

Table 2.11: UNION MEMBERSHIP BY AFFILIATION, CANADA, 1978, –80, –85, –90

Central Labour Body	1978		1980		1985		1990	
	Number	Percent	Number	Percent	Number	Percent	Number	Percent
CLC (Canadian Labour Congress)	1,102,812	67.2	2,329,067	68.5	2,119,724	57.8	2,360,656	58.6
CNTU (Confederation of National Trade Unions)	177,755	5.4	187,186	5.5	211,017	5.8	211,810	5.3
CSD (Centrale des syndicates democratiques)	38,083	1.2	43,824	1.3	39,885	1.1	60,596	1.5
CCU (Confederation of Canadian Unions)	26,007	0.8	27,350	0.8	37,155	1.0	32,394	0.8
AFL-CIO (American Federation of Labor—Congress of Industrial Organizations)	10,573	0.3	3,441	0.1	354,507[a]	9.7	388,882[b]	9.6

Unaffiliated Unions

Unaffiliated International Unions	96,278	3.0	100,506	3.0	104,067	2.8	15,597	0.4
Unaffiliated National Unions	665,088	20.3	613,813	18.1	703,889	19.2	719,610	17.9
Independent Local Organizations	60,372	1.8	91,534	2.7	95,444	2.6	135,900	3.4
TOTAL	3,277,968	100.0	3,396,721	100.0	3,665,688	100.0	4,030,759[c]	100.0[c]

SOURCE: Labour Canada, *Directory of Labour Organizations in Canada*, Bureau of Labour Information, 1978, 1980, 1985, 1990. Table 2.
[a] Relates to AFL–CIO/CFL. Only AFL–CIO=144, 626 (4%).
[b] Relates to AFL–CIO/CFL. Only AFL–CIO=177, 568 (4.4%)
[c] Includes figures for CEQL–103, 141 (2.6%) and CNFIO 2,173 (0.1%).

not affiliated to any central body. The unaffiliated unions consist primarily of professional bodies of nurses, teachers, etc.

Since the early unions in Canada were craft unions organized by the AFL, women, as unskilled workers, were largely excluded from them. With industrialization came the industrial unions in the 1930's and 1940's. These were international and organized by the CIO in the Canadian branch plants of American industry. As industrial jobs were "men's jobs", women were, by and large, excluded from these unions also.

For each one of the three categories—female, male and total—both national unions and government employee organizations increased their share of union membership between 1962 and 1976, while the international unions have slipped back, as seen from Table 2.12. In 1976, internationals still had the major share (61.9 percent) of the male membership while the national had 44.9 percent of the female membership.

The decline in 1988 in the case of international unions and government employee organizations is probably due to the economic recession that hit the western world, especially Canada, during 1981–85 since economic decline always adversely affects union membership levels.

The Canadian Unions are a recent phenomenon. By and large, it is these unions, not the international unions, that have been organizing women workers in Canada. As seen from Table 2.13, female membership in national unions increased from 23.45 percent in 1962 to 44.3 percent in 1988, in government employee organizations from 23.93 to 44.2 percent, while in internationals from 11.70 to 23.9 percent.

Table 2.14 gives data on the 12 unions with the highest number of female members. Seven of them are Canadian, showing a clear concentration on the public sector (public administration, teaching and nursing), while the five internationals are concentrated on garment and clothing, service, retail trade and meat cutting.

Women's representation in the Canadian organized labour force was 16.4 percent in 1962; it increased to 37.5 percent in 1988, as Table 2.15 shows. However, this growth has been

Table 2.12: DISTRIBUTION OF UNION MEMBERSHIP BY TYPE OF UNION AND SEX, CANADA, 1962, 1976 AND 1986

	1962			1976			1986		
	Female	*Male*	*Total*	*Female*	*Male*	*Total*	*Female*	*Male*	*Total*
International Unions	47.8	69.2	65.9	34.5	61.9	54.5	21.0	40.4	33
National Unions	33.8	20.2	22.3	44.9	24.3	24.9	62.5	47.2	53
Government Employee Organizations	18.4	10.6	11.8	20.6	13.8	15.6	16.5	12.4	14
TOTAL	100.0	100.0	100.0	100.0	100.0	100.0	100.0	100.0	100

SOURCE: Annual Report of the Minister of Trade and Commerce, *Corporations and Labour Unions Returns Act* (CALURA), 1962. Statistics Canada, *Corporations and Labour Unions Returns Act* (CALURA), 1976, part 2, cat. no. 71–202, p. 49, table 18.

Table 2.13: **PERCENTAGE OF FEMALE MEMBERSHIP OF REPORTING LABOUR ORGANIZATIONS IN CANADA, 1962, 1976 AND 1988**

Type of Union	*Percentage of Female Membership*		
	1962	1976	1988
International Unions	11.70	17.07	23.9
National Unions	23.45	40.67	44.3
Government Employee Organizations	23.93	35.56	44.2

SOURCE: Annual Reports of the Minister of Trade and Commerce, Corporations and Labour Unions Returns Act, 1962 and 1988. Statistics Canada, *Corporations and Labour Unions Returns Act*, part 2, cat. no. 71–203, p. 49, table 18.

regionally uneven as Chart 2-A indicates. In 1979, percentage of unionized women was 34.5 percent in Ontario, 31.8 percent in Quebec and 12.6 percent in British Columbia. The prairie region ranged from 3.8 percent in Saskatchewan to 6.7 percent in Alberta. In the maritimes it varied from 0.4 percent in Prince Edward Island to 1.8 percent in New Brunswick. The obvious conclusion is: unionization takes place where the action is.

In terms of growth rates, during the period 1971–79, the internationals have been almost static. Government employees' associations have registered the highest growth rate with national unions following very closely. This is indicated by the trend lines in Chart 2-B and the histograms in Chart 3. Meanwhile, Table 2E in the Appendix gives more detailed information on union growth for the period 1968–79.

In the international unions, the percentage of Canadian unionized women increased from 13.7 percent in 1968 to 18.3 percent in 1979. In the national unions, this percentage increased from 35.4 in 1968 to 42.4 in 1979. In the Government Employees' Organizations, the figure stood at 22.8 percent in 1968 and increased to 39.0 percent in 1979, an almost 70 percent increase over the period.

Table 2.14: THE 12 UNIONS WITH THE HIGHEST NUMBER OF FEMALE MEMBERS, CANADA, 1976

Union and Type of Union	Total Membership	Female Membership	Women as Percentage of Total Membership
Canadian Union of Public Employees (National)	218,606	89,183	40.8
Quebec Teachers Corporation (National)	97,405	61,373	63.0
Public Service Alliance of Canada (Government)	145,141	51,761	35.7
Social Affairs Federation (National)	60,625	41,810	68.9
Service Employees; International Union (International)	52,071	34,949	67.0
Ontario Public Service Employees Union (Government)	57,346	27,504	48.0
Retail Clerks International Association (International)	48,447	21,892	45.2
Amalgamated Meat Cutters of North America (International)	57,605	20,713	36.0
International Ladies Garment Workers Union (International)	22,582	19,101	84.6
Registered Nurses Association of British Columbia (National)	18,849	18,849	100.0
Amalgamated Clothing and Textile Workers Union (International)	30,127	18,660	61.9
Alberta Union of Provincial Employees (Government)	34,175	17,783	52.0

PRIMARY SOURCE: Statistics Canada, *Corporations and Labour Unions Returns Act*, Part 2, Cat. no. 71–202, 1976, p. 49.
SECONDARY SOURCE: Julie White: *Women and Unions*, 1980.

Table **2.15: WOMEN'S REPRESENTATION IN THE ORGANIZED LABOUR FORCE, CANADA, 1962–1988**

	Number of Women Members	Percentage of all Members
1962	248,884	16.4
1963	260,567	16.6
1964	276,246	16.7
1965	292,056	16.6
1966	322,980	17.0
1967	407,181	19.8
1968	438,543	20.4
1969	469,235	21.2
1970	513,203	22.6
1971	558,138	23.5
1972	575,584	24.2
1973	635,861	24.6
1974	676,939	25.2
1975	711,102	26.0
1976	750,637	27.0
1977	792,282	27.7
1978	835,263	28.7
1979	890,365	29.3
1980	932,883	30.2
1981	979,862	31.0
1982	985,376	32.3
1983	1,179,233	34.8
1984	1,219,065	35.5
1985	1,264,883*	36.2
1986	1.31 million	36.4
1987	1.36 "	37.2
1988	1.40 "	37.5

SOURCE: *Corporations and Labour Unions Returns Act,* Canada, reports of
relevant years.
* From 1985 on, only graphical representations have been provided.

One of the main characteristics of the Canadian labour market is that there have always been men's jobs and women's jobs. As we have seen earlier, women were virtually excluded from the skill-intensive craft jobs through the 19th century and later from industrial blue collar jobs. Women have been pushed to the residual tertiary sector jobs, rightly called

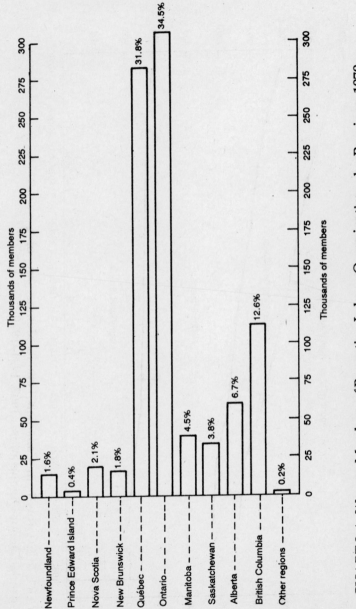

CHART 2-A: Women Members of Reporting Labour Organizations, by Province, 1979

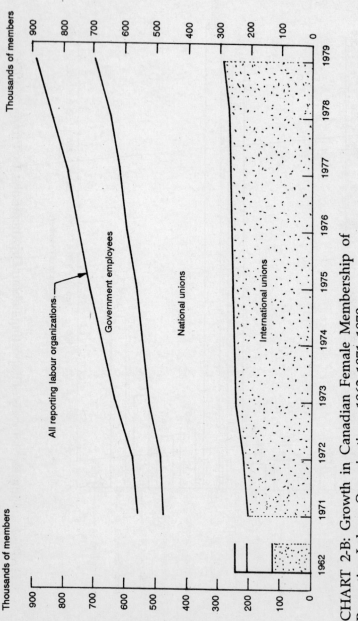

CHART 2-B: Growth in Canadian Female Membership of Reporting Labour Organizations, 1962, 1971–1979

SOURCE: *CALURA*, part II, 1979, Cat. #71–202

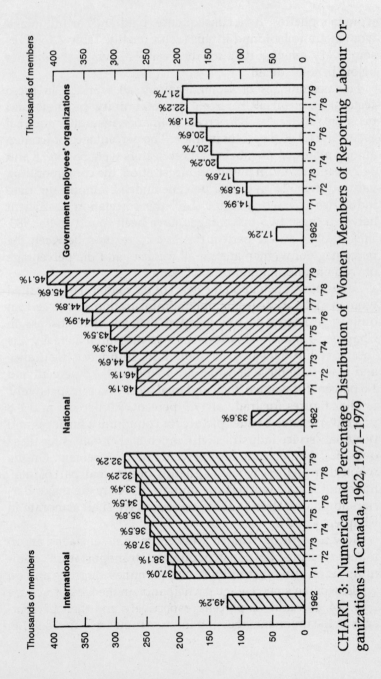

CHART 3: Numerical and Percentage Distribution of Women Members of Reporting Labour Organizations in Canada, 1962, 1971–1979

SOURCE: *CALURA*, Part II, 1979, Cat. #71–202.

women's ghettos. As a consequence, paid and/or unionized women are to be found in this sector mostly. Table 2.16 gives some very relevant data for the year 1977 which we discuss below in some detail.

The percentages of women among all workers in these sectors were: (a) 59.8 percent in community, business and personal service, (b) 58.5 percent in finance, insurance and real estate and (c) 40.6 percent in trade. The percentages of women among all union members in these sectors were 55.8, 63.8 and 34.7, respectively. In public administration, the corresponding values were 32.5 and 33.0 percent. Indeed, among the nine industries covered in Table 2.16, the correlation coefficient between these two percentages have been found to be .983. This implies a near perfect positive correlation between the percentage of women among all workers and the percentage of women among unionized workers.

Let us now touch upon the heart of the matter. The so-called women's jobs, aside from public administration, have a certain built-in resistance to unionization that we shall discuss in Chapters 4 and 5. This resistance is measured here by the "membership densities" in Table 2.16. In finance, insurance and real estate these densities are 1.7 percent, 1.3 percent and 1.5 percent for women, men and total work-force, respectively. Similar figures for trade are 7.5 percent, 9.6 percent and 8.8 percent. We have a better picture for community, business and personal service industries with much higher values for these densities: 30.2 percent, 35.6 percent and 32.3 percent. On the whole then, in these women's ghettos, only a small part of total, male and female workers are unionized. There are major barriers to unionization in these sectors as we shall elaborate in Chapters 4 and 5.

Now a word on women workers in male enclaves. In (a) manufacturing, (b) construction, (c) transportation, communication and other utilities, and (d) mines, quarries and oil wells, women's percentage participation in the work-force are 25.0, 7.4, 19.9 and 9.3 percent respectively, and their percentages in the union membership in these industries are 18.9, 1.0,

Table 2.16: NUMBER OF PAID WOMEN WORKERS, WOMEN AS A PERCENTAGE OF TOTAL WORKERS, UNION DENSITY BY SEX, AND WOMEN UNION MEMBERS AS A PERCENTAGE OF TOTAL UNION MEMBERS, BY SELECTED INDUSTRIES, CANADA, 1977

Industry	Number of Paid Women Workers '000	Women as a Percentage of Total Workers	Union Membership Density[2]			Women Union Members as a Percentage Total Unions Members
			Women percent	Men percent	Total percent	
Agriculture	39	27.3	1.2	2.4	2.1	16.0
Mines, quarries and oil wells	14	9.3	10.6	45.6	42.1	2.3
Manufacturing	467	25.0	35.2	50.4	46.6	18.9
Construction	41	7.4	7.5	61.3	57.2	1.0
Transportation, communication and other utilities	155	19.9	49.1	58.0	56.3	17.3
Trade	611	40.6	7.6	9.6	8.8	34.7
Finance, insurance and real estate	301	58.5	1.7	1.3	1.5	63.8
Community, business and personal service industries	1445	59.8	30.2	35.6	32.3	55.8
Public administration	227	32.5	66.9	65.3	65.8	33.0
All industries	3305[1]	38.1	26.8	41.1	35.7	28.6

[1]Figures do not add to total due to rounding.
[2]Density refers to: actual union membership/potential union membership x 100.
SOURCE: Canada, *Women in the Labour Force: Facts and Figures, 1977 ed. Part III, Miscellaneous*. Ottawa: Labour Canada, Women's Bureau, 1980. Table 4, p. 11.

17.3 and 2.3, respectively. These are the sanctuaries of industrial unions. Men do production jobs in these industries
and the women are, typically, clerks. Although highly
unionizable, as shown by high total union membership densities, female union membership densities in these industries
are significantly lower than those for males. The initiative for
unionization naturally comes from the men in these jobs.
Women's lower union membership density here is due, in part,
to the male unionists' lack of interest in these secretarial
women—the typists. It may partly be due also to lack of
interest among the typists themselves. We will come back to
this issue in Chapter 5.

Public administration is a category by itself. Both legislation
and the relatively higher level of education in this section than
elsewhere are responsible for highly vigorous female
unionization in this sector with a surprisingly high union
membership density of 66.9 percent for females as against 65.3
percent for males.

Finally, in Table 2.17 we have information on women's
leadership roles in the trade union movement. The percentage
of women on the executive boards of international unions was
2.8 percent in 1970 and increased to 4.5 percent in 1977. In the
national unions, the percentage was 13.1 percent in 1970 and
increased to 24.4 percent in 1977. In the government
employees' organizations, the figure increased from 6.5 percent in 1970 to 8.8 percent in 1977. Though not rich in coverage,
this is an important table and, together with our primary data
collected from interviews and mail order survey of union
executives, will help clarify the issues concerning barriers to
unionization of women.

The data and discussion in this chapter have led us to a
historical picture of women's increasing involvement in the
labour market in Canada. The percentages of women in the
labour force and in union membership have been secularly
rising and have reached the levels of 40.0 percent and 30.2

Table 2.17: EXECUTIVE BOARD MEMBERS OF UNIONS: BY TOTAL NUMBER OF MEMBERS, BY PERCENT WOMEN EXECUTIVE MEMBERS AND BY OVERALL TOTAL NUMBER OF EXECUTIVE MEMBERS, 1972, 1975, 1976, 1977

Union	INTERNATIONAL		NATIONAL		GOVERNMENT EMPLOYEES			
	Total no. of Members	% Women of Total Members	Total no. of Members	% Women of Total Members	Total no. of Members	% Women of Total Members	Overall Total no. of Board Members	Overall percent of Women of Total Board Members
1970*	-	2.8	-	13.1	-	6.5	-	9.8
1972	132	3.8	460	14.1	413	5.8	1,005	9.4
1975	142	4.2	541	13.7	483	7.5	1,166	9.9
1976	158	5.1	589	16.8	402	7.2	1,149	11.8
1977	112	4.5	636	24.4	443	8.8	1,191	16.7

*The figures for 1970 have been taken from Julie White, op. cit., Table 7, p. 23.
SOURCE: Women's Bureau, Labour Canada, Women in the Labour Force: Facts and Figures, 1975 edition, Table 3, p. 289, 1976 ed. part III, table 3, p. 9 and 1977 ed., table 2, p. 7.

percent in 1980. But women have yet a long way to go. They are still crowded in low-paying, unstable market segments and face ideological, institutional and structural barriers to labour participation and unionization. To these issues, we now turn.

NOTES

[1] Tables 2A through 2E are placed at the end of the Chapter as an Appendix.
[2] Labour Canada, *Labour Organizations in Canada*, 1978, p. 12, table 3.
[3] Julie White, *Women and Unions*, The Canadian Advisory Council on the Status of Women, Ottawa, 1980, p. 76.
[4] Julie White, ibid., p. 77.
[5] Julie White, ibid., p. 80.

APPENDIX

to

Chapter Two

78   WOMEN, UNIONS AND THE LABOUR MARKET

Table 2A: **PERCENTAGE DISTRIBUTION OF FEMALES IN THE LABOUR FORCE, CANADA, 1911–82 (SELECTED YEARS)**

Years	Total Both Sexes in Labour Force[1] 000's	Total Females in Labour Force 000's	Percent Females in Labour Force
1911	2724	365	13.4
1921	3164	489	15.4
1931	4151	794	19.1
1936	4468	895	20.0
1941	4466	998	22.3
1945	4520	1418	31.4
1946	4755	1106	23.2
1949	5006	1114	22.2
1951	5172	1179	22.8
1953	5283	1186	22.4
1960	6041	1639	27.1
1963	6748	1870	27.7
1964	6933	1972	28.4
1965	7141	2076	29.1
1967	7694	2357	30.6
1968	7919	2476	31.3
1969	8162	1602	31.9
1970	8374	2690	32.1
1971	8631	2831	32.8
1972	8891	2953	33.2
1973	276	3303	35.6
1974	9639	3477	36.1
1975	9974	3680	36.9
1976	10206	3837	37.6
1977	10498	3994	38.0
1978	10882	4232	38.9
1979	11207	4408	39.3
1980	11522	4613	40.0
1981	11830	4811	40.7
1982 (av.)	11667	4799	41.1

[1] 1911 to 1970, 14 years and over; 1971 forward, 15 years and over.

Figures for 1911 and 1921 from series C36–46, p. 60 in *Historical Statistics of Canada*, ed. by M.C. Urquhart and K. Buckley, 1965, Toronto: Macmillan Co. of Canada. Includes "Gainfully employed".
Figures for 1931 to 1960 from Series 56–69, p. 62 in the above reference.
1963 to 1972 from *Canada Year Book*, 1979. Table 8.1 and 8.2.
1973 to 1978 from *Canada Year Book*, 1980–81, Table 7.2 and 7.1.

1979 from *The Labour Force*, 1979, Annual Average, Cat. 71–001, Table 56, p. 70.

1980 from *The Labour Force*, 1980, Annual Average, Cat. 71–001, Table 57, p. 75.

1981 from *The Labour Force*, 1981, Annual Average, Cat. 71–001, Table 57, p. 80.

1982 from *The Labour Force*, Jan. through May issues, averaged, Table 3, Cat. 71–001.

Table 2B: MARITAL STATUS OF FEMALES IN THE LABOUR FORCE BY SELECTED YEARS, 1931–81

Year	Total Females in Labour Force (000's)	Married		Single		Other (Widowed, Divorced, Separated)	
		Number	Percent	Number	Percent	Number	Percent
1981	4,811	2,883	60.0	1,435	29.8	493	10.2
1980	4,613	2,764	60.0	1,380	30.0	469	10.0
1975	3,697	2,204	59.6	1,146	31.0	347	9.4
1970	2,690	1,525	56.7	925	34.4	240	8.9
1965	2,076	1,073	51.7	807	38.9	196	9.4
1960[1]							
1955	1,238	463	37.4	650	52.5	125	10.1
Census 1951	1,164	349	30.0	723	62.1	92	7.9
1950	1,071	311	29.0	656	61.3	104	9.7
1945	1,062	309	29.1	667	62.8	86	8.1
Census 1941 1940[1]	833	106	12.7	666	80.0	61	7.3
Census 1931	666	68	10.2	537	80.6	61	9.2

[1]Figures unavailable for the non-census years 1932–40 in any of the sources listed below.

1980–81, Statistics Canada, 71–001, *The Labour Force*, Table 60, 1980, p. 78, 1981, p. 83, pop. 15 yrs. and over (in the Labour Force).

1965, 1970, 1975 *Women in the Labour Force Facts and Figures*, Part 1, Labour Force Survey, 1976, Table 14, p. 38. 1975, pop. 15 yrs. and over (in Labour Force). 1965, 1970—pop. 14 yrs. and over (in Labour Force).

1931, 1941, 1951, *Women at Work in Canada*, 1958, Table 10, p. 15, pop. 14 yrs. and over (in Labour Force). N.B.—married includes permanently separated; 1941 does not include those on active service.

1945–1958, *The Labour Force*, November 1945—July 1958 Reference Paper No. 58, 1958 Revision, Cat. No. 71–502. Dominion Bureau of Statistics, Special Surveys Division, Table 9, p. 100. N.B.—only females with jobs (employed)—1951 census figures from source listed above (Labour Force Participation Rates).

—unable to find any reliable sources for 1959, 1960 or 1932–1944 (excluding 1941).

—all years except 1945–1958 are total labour force—employed and unemployed.

Table 2C: FEMALE LABOUR FORCE BY AGE FOR CANADA BY SELECTED YEARS, 1953–75, CALCULATIONS OF PERCENTAGE OF FEMALE LABOUR FORCE OF TOTAL FOR THESE YEARS

Age	1953 Percent	1955 Percent	1960 Percent	1965 Percent	1970 Percent	1975 Percent
14–24 years	36.9	37.2	39.0	40.3	41.6	42.0
25 years and over	17.5	18.3	22.2	25.6	28.8	32.4
45 years and over	14.3	15.8	21.2	25.8	28.4	30.1
25–54 years	18.8	19.4	23.0	26.3	29.6	33.4
55 years and over	11.6	13.3	18.6	22.8	25.5	27.2
14–19 years	39.1	40.5	42.7	43.1	42.9	42.6
20–24 years	35.2	34.8	35.9	38.2	40.9	41.8
25–44 years	19.6	20.0	22.8	25.5	29.2	33.9
45–64 years	15.1	16.5	21.8	26.3	29.0	30.5
65 years and over	9.3	10.8	16.1	20.3	20.9	24.3
TOTAL	22.1	22.6	25.8	29.1	32.1	35.1

NOTE: Age ranges during these years includes labour force at 14 years of age.
SOURCE: Statistics Canada, *The Labour Force*, cat. #71–001, December issues, 1953–75.

Table 2D: **FEMALE LABOUR FORCE, CANADA, BY AGE, 1976 AND 1981**[*]

Age	1976			1981		
	Total	*Female*	*Percentage*	*Total*	*Female*	*Percentage*
15–24 years	2,785	1,253	45.0	3,095	1,421	45.9
25 years and over	7,523	2,605	34.6	8,736	3,390	38.8
45 years and over	2,908	952	32.7	3,122	1,108	35.5
25–54 years	6,326	2,246	35.5	7,417	2,960	39.9
55 years and over	1,198	359	30.0	1,319	430	32.6
15–19 years	1,147	531	46.3	1,246	582	46.7
20–24 years	1,638	722	44.1	1,849	839	45.4
25–44 years	4,616	1,653	35.8	5,614	2,282	40.6
45–64 years	2,730	908	33.3	2,933	1,053	35.9
65 years and over	178	44	24.7	189	55	29.1
TOTAL	10,308	3,859	37.4	11,830	4,811	40.7

[*]This is basically a continuation of Table 2C which provides the data only up to 1975.
SOURCE: Statistics Canada, *The Labour Force*, Cat. 71–001, December issues 1976, 1977, 1979, 1980, 1981.
NOTE: Figures to the 1,000th.

Table 2E: FEMALE UNION MEMBERSHIP BY YEARS, CANADA, 1968–79

Year	Percentage of Women in Following Unions			Percentage of Women in Unions	Total Number of Women in Unions	N = Total Union Members (Male + Female)
	International	National	Government Employees			
1968	13.7	35.4	22.8	20.4	438,314	2,143,422
1969	14.0	36.3	24.3	21.2	469,020	2,214,397
1970	14.3	39.1	27.5	22.7	512,920	1,163,931
1971	14.6	40.0	28.5	23.5	557,742	2,371,643
1972	15.2	42.3	29.6	24.2	574,889	2,372,889
1973	15.9	40.3	31.1	24.7	634,849	2,574,707
1974	16.6	36.7	34.4	25.2	676,217	2,678,700
1975	16.9	38.5	34.9	26.0	710,319	2,731,479
1976	17.1	40.7	35.6	27.0	749,378	2,773,434
1977	17.3	40.8	38.0	27.7	780,732	2,816,703
1978	17.6	42.4	38.4	28.7	833,217	2,901,081
1979	18.3	42.4	39.0	29.3	888,220	3,028,991

SOURCE: *Corporations and Labour Unions Returns Act*, Statistics Canada, cat. #71–202. Supplement, part 2, 1970–1979, and the annual report of the above publication, 1968–1969.

Chapter 3
Patriarchy and Sex-role Ideology

UNTIL RECENTLY, women were confined to the family, the private sphere of reproduction, and excluded from the public sphere of social production. This was the broad sexual division of labour. During the last few decades, without being relieved of their domestic chores, and facing discrimination in the labour market, women have been participating increasingly in wage-labour. A working woman thus has a "double day of labour". Sometimes she is also oppressed at home by her dominating husband. More frequently, she faces discrimination in the workplace both from her male co-workers and her male employer. She, like her male co-worker, is of course also subject to economic exploitation by her capitalist employer. The "woman question" comprises this sex phenomenon (patriarchy) and the economic class phenomenon (capitalism). As she tries to (a) enter the labour market and (b) unionize upon entry, she faces barriers arising out of patriarchy and the associated "sex-role ideology". In this chapter, we examine these institutional barriers.

The first attack on patriarchy was launched by "radical feminists". Radical feminism dates from the beginnings of the second wave of the women's liberation movement around 1969–70. This brand of feminism is an extension of the liberal feminism of an earlier generation led by Mary Wollstoncraft, Elizabeth Cady Stanton, Harriet Taylor Mill, etc., who spoke of "sexual politics" long before Kate Millett. While these forerunners understood male power, they did not (or could not) relate it to the economic foundation of capitalist society. Today, radical feminists, such as Shulamith Firestone,[1] are more sophisticated in the sense that they give a clarion call for the destruction of patriarchy whereas their earlier liberal sisters only wanted the right to vote and some legal reforms. The radical feminists want nothing short of an overhaul, and better still abolition, of the "biological family", the "hierarchical sexual division of society" and "sex roles" themselves. Sexual division of labour and society, expressing as it does the basic hierarchical division of society into male-female roles, is the control mechanism of "patriarchal culture". It expresses the notion that roles, purposes, activities, social functions, individual power, etc., are determined sexually.

These women are equally disenchanted with the traditional radical left, including the Marxists of various shades. They are dissatisfied with the "Marxist definition of power" and the Marxists' alleged "equation between women's oppression and exploitation". For them, economic categories, such as class and class struggle, are of no significance. All history is the history of sex struggle and not class struggle. In their view, the battle lines are drawn between males and females and not between capitalists and workers; the basic relations are those of "reproduction" and not of "production".

They define patriarchy as a sexual system of power in which men possess superior power and privilege. Patriarchy is the male hierarchical ordering of society. It is a universal system rooted in biology and independent of history and economy. It is auto-structured, auto-regulated. In the past, its "legal-institutional base" was more explicit than today. Yet it is preserved through marriage and family. In this system, sex as personal also becomes political, and women are the victims of oppression because of the sexual politics of men. The intellectual leader of this group, Shulamith Firestone, has developed "a materialist view of history based on sex itself".[2]

An independent attack on the concept of patriarchy, a sexual hierarchy, was made by an Althusserian Marxist, Juliet Mitchell, who found women's powerlessness in capitalist society rooted in four "structures": production, reproduction, sexuality, and socialization of children.[3] Women's emancipation would need the transformation of all four of these structures.

Marxist-feminists[4,5] reject both the radical feminists and Mitchell for their ahistorical approach to the woman question and their inability to organically link patriarchy with capitalism and ideological superstructure with the economic structure. Marxist-feminists, in their turn, have not gone beyond this criticism. We try to help fill this gap in this chapter through a historical analysis of the evolution of the institution of family and patriarchy.

Patriarchy: A Historical Perspective

Engels generalizes Morgan's periodization of the history of human development: savagery, barbarism and civilization.[6] Savagery is the period in which the appropriation of products of nature, that is, products which are directly usable, predominated; furthermore, things produced by human beings were mainly instruments that facilitated this appropriation. Barbarism is the second stage of human history in which, on the one hand, knowledge of cattle breeding and land cultivation was acquired and, on the other, methods of increasing the productivity of nature through human activity were learned. Finally, civilization is the period in which knowledge of further processing of natural products, of industry proper, and of art was acquired. The institution of family is classified similarly: group marriage for savagery, pairing marriage for barbarism and finally, monogamy, supplemented by adultery and prostitution, for civilization. The study of the history of primitive society reveals conditions in which men lived in polygamy and, simultaneously, their wives in polyandry; the children were common to all. These conditions underwent a whole series of modifications until they were dissolved ultimately in monogamy. The modifications involved the progressive narrowing down of the circle of people embraced by the tie of common marriage until finally only the single couple was left constituting, as it still does, the predominant pattern today: the molecule with two atoms—husband and wife.

According to Morgan, out of a very early original stage of promiscuous intercourse, in which the whole tribe consisted of husbands and wives in a communistic family community, the institution of family evolved successively through three stages. The first two were characterized by the group marriage of savagery, and the third by the "pairing family" of barbarism, which would eventually yield to monogamy. The "consanguine family" was the first stage, when the marriage groups were ranged according to generations: all the grandfathers and grandmothers, within the limits of the family, were all mutual husbands and wives. They formed the first circle. The second circle consisted of fathers and mothers, i.e., children of the first circle. Sons and daughters constituted the third circle of mutual husbands and wives; grandsons and granddaughters the fourth circle. No vertical marriage took place, i.e., marriage between successive generations—ancestors and descendants, parents and children. In this sense, it was the first advance over the earlier system of universal promiscuity. Horizontally, however, brothers and sisters, male and female cousins of the first, second and more remote degrees were all mutually brothers and sisters and, precisely because of this, were husbands and wives.

The "punaluan family" marks the second and more advanced stage that prohibits sexual intercourse, and marriage, between natural brothers and sisters and, gradually, between "collateral brothers and sisters", i.e., first, second and third cousins. Engels gives two explanations for the transition to the punaluan family.[7] The material explanation is that inbreeding hinders physical and mental development. The moral explanation is the "conception of the impropriety of sexual intercourse between the children of a common mother". Tribes among whom this system evolved rapidly developed the institution of "gens"—the social foundation of most, if not all, barbarian peoples of the world.

Every consanguine family had to split up after a couple of generations or so because of the limit on the number of members the original communistic common household could accommodate. This upper limit on the size of the family community was more or less the same within a given locality. This process of division of the old and creation of new

households was profoundly affected by the introduction of the
new moral code—prohibition of marriage between brothers
and sisters, natural or collateral. In the punaluan family, one
or more groups of sisters became the nucleus of one household,
their natural brothers the nucleus of another. As in Hawaii, a
number of sisters, natural or collateral, were the common
wives of their common husbands—their brothers (natural or
collateral) being excluded from this relationship. Similarly, a
number of brothers had common wives not including their
sisters. These husbands/wives no longer called each other
brothers/sisters but, *punalua*—partner. All children in the
family are brothers and sisters to each other. While a woman
would call her sister's children her own, her brother's children
she would call her nephews and nieces. Similarly for a man.

In all forms of group family, it is never certain who the father
of a child is, but everyone knows who the mother is. Descent
is thus traceable through the mother. The female line alone is
recognized. This exclusive recognition of lineage through the
mother and the inheritance relations arising therefrom was
called "mother-right" by Bachofen.[8]

One of the typical groups in the punaluan family consists of
a number of natural and collateral sisters (i.e., those descend-
ent from natural sisters in the first, second and more remote
degrees) together with (*a*) their children and (*b*) their natural
or collateral brothers on their mother's side (at this stage of
human development these brothers are not their husbands).
This group is the first circle of persons who will later on appear
as members of a "gens" in the original form of that basic
institution of gentile society of barbarism: The tribe will be
divided into a number of "gentes". These sisters all have a
common ancestress whose female descendants, generation by
generation, are sisters by virtue of descent from her. These
sisters' husbands can no longer be their brothers, i.e., cannot
be descendants of the same ancestress and therefore do not
belong to their (the sisters') consanguineous group. Once the
proscription of marriage between sisters and brothers, including the most remote collateral relations on the mother's side,

is established, the above-mentioned group becomes a gens—a rigidly limited circle of blood relatives in the female line—within which intermarriage is not permissible. This group gradually consolidates itself with the help of social and religious institutions and distinguishes itself from other gentes of the same tribe. In other words, the whole tribe would now consist of several gentes.

The punaluan family was built on the form of group marriage that was coming to an end in the later days of savagery, gradually succumbing to the pairing family, which is identifiable with the period of barbarism. This transition is of crucial importance for our purpose in this study, as will be evident later. Let us give some details. According to Engels, a certain amount of pairing had already taken place under group marriage—among his numerous wives, a man had a principal wife and vice versa. Gradually, as the gens developed and more classes of "brothers" and "sisters" were prohibited from intermarriage, these "pairings" increased. Engels then gave an example of the Iroquois and other Indian tribes during the lower stage of barbarism, among whom marriage was prohibited between *all* relatives recognized as such (which numbered hundreds). Basically then, this growing number of prohibitions made group marriages very difficult and they were increasingly succeeded by the *pairing family*. Expanded Engels:

At this stage one man lives with one woman, yet in such a manner that polygamy and occasional infidelity remain men's privileges, even the former is seldom practised for economic reasons; [simultaneously], the strictest fidelity is demanded of the woman during the period of cohabitation, adultery on her part being cruelly punished. The marriage tie can, however, be easily dissolved by either side, and the children belong solely to the mother, as previously...[9]

Thus the evolution of the family in prehistoric times consisted in the continual narrowing of the circle—originally embracing the whole tribe—within which marital community between the two sexes prevailed. By the successive exclusion, first of closer, then of ever remoter relatives, and finally even of those merely related by marriage, every kind of group marriage was ultimately rendered practically impossible; and in the end there remained only the one, for the moment still loosely united, couple—the two-atom molecule—with the dissolution of which marriage itself completely ceases. This fact alone shows how little individual sexual love, in the modern sense of the word, had to do with the origin of monogamy. Engels expanded, "Whereas under previous forms of the family, men were never in want of women but, on the contrary, had a surplus of them, women now became scarce and were sought after. Consequently, with pairing marriage begins the abduction and purchase of women—widespread *symptoms*, but nothing more, of a much more deeply rooted change that had set in.[10]

It is, of course, understandable that, with the increasing restrictions on taking relatives as marriage partners, the number of women available to a man as potential wives declined and women became scarce. This scarce resource had to be allocated judiciously. The man was not left alone trying to woo a girl to a tie similar to the so-called "love marriage" of the bourgeois state that was to evolve several centuries later. An "arranged marriage" was settled by the mothers of the two young persons involved. It was a deal. The bridegroom had to present gifts, prior to the marriage, to the gentile relatives of the bride on her mother's side. The presents served as purchase gifts for the ceded girl. We note here that the girl was sold to the boy and not vice versa. Was this an unequal relationship between men and women? If so, why did the women, the heads of communistic households, agree to it? Also, why was it the case that "polygamy and occasional infidelity" remained men's privileges while "the strictest fidelity [was] demanded of the woman during the period of cohabitation, adultery on her part being cruelly punished"? Why did women become party to the "successive exclusion" of relatives from marriage and, more fundamentally, why did they at all create the gens and the gentile system?

Elaborating on Bachofen, Engels would later argue that the transition from group marriage to pairing was effected by women. If so, they gained from it in spite of the inequality which is implied by the double standard in the sphere of infidelity. Before assessing this question, let us probe what Engels meant by "widespread *symptoms,* but nothing, more, of a much more deeply-rooted change that had set in".

The pairing family emerged on the borderline between savagery and barbarism: it is the form of family characteristic of barbarism. At the earlier stage of savagery, the savage lived in the forest and ate wild fruits, nuts and roots. At the middle stage fish for food and fire are discovered and, following the rivers, the savage population spread over the greater part of the earth's surface. With uncertainty in food supply, cannibalism arises at this stage. In the third and final stage of savagery, bow, sling and arrow are discovered and hunting becomes a normal occupation and one finds beginnings of settlement in villages and a certain mastery of means of subsistence: Wooden vessels, utensils, finger weaving, baskets, polished stone implements, dug-out canoes and, in some races, timber and planks for housebuilding. Barbarism dates from the introduction of pottery and, in its middle stage, domestication of animals and cultivation of edible plants begin. This is the "deeply-rooted change" that Engels must have meant, out of which emerged private property, towards the end of barbarism, and which brought about the transformation of pairing marriage into monogamy and the replacement of mother-right by father-right.

By the end of savagery, a wealth of accumulated experience and sharpened mental powers ushered in material changes in tribal life. As we have seen, the tribe was now composed of gentes and the family form of the pairing type. Meanwhile, the pairing family, too weak to become an independent household, still retained characteristics of the communistic household of earlier times. And, as implied previously, a communistic household suggests supremacy of women in the house by virtue of the fact that their exclusive recognition as natural mother signifies high esteem for them. In the words of Engels, "That woman was the slave of man at the commencement of society is one of the most absurd notions that have come down to us from the Enlightenment of the eighteenth century."[11] On the contrary, women had freedom and a highly respected position among all savages and all barbarians of the lower and middle stages, and partly even of the upper stage. As quoted by Engels, Arthur Wright, a missionary for many years among the Seneca Iroquois, reinforced this finding about woman's place in the pairing family:

> As to their family system, when occupying the old long houses [communistic households embracing several families]... it is probable that some one clan [gens] predominated, the women taking in husbands from other clans [gentes].... Usually the female portion ruled the house; the stores were in common; but woe to the luckless husband or lover who was too shiftless to do his share of the providing. No matter how many children or whatever goods he might have in the house, he might at any time be ordered to pack up his blanket and budge; and after such orders it would not be *healthful* for him to attempt to disobey. The house would be too hot for him; and he had to retreat to his own clan [gens]; or, as was often done, go and start a new matrimonial alliance in some other. The women were the great power among the clans [gentes], as everywhere else. They did not hesitate, when occasion required, to knock off the horns, as it was technically called, from the head of the chief and send him back to the ranks of the warriors.[12]

Basically then, the communistic household was the foundation upon which a majority of women, in primitive times, were able to acquire high degrees of independence and respectability. In other words, women did not lose their erstwhile power after group marriage had been replaced by pairing marriage, because the former communistic household was preserved; in fact, the only difference was that the marriage partners were now on a one-to-one basis. Engels explained that the penance with which the woman buys her right to chastity—for infringing the commandments of the gods (Bachofen)—was, in fact, a means by which she could purchase her "redemption from the ancient community of husbands and acquire the right to give herself to *one* man only."[13] He elaborated that this penance was a "form of limited surrender"—the Babylonian women surrendered themselves once a year at the Temple of Mylitta; the Middle Eastern girls were sent for years to the Temple of Ansistis, where they practised free love with their own favourites before being allowed to marry; the Asiatic peoples between the Mediterranean and the Ganges also have similar customs, usually under a religious guise.[14] Gradually, this sacrifice to placate the gods for redemption becomes lighter, until a time when "the annually repeated offering yields place to the single performance: the hetaerism of the matrons is succeeded by that of the maidens, its practice during marriage [succeeded] by practice before marriage, the indiscriminate surrender to all [succeeded] by surrender to certain persons.[15]

Let us recall the "predominancy of women" in the communistic household at this period, and also the premise that women effected the transition to the pairing family. By doing the latter, according to Bachofen, the woman bought "her right to chastity" and thereby infringed the "ancient commandments of the gods". To appease the gods, she had to make penance by limited hetaerism, replacing post-marital hetaerism with pre-marital hetaerism. For Engels, however, this implied that, with this penance, she bought her "right to give herself to *one* man only" and, consequently, purchased "her redemption from the ancient community of husbands" rather than the "ancient commandments of the gods".

The answer offered to our question why women brought about pairing marriage then is her need either for "chastity" or for "one man". Why did this need arise? Up to this point in the argument, Engels relies on Natural Selection as the explanation of the evolution of the family. However, according to Engels, as we shall see later, Natural Selection terminates with the introduction of the pairing family. Further on, Engels agrees with Bachofen that the transition from pairing marriage to monogamy was brought about by women basically because the greater the "development in the economic conditions of life" (characterized by the decline of the old communism and increase in the population), the more degrading and oppressive did women find the old, traditional sexual relations to be. This in turn gave added impetus to their demand for a right to chastity and monogamy as a liberation. According to Engels, this "progress" could not have been initiated by men, "if only for the reason that they had never... dreamt of renouncing the pleasures of actual group marriage. Only after the transition to pairing marriage had been effected by women could the men introduce strict monogamy—for the women only, of course."[16]

Here is the point where Engels parts company with nature and its "selection" and begins to look for social causation for the emergence of monogamy. Finding evidence that the pairing marriage began declining and, by the middle stage of barbarism, was coming to an end, Engels concluded that, if no new *social* driving forces had come into operation, no new form of the family would have arisen out of the pairing family. But these driving forces did start operating,[17] and hence the transition from pairing marriage to monogamy.[18] Thus, did he justify his belief in social causation for the emergence of monogamy.

Engels finds these "social driving forces" in the Old World, in Europe and Asia, where "the development of the economic conditions of life" and "the undermining of the old communism and the growing density of the population" took place. In America, there was no evidence that pairing marriage ever advanced to strict monogamy until the continent was discovered and conquered by the Europeans. During the middle stage of barbarism, domestication of animals and the breeding of herds were characteristic of the Old World while cultivation of edible plants was the distinguishing feature in North America. The domestication of animals and breeding of herds needed only elementary care and supervision for ensuring an ever-increasing supply of milk and meat, whereas the wild buffalo had to be hunted down. The implication here is that, in the Old World, there was the "development of the economic conditions of life" mentioned earlier, whereas in North America life still retained some of the "naive and primitive jungle" character typical of the communistic household of earlier times.

According to Engels, the "*first great social division of labour*" took place when the "pastoral tribes separated themselves from the general mass of the barbarians".[19] These tribes not only produced more, but in greater variety too, thus making possible more regular exchanges of goods. Prior to this, there had only been occasional exchanges; specifically, some exceptional talent in making weapons and tools may have led to some brief division of labour, thus accounting for the stone implements found in many places. Their creators had probably worked for the community. At any rate, that was probably the only mode of exchange. However, expanded Engels, "after the crystallization of the pastoral tribes, ...[there existed] all the conditions favourable for exchange between members of different tribes, and for its further development and consolidation as a regulation institution."[20] Originally, exchanges between tribes were made through the chiefs. Gradually, as the herds became personal property, exchange between individuals predominated and, eventually, became the primary form of exchange. The principal article of exchange was cattle; basically, it assumed the function of money.[21] Thus, Engels explained the origin of private property.

Who owned the herds and flocks? At the beginning they were the common property of the tribe or gens. But on the threshold of authenticated history, they are already the separate property of the family chiefs—men. A revolution has taken place; women have been dethroned as head of the household. Mother-right has succumbed to father-right. Slavery has already come into being and the family chief owned the slaves also. How did this happen?

So far, human labour power did not produce any surplus above the cost of its maintenance. With cattle-breeding, metal-working, weaving and finally field cultivation, a surplus was beginning to arise and riches began to be the private possession of the families. Family labour became inadequate for these multifarious activities. Captives taken in inter-tribal warfare were now converted into slaves to work the fields, tend the cattle, etc. Pairing marriage had already introduced a new element in the barbarian family. The father, even if his paternity is not yet certain at this stage, is identifiable as the only husband of the child's mother. He is "natural" in this sense. As, according to the "natural division of labour" prevailing in the family till then, the man was responsible for procuring food and producing the means of procuring food, he therefore owned these means and took them with him in case of separation, just as the women kept the household goods. Thus, by prevailing custom, man became the owner of the new means of food procurement, i.e., the cattle and the slave. But by custom again, his children could not inherit these properties from him because they belonged to his wife's gens, and not his, and his property, upon his death, had to remain in his gens. His property passed to his brothers and sisters and to his sisters' children or to the descendants of his mother's sisters.

With the increase in wealth, man's status in the family increased and woman's declined. This inspired man to overthrow the traditional order of inheritance. Mother-right was now replaced by father-right. According to Engels, this was done rather easily and without any protest from women because this revolution, one of the most decisive ever experienced by mankind, need not have disturbed one single living member of a gens. In his words,

All the members could remain what they were previously. The simple decision sufficed that in future the descendants of the male members should remain in the gens, but that those of the females were to be excluded from the gens and transferred to that of their father. The reckoning of descent through the female line and the right of inheritance through the mother were hereby overthrown and male lineage and right of inheritance from the father instituted...[22]

For example, among the Shawnees, Miamis and Delawares of North America it has become the custom to transfer children to the father's gens by giving them gentile names obtaining therein, in order that they may inherit from him. According to Engels, "The overthrow of mother-right was the *world-historic defeat of the female sex*. The man seized the reins in the house also, the woman was degraded, enthralled, the slave of the man's lust, a mere instrument for breeding children.... The first effect of the sole rule of the men that was now established is shown in the intermediate form of the family which now emerges, the patriarchal family."[23]

It must be emphasized that Engels here calls the patriarchal family the "intermediate form of the family". He views it as a transitional form between the pairing family and the monogamian family characteristic of civilization, i.e., the period from the end of barbarism to the present day. This intermediate form maintains the polygamy aspect of pairing but its chief attribute is "the organization of a number of persons,... into a family, under the paternal power of the head of the family. In the Semitic form, this family chief lives in polygamy, the bondsman has a wife and children, and the purpose of the whole organization is the care of flocks and herds over a limited area."[24]

The essential feature of the patriarchal family is the incorporation of paternal power and bondsmen—slaves acquired through both tribal warfare and commodity exchange. In order to guarantee the fidelity of the wife and the paternity of the children, the woman is placed within the absolute power of the man. It is a family community embracing several generations of descendants of one father and their wives who all live together in one household and have common land ownership and common tillage. The head of the household and probably a couple of his sons exercise polygamy with their wives procured mostly through the purchase of female slaves. The rest, mostly male slaves, have to be content with one wife each.

The patriarchal family converges to the monogamian family in which the polygamy aspect is formally eliminated but, in essence, it remains the pairing family but with tighter rules of dissolution of marriage. In this form, as a rule, only the man can dissolve the marriage and cast off his wife. The old promiscuity is now practised secretly and extra-maritally. The monogamian marriage is a marriage of convenience, an instrument to beget heirs to man's private property. Comments Engels:

> Thus, monogamy does not by any means make its appearance in history as the reconciliation of man and woman, still less as the highest form of such a reconciliation. On the contrary, it appears as the subjection of one sex by the other, as the proclamation of a conflict between the sexes entirely unknown hitherto in prehistoric times.... The first class-antagonism which appears in history coincides with the development of the antagonism between man and woman in monogamian marriage, and the first class-oppression with that of the female sex by the male.[25]

The old communistic household embraced several families, a number of couples and their children. The administration of such a "large enterprise" by the women was as much a public affair, as much a socially necessary industry, as the providing of food by men. This situation began to be changed in the patriarchal family and was finally abolished in the monogamian individual family. The administration of the household lost its public character; it was no longer the concern of society. It now became a private *service*. The wife now became "the first domestic servant, pushed out of participation in social production."[26]

Thus we find the exclusion of women from the world of material production at the very end of barbarism and at the dawn of civilization. From then on women were to remain "hidden in the household" for over three thousand years. Tribal society passed on to "civil society". With the rise of private property, there also rose the phenomenon of unequal private property and the contradiction between the private interest and the common interest. To mediate between the two, the institution of "state" was devised. Society now became class society and the state, seemingly neutral, became the instrument of the dominant class for facilitating surplus extraction from the labour of the toiling masses: the slaves under slavery and, later, the serfs under feudalism. Throughout these two epochs of history, the sexual division of labour prevailed, with women confined to the home and men dominating the outside world of material production.

If private property is the basis of monogamy (for women) and male domination, then the nature of this monogamy and male domination, patriarchy in short, will have to vary with the form of property relations, nay, the mode of production. Patriarchy will have to be considered an aspect of the superstructure which is not an independent entity but corresponds to an underlying mode of production. As such, there will be, in theory, as many forms of patriarchy as there are modes of production. Within each mode of production, again, there may not be a homogeneous pattern of patriarchy; it will vary from propertied class to propertied class. In pre-capitalist modes of production, especially in the feudal mode, the direct producer, for instance the serf, had some private property in the means of production and the feudal lord exercised an indirect control over the primary means of production—the land—and collected rent from the peasant in different forms under different stages of feudalism. As serf, the peasant paid labour-rent by working on the lord's manor for a specified part of the week; only during the rest of the week did he work on the plot allotted to him by the lord for his own and his family's subsistence. Under a later development, he paid rent in kind and subsequently in cash for his parcel of land. In this sense, he had private property and exercised his domination over his wife and children as the possessor and owner of it. Similarly, the artisan owned his tools and his wife and children worked under him in a dominance–dependence relation.

With the rise of capitalism during the sixteenth through the eighteenth centuries, patriarchy changed with the division of society into two economic classes, the capitalist and the proletariat. Concerning the form of family in this mode of production, Engels has this to say:

> The modern individual family is based on the open or disguised domestic enslavement of the woman; and modern society is a mass composed solely of individual families as its molecules. Today, in the great majority of cases, the man has to be the earner, the bread-winner of the family, at least among the propertied classes, and this gives him a dominating position which requires no special legal privileges. In the family, he is the bourgeois; the wife represents the proletariat.[27]

Notice Engels' emphasis here on "the propertied classes". Man is the bread-winner "at least among the propertied classes" and, as such, exercises hegemony over his family. One is forced to ask about the nonpropertied class—the proletariat. The worker in capitalist society, in its pure form, owns nothing but his labour power, a commodity whose exchange-value is the only source of his and his family's subsistence. Does he dominate over his family?

Now, as capitalism began, a change in the division of labour began to take place. Capitalism began to draw on the cheapest source of labour in the artisan family, the women and the children. Marx and Engels considered this tendency to be a characteristic law of capitalism. Women who were confined to the (private) domestic sphere in the earlier modes of production would from then on be fully drawn into social production side by side with the male members of the proletariat. Let us hear Engels on this:

> Only modern large-scale industry again threw open to her—and only to the proletarian woman at that—the avenue to social production; but in such a way that, when she fulfils her duties in the private service of her family, she remains excluded from public production and cannot earn anything; and when she wishes to take part in public industry and earn her living independently, she is not in a position to fulfil her family duties. What applies to the woman in the factory applies to her in all the professions, right up to medicine and law.[28]

This is a profound statement of the mature Engels; essentially, capitalism "threw open" to woman the "avenue" to social production. But she had a dilemma; she was not fully emancipated from her household chores. For the first time in history, Engels here raises the modern question, the concern of this dissertation, women's work: their domestic labour and wage labour. Engels does not pursue this matter but he raises today's so-called "domestic labour debate" and the question of women's participation in the labour market. This matter will be elaborated in the next two chapters.

Meanwhile, in reference to the proletarian family, all the foundations of classical monogamy are removed. Here there is a complete absence of all property for the safeguarding and inheritance of which monogamy and male domination were established. Therefore, there is no stimulus whatever here to assert domination. In the Communist Manifesto, Marx and Engels maintained that, "The proletarian is without property; his relation to his wife and children has no longer anything in common with the bourgeois family relations."

Later in the *Origin*, Engels asserts that the proletariat's private property, which, in the first place, at the dawn of civilization, had forced monogamy on women, has long since parted company with him. Consequently, the real basis of monogamy is non-existent for the proletariat. As we shall see later, it is not true that "the proletarian is without property"; on the contrary, today he possesses property and thus he has something in common with the bourgeois. This then was one of the first mistakes of Marx and Engels. Another mistake manifests itself in the following statement by Engels:

> Moreover, since large-scale industry has transferred the woman from the house to the labour market and the factory, and makes her, often enough, the bread-winner of the family, the last remnants of male domination in the proletarian home have lost all foundations—except, perhaps, for some of that brutality towards women which became firmly rooted with the establishment of monogamy. Thus, the proletarian family is no longer monogamian in the strict sense, ... The two eternal adjuncts of monogamy— hetaerism and adultery—therefore, play an almost negligible role here; the woman has regained, in fact, the right of separation, and when the man and woman cannot get along they prefer to part. In short, proletarian marriage is monogamian in the etymological sense of the word, but by no means in the historical sense.[29]

Large-scale industry has not "transferred the woman from the house to the labour market and the factory". Marx and Engels did not live to see that capitalism would later shunt them back to the household for a long time and again call them back only up to a point and restrict them to a certain kind of work-ghetto. What happened is briefly this. The first phase of capital accumulation was the primitive accumulation of labour-intensive methods. Marx called it the extraction of absolute surplus value by lengthening the working day and by exploiting cheap female and child labour. The far-sighted sections of the bourgeoisie, especially the non-industrialists and the professionals-cum-intellectuals, raised the hue and cry of a "normal family life" which meant that women's place was in the home and that a single wage should cover the subsis-

tence of the entire proletarian family. The legislation that followed (a) curbed child labour and limited adult female labour,
(b) reduced the normal working day from twelve to ten to eight
hours, (c) introduced minimal health standards and working
conditions in the factory, (d) rationalized welfare provisions,
and (e) provided for compulsory universal public schooling.
Through these reforms, the male workers became "primary
bread-winners"—"good providers"—and their wives become
"good mates" to themselves and "good mothers" to their
children.

This single family wage gave the male worker what Wally
Seccombe has called the "bread-winner power".[30] His wages
began to play the role of private property of earlier times. But
worse still, a part of the single wage was indeed converted to
private household property. Marx assumed that the worker
would be paid the equivalent of his labour power exhausted
in the course of the labour process. That was, of course, based
on the competitive promise of quid pro quo—exchange of
equivalents. But capitalism became oligopolistic. Worker
productivity rose tremendously due to capital-intensive
modern technology (relative surplus value). Through
protracted struggles via the trade union movement, the working class was able to partake of a share in this increased
productivity. The male worker was now able to save a part of
his wages and accumulate property in the form of a house, a
car, a cottage and consumer durables. This private property
was his and that entitled him to be the head/patriarch of the
family. The proletarian family thus became monogamian "in
the historical sense" and not simply "in the etymological
sense".

Thus a sex-role ideology emphasizing the public–private
dichotomy and glorifying the mothering role of women has
been enshrined by males, both capitalist and proletarian.
Herein lies the secret of the so-called "ambivalence" of the
male trade unionists towards women workers' unionization.
We now present an analysis of this "sex-role ideology"

prevalent in the capitalist mode of production which Marx and Engels could not forecast correctly.

Mothering*

Friedrich Engels divided the material basis of society into two spheres: that of material production and that of human reproduction. The organic connection between the two determined the nature of any particular society. They are not developed in any biologically self-evident or unmediated ways; each has its respective social form—the social form of the production of the means of subsistence is labour and that of the production of people is family. Extending Engels' framework, Gale Rubin argues that every society has, besides a mode of production, a "sex-gender system" that systematically deals with sex, gender and babies.[31] The sex-gender system includes ways in which biological sex becomes cultural gender, a sexual division of labour, social relations for the production of gender and of gender-organized social worlds, rules and regulations for sexual object choice, and concepts of childhood. Like the mode of production, the sex-gender system is a fundamental determining and constituting element of society, socially constructed and subject to historical change and development. Kinship and family organization form the locus of any society's sex-gender system. Kinship and family organization consist in and reproduce socially organized gender and sexuality.

The mode of production and the sex-gender system of capitalist society have several features. First they assign to women primary parenting functions, as did all earlier societies. They create two—and only two—genders out of the panoply of morphological and genetic variations found in infants and maintain a heterosexual norm. Capitalist family

*This section draws heavily on Nancy Chodorow: "Mothering, Male Dominance, and Capitalism" in Zillah R. Eisenstein ed.: *Capitalist Patriarchy and the Case for Socialist Feminism*, New York, Monthly Review Press, 1979, pp. 83–106.

structure is largely nuclear, and its sexual division of labour locates women first in the home and men first outside of it. It is male-dominant, not sexually egalitarian, in that husbands traditionally have rights to control wives and power in the family; women earn less than men and have access to a narrower range of jobs; women and men tend to value men and men's activities more then women and women's activities.

In capitalist society, material production has progressively left the home, the family has been eliminated as a productive economic unit, and women and men have in some sense divided the public and domestic spheres between them. The distinction between the economy ("men's world") and the family ("women's world") and the separation of the mode of production and the sex-gender system does not mean that these two spheres are not structurally connected. Rather, they are linked, and inextricably intertwined, in numerous ways. Of these ways, women's mothering, that pivotal structural feature of the social organization of gender and ideology about women, is the most significant link between the sex-gender system and the mode of production.

In all societies there is a mutually determining relationship between women's mothering and the organization of production. Women's work has been organized to enable them to care for children and, conversely, childbirth, family size and child-tending arrangements have also been organized to enable women to work. Sometimes, as seems to be happening in industrial societies today, women must care for children and work in the labour force simultaneously.

As Michelle Rosaldo has argued, women's responsibility for child care has led, for reasons of social convenience rather than biological necessity, to a structural differentiation in all societies of a "domestic" sphere that is predominantly women's and a "public" sphere that is men's.[32] The domestic sphere is the sphere of the family; it is organized around mothers and children. Domestic ties are particularistic, that is they are based on specific relationships between members, and are often inter-generational and assumed to be natural and biological. The public sphere is non-familial and extra-domestic. Public institutions, activities and forms of association are defined and recruited normatively, according to universalistic criteria in which the specific relationships among participants are not a factor. The public sphere forms "society" and "culture"—constructs that take humanity beyond nature and biology. And the public sphere, and therefore society itself, is masculine.

Societies vary in the extent to which they differentiate the public and the domestic spheres. In small hunter and gatherer bands, for instance, there is often minimal differentiation. Even here, however, men tend to have extra-domestic distribution networks for the products of their hunting, whereas what women gather is shared only with the immediate family.[33]

The structural differentiation between public and domestic spheres has been sharpened through the course of industrial capitalist development, producing a family form centred on women's mothering and maternal qualities. In pre-capitalist and early capitalist times, the household was the major productive unit of society. Husband and wife, with their own and/or other children, were a cooperative productive unit. A wife carried out her child care responsibilities along with her productive work, and these responsibilities included training girls—daughters, servants and apprentices—for this work. Children were integrated early into the adult world of work, and men took responsibility for the training of boys once they reached a certain age. This dual role, productive and reproductive, is characteristic of women's lives in most societies and throughout history. Until most recently, women everywhere participated in most forms of production. Production for the home was in, or connected to, the home.

With the development of capitalism, and the industrialization that followed, production outside the home expanded greatly, while production within the home declined. Women used to produce food and clothing for the home. Cloth, and later food and clothing, became mass-produced commodities. Because production for exchange takes place only outside the home and is identified with work as such, the home is no longer viewed as a workplace. Home and workplace, once the same, are now separate.

This change in the organization of production went along with and produced complex, far-reaching changes in the family. In addition to losing its role in production, it has lost many of its educational, religious and political functions, as also its role in the care of the sick and aged. These losses have made the contemporary nuclear family a quintessentially relational and personal institution, and a personal sphere of society. The family has become the place where people go to rest after work, to find personal fulfilment and a sense of self, and remains the place where children are borne and nurtured.

This split between social production, on the one hand, and domestic reproduction and personal life, on the other, has deepened the pre-industrial sexual division of spheres. Men have become less and less central to the family, becoming primarily "bread-winners". They continued to maintain authority in the family for a while, but as their autonomy in the non-familial world decreased, their authority in the family itself has declined, and they have become increasingly non-participant in family life itself.[34] Hence, as women lost their productive economic role both in social production and in the home, men tended to be increasingly sidelined in the domestic sphere.

This extension and formalization of the public–domestic split brought with it increasing sexual inequality. As production left the home and women ceased to participate in primary productive activity, they lost power both in the public world and in their families. Women's work in the home and the maternal role are devalued because they are outside the sphere of monetary exchange and unmeasurable in monetary terms, and because love and care, though supposedly valued, are valued only within a devalued and powerless realm, a realm separate from and not equal to profits and achievement. Women's and men's spheres are distinctly unequal, and the structure of values of industrial capitalist society has reinforced the ideology of inferiority and relative lack of power vis-a-vis men which women brought with them from pre-industrial, pre-capitalist times.

Simultaneously, as Wells has shown, women's reproductive role has changed.[35] Two centuries ago, marriage was essentially synonymous with childbearing. One spouse was likely to die before the children were completely reared, and the other spouse's death would probably follow within five years of the last child's marriage. Parenting lasted from the inception of a marriage to the death of the marriage partners. But over the last two centuries, fertility and infant mortality rates have declined, longevity has increased, and children spend much of their childhood years in school.

Just as the actual physical and biological requirements of childbearing and child care were decreasing, women's mothering role gained psychological and ideological significance and came increasingly to dominate women's lives, outside the home as well as within it. In capitalist society, as in all other previous societies, it is not considered that the work women do as mothers and wives, as part of their routine contribution to their families, is productive or income-generating, even though the factual basis for this assumption is fast being eroded. The number of wives and both married and single mothers in the paid labour force soars, but the ideology remains. Whatever their marital status and despite evidence to the contrary for both married and unmarried women, women are generally assumed to be working only to supplement a husband's income in a non-essential way. This assumption justifies discrimination, less pay, layoffs, higher unemployment rates than for men, and arbitrary treatment.

The kind of work women do also tends to reinforce stereotypes of women as wives and mothers. This work is relational and often an extension of women's wife-mother roles in a way that men's work is not. Women are clerical workers, service workers, teachers, nurses, salespeople. If they are involved in production, it is generally in the production of non-durable goods like food and clothing, not in "masculine" machine industries like steel and automobiles. All women, then, are affected by an ideological norm that defines them as members of conventional nuclear families.

This ideology is not merely a statistical norm. It is transformed and given an "explanation" in terms of *natural differences* and *natural causes*. Sexual division of labour is explained as an outgrowth of physical differences. Family is seen to be a *natural* rather than a social creation. In general, the social organization of gender is not seen to be a product or aspect of social organization at all. The hypostatization of gender, then, involves disregarding the importance of historical authenticity and the fact that people produce and have produced its social forms.

According to Sherry Ortner, an ideology that sees women as closer to nature than men, or as anomalies—neither natural nor cultural, remains fundamental.[36] In capitalist society, moreover, the particular ideology of nature that defines the social organization of gender generally, and women's lives in particular, bases itself especially upon interpretations and extensions of women's mothering functions and reproductive organs. Historians have described how industrial development in the capitalist United States relegated women to the home and elevated their natural qualities as nurturant supporters and moral models for both children and husbands. Ruth Block has examined American magazines from the latter part of the eighteenth century to trace the origins of this nineteenth century ideology.[37] During the late colonial period, magazines assigned no special weight to the role of mother, either in relation to women's other roles or in contrast to the role of father. Women were rational mothers, part of a rational parenting pair, along with their other housewifely duties. Around 1790, however, in conjunction with the growth of increasingly impersonal competitive work engaged in by husbands, a sentimental image of the "moral mother" came to dominate and take over from previously dominant images of women, images Block calls the "delicate beauty" and the "rational housewife". The moral mother incorporated some of the traits of her predecessors while giving them new meaning:

> Like the rational housewife, she was capable, indispensable, and worthy of respect. Like the delicate beauty, however, she was wonderfully unlike men, intuitive as opposed to rational, and therefore, also the subject of sentimental idealizations. Magazines extolled the involvement and importance of mothers in the production of worthy sons. But they also suggested that women play a similar maternal role for their husbands.[38]

Block concludes: "This view of man's wife as providing him with crucial emotional support fed into a conception of woman as essentially 'mother', a role which in the magazines of the 1790's began to receive effusive praise for its indispensable and loving service to the human race."

Thus the virtues of mother and wife collapsed into one, and that one was maternal: nurturant, caring, and acting as moral model. This maternal image of women, moreover, reinforced the assumption regarding women as "sexless", pointing further to the assimilation of wife to mother in the masculine psyche.

The moral mother was a historical product. She "provided the love and morality which enabled her husband to survive the cruel world of men". As this world grew crueller with nineteenth century industrial development, both the image of the moral mother and attempts to instil it grew. Barbara Welter describes its apogee in the "cult of true womanhood".[39] Women's magazines and books expanded on this cult, and women discussed it in diaries, memoirs, and novels. Bourgeois women of the nineteenth century were expected to be pious, pure, submissive, and domestic—again, to provide a world of contrast to the immoral, competitive world of their husband's work, and a place where their own children (more especially their sons) could develop proper moral qualities and character. Because of this, compliance with the requisites of maternal morality was not left to chance. Medical practices treated bourgeois women as sexless and submissive by nature. They explained deviation from this norm (women's resistance and assertions of self) as being medically caused. Doctors, upon husbandly suggestion or on their own, extirpated sexual and reproductive organs of women who were too sexual and aggressive and who thereby threatened men's control of women and the careful delineation of sexual spheres.

During the present century the ideology of natural gender differences and of women's natural maternal role has lost some of its Victorian rigidity. The dichotomy, however, between what is social and public and what is natural and private takes on ever increasing psychological weight. In today's capitalistic society which is characterized by, and organized around, socially constructed, universalistic variables (such as a market for labour, alienation, bureaucratic norms, citizenship, and formal equality of access to the political sphere and before the law), people retain at least one sphere where membership and attribution seem to be entirely independent of social construction. People continue to explain the sexual division of labour and the social organization of gender as an outgrowth of physical differences and to see the family as a natural, rather than a social, creation.

The ideology of women as natural mothers has also been extended within the home. In the last fifty years, the average birth rate has fallen but, during this same period, studies (e.g. Vanek[40]) show that women have come to spend more time on child care. Women in the home used formerly to do productive work and more physical labour along with their mothering. They used to have more children, which meant they were involved in actual physical care and nursing for most of their adult lives. In pre-industrial societies, and in traditional communities, children and older people often helped and continue to help in child care. Now, in industrial societies, homes contain few children, and these children enter school at an early age. They are not available as aides to their mothers.

The Western family has been largely "nuclear" for centuries, households have usually contained only one married couple with children. But some of their children could be grown and not married, and households often contained a number of other members—servants, apprentices, boarders and lodgers, and grandparents—as well. The rise of capitalist industrialization has made the household an exclusive parent-and-small-child realm. It has removed men from the household and parenting responsibilities. Infant and child care has become the exclusive domain of biological mothers, who are increasingly isolated from other kin, with fewer social contacts during their parenting time. Participation in the paid labour force does not change this. When women are home, they still have nearly total responsibility for the children.

Ironically, biological mothers have come to have more and more exclusive responsibility for child care just as the biological components of mothering have lessened, as women have borne fewer children and bottle feeding has become available. Post-Freudian psychology and sociology have provided new rationales for the idealization and enforcement of women's maternal role, as it has emphasized the crucial importance of the mother–child relationship for the child's development.

This crucial mothering role contributes not only to child development but also to the reproduction of male supremacy. Because women are responsible for early child care and for most later socialization as well, because fathers are more absent from the home, and because men's activities generally have been removed from the home while women's have remained within it, boys have difficulty in attaining a stable, masculine gender role identification. They fantasize about and idealize the masculine role, and their fathers and society define it as desirable. Freud first described how a boy's normal oedipal struggle to free himself from his mother and become masculine generated "the contempt felt by men for a sex which is the lesser". Psychoanalyst Grete Bibring argues from her own clinical experience that "too much of mother", resulting from the contemporary organization of parenting and extra-familial work, creates men's resentment and dread of women, and their search for non-threatening, undemanding, dependent, even infantile women, women who are "simple", and thus "safe and warm".[41] Through these same processes, she argues, men come to reject, devalue, and even ridicule women and things feminine. Thus women's mothering creates ideological and psychological modes which reproduce orientations to, and structures of, male dominance in individual men and builds an assertion of superiority into the very definition of masculinity.

Women's mothering has traditionally been and continues to be a pivotal feature in the social organization and social reproduction of gender and sexual inequality. In bourgeois society it is pivotal also to the reproduction of the capitalist mode of production and the ideology which supports it. To begin with, women, now as always, reproduce the species biologically. Apart from this biological universal, women in bourgeois society perform specific tasks for the daily and generational reproduction of the capitalist mode of production.

The capitalist organization of production sustains conditions that ensure a continually expanding labour force whose wages can maintain its members and their families but are not sufficient to enable them to become capitalists. Legitimating ideologies and institutions—the statutes, schools, media, families—contributes to the reproduction of capitalism. Finally, workers themselves, at all levels of the production process, are reproduced, both physically and in terms of requisite capacities, emotional orientations, and ideological stances. The family is a primary locus of this last form of reproduction, and women, as mothers and wives, are its primary executors. Therefore, women's role and work in the family contribute to the social reproduction specific to capitalism.

With the development of capitalism and the separation of work and family life, women continued to have primary home responsibilities as a heritage from the pre-capitalist past and as an extension of the domestic–public division found in this

Patriarchy and Sex-role Ideology   115

earlier period. This did not mean that the factory system and
industrialization automatically drew men, and not women,
into its labour force: women and children were prominent
among the first factory workers. In the United States, most men
engaged in agricultural production as the factory system was
developing, and in England women and children were a
cheaper source of labour than men. Moreover, the first factories
produced cloth, which used previously to be produced in the
home by women. Significantly, however, the development of
labour outside the home (a development that would subsequently be reversed) did not affect the division of labour
within it. Women of all classes retained, and continue to retain,
home responsibilities.

Women, to begin with, are responsible for the daily
reproduction of the (by implication, male) adult participant in
the paid work world. This responsibility, apart from being
physical, is also psychological and emotional. Talcott Parsons
claims that the "stabilization and tension-management of
adult personalities" is a major family function.[42] The
wife/mother is her family's "expressive" or "social-emotional" leader; she does the tension-managing and stabilizing and
the husband/father is thereby soothed and steadied.

Tension-management and stabilization constitute the support necessary to masculine participants in the extra-domestic
work world. These participants need much support because
their work is alienating and inaffective, and would be otherwise unbearable. Women's role in the family, then, serves as an
important anodyne for work discontent and tends to ensure
worker stability. It also lessens the need for employers themselves to attend to such stability and to create contentedness.
Sociologists Peter Berger and Mansfried Kellner put this well:

> The public institutions now confront the individual as an
> immensely powerful and alien world, incomprehensible in
> its inner workings, anonymous in its human character.... The
> point, however, is that the individual in this situation, no
> matter whether he is happy or not, will turn elsewhere for

the experience of self-realization that does have importance for him: The private sphere, this intervening area created (we would think) more or less haphazardly as a by-product of the social metamorphosis of industrialism, is mainly where he will turn. It is here that the individual will seek power, intelligibility and, quite literally, a name—the apparent power to fashion a world, however Lilliputian, that will reflect his own being: a world that, seemingly having been shaped by himself and thus unlike those other worlds that insist on shaping him, is translucently intelligible to him (or so he thinks); a world in which, consequently, he is somebody—perhaps even, within its charmed circle, a lord and master.[43]

This social-emotional role of women is work. This effective work, sometimes called ego-building, is one part of that work of women in the home that reconstitutes labour power in capitalist society. This work includes the actual physical labour of housework ignored by Parsons and other family theorists. Mariarosa dalla Costa, carrying the socialist–feminist argument to its extreme, says that the home in capitalist society is a factory producing capitalism's most crucial commodity—labour power.[44]

Women also reproduce labour power in their specific role as mothers. Theorists of the Frankfurt Institute for Social Research and Parsonians have drawn on psychoanalysis to show how the relative position of fathers and mothers in the family produces men's psychological commitment to capitalist domination: the internationalization of subordination to authority, the development of psychological capacities for participation in an alienated work world, and achievement orientation.[45]

Women resuscitate adult workers, both physically and emotionally, and rear children who have particular psychological capacities which workers and consumers require under capitalism. Most of these connections are historical and not inevitable. The physical reproduction of workers must occur, but there is nothing in the nature of physical reproduction that *requires* its occurrence in the family. Rather, capitalist development, and the separation of work from the home, built on pre-capitalist forms in a way that has certainly been convenient to capitalists. People argue that housework as it is currently organized creates greater profits, since direct market payment for all of a worker's physical requirements and for day care is unquestionably more expensive than the marginal addition to a worker's salary to support his family. Today, however, wives continue to do this unpaid work even while earning their own support in the paid labour force. But all this is a question of history, convenience, and profitability, but not a logical requirement. As more and more women enter the work-force, the extra-domestic economic sector may take over more aspects of physical reproduction.

As mentioned earlier, the reproduction of workers is not exclusively a physical or physiological question in capitalist society. Capitalist achievement, and properly submissive, organized, and regular work habits in workers have never been purely a matter of money. Inner direction, rational planning and organization, and a willingness to come to work at certain hours steadily, whether or not money is needed that day, certainly facilitated the transition to capitalism. Additional psychological qualities play a major part in late capitalism: specific personality characteristics and interpersonal capacities are appropriate to the bureaucrat, the middle manager, the technician, the service worker, and the white collar worker. The increasingly nuclear, isolated, family in which women do the mothering is suited to the reproduction in children of personality commitments and capacities appropriate to these forms of work and domination.

This internal connection, rather than a connection of capitalist convenience, is also true of wives' material support of husbands and of their denial of threatening sexuality. Thus, a wife's role draws not only upon the heterosexual elements of ideology about women, but also upon the expectations of women. Sex is undoubtedly a source of masculine self-esteem, and *sexual dominance* helps a man to work out frustration encountered on the job and to exercise in his own sphere the control he feels exercised over him at work. Women's dependent and passive behaviour toward their husbands, however, also masks the nurturant controlling that is going on. As long as women continue to provide emotional support and ego-building to their husbands, they are mothering them.

Women's mothering as a basis of family structure and of the male dominance has thus developed an internal connection with the reproduction of capitalism. But while mothering contributes to the reproduction of sexual inequality, the social organization of gender, and capitalism, is also in profound contradiction to another consequence of recent capitalist development—the increasing labour force participation of mothers. This problematique, i.e., domestic labour *vs.* wage labour will be our concern in the next chapter.

The domination of women by men has been traced in our discussion to the rise of private property at the dawn of civilization. Man had the historical opportunity to be the owner of private property as a result of the prehistoric "natural division of labour" which assigned to men the task of providing for the family and to women the role of managing the household. Why it came about this way and not the other way around cannot be answered; it was natural, nature-determined, at least to Marx and Engels. Through the development of society via various modes of production, the form of male dominance—patriarchy—has also evolved as a relation of the superstructure, which itself changed with the mode of production.

The radical-feminist view that patriarchy is an independent structure is untenable. If it were tenable, it would imply that male domination over women is naturally determined and cannot be removed without insulating men and women from nature, which cannot be "naturally" done. The radical-feminist thesis that technology will liberate woman from her "sex" is an indirect admission that the problem is social and hence also economic, for technology is a socio-economic phenomenon.

The structuralist-Marxist thesis that the women's problem is located in several "structures" is certainly true but needs clarification. These theorists place major emphasis on the superstructure, with patriarchy, male domination, being an aspect of it.

Marx and Engels located the law of motion of the capitalist mode of production in the contradiction between wage-labour and capital. That is the "primary contradiction". Capitalist society has many other contradictions, including the contradiction between manual and mental labour, between town and countryside. The contradiction between male and female is one such "secondary contradiction". The primary contradiction is the "essence" and it "appears" in so many different "forms", depending on the stage of development of the mode of production in question. The "male–female contradiction"— patriarchy—has come into prominence in the last decade or so in capitalist societies. It may be the *avatar*, to use an Althusserian term, of the principal contradiction of capitalism today. Maybe, struggling through this contradiction, the proletarian cause will be advanced. It may be the contemporary battleground in a historical series of battles through which the primary contradiction is fought out.

REFERENCES

1. Shulamith Firestone, *The Dialectic of Sex.*
2. Ibid.
3. Juliet Mitchell, *Women's Estate.*
4. Zillah R. Eisenstein, ed., *Capitalist Patriarchy and the Case for Socialist Feminism.*
5. Charnis Guettel, *Marxism and Feminism.*
6. Friedrich Engels, "The Origin of the Family, Private Property, and the State" from Marx and Engels: *Selected Works.*
7. Ibid.
8. Ibid. *NB:* This term by Bachofen is quoted by Engels in the work referred to.
9. Ibid., p. 487.

10. Ibid., p. 488.
11. Ibid., p. 489.
12. Ibid., p. 489.
13. Ibid., p. 491.
14. Ibid., p. 491.
15. Ibid., p. 491.
16. Ibid., p. 492.
17. Ibid., p. 489.
18. Ibid., p. 493.
19. Ibid., p. 478.
20. Ibid., p. 478.
21. Ibid., p. 478.
22. Ibid., p. 495.
23. Ibid., p. 496.
24. Ibid., p. 496.
25. Ibid., p. 498.
26. Ibid., p. 498.
27. Ibid., p. 510.
28. Ibid., p. 510.
29. Ibid., p. 508.
30. Wally Seccombe, "Domestic Labour and the Working Class Household" in Bonnie Fox ed.: *Hidden in the Household*.
31. Gale Rubin, "The Traffic in Women: Notes on the Political Economy of Sex " in *Anthropology of Women*, ed. Rayma Reiter.
32. Michelle S. Rosaldo, "Women, Culture and Society: A Theoretical Overview", in Michelle Rosaldo and Louis Lampline: *Women, Culture and Society*.
33. Ibid.
34. Ibid.
35. Robert V. Wells. "Demographic Change and the Life Cycle of American Families" in *Journal of Interdisciplinary History*, Vol. 2, No. 2 (1971), pp. 273–82.
36. Sherry Ortner, "Is Female to Male as Nature is to Culture?" in Rosaldo and Lampline's *Women, Culture and Society*.
37. Ruth Block, "Sex and Sexes in Eighteenth Century Magazines", 1972.
38. Ibid.
39. Barbara Welter, "The Cult of True Womanhood: 1820–1860" in Michael Gordon ed., *The American Family in Social–Historical Perspective*.
40. Joan Vanek, "Keeping Busy: Time Spent in Housework, United States, 1920–1970", 1973.
41. Grete Bibring, "On the Passing of the Oedipus Complex in a Matriarchal Family Setting", in *Drives, Affects and Behaviour*, ed. Rudoph M. Lowenstein, pp. 278–84.
42. Talcott Parsons, and Robert F. Bales, *Family, Socialization and Interaction Process*.
43. Peter L. Berger, and Mansfried Kellner, "Marriage and the Construction of Reality" in Rose Lamb Cosner ed., *The Family: Its Structure and Functions*.

44. Mariarosa dalla Costa, *The Power of Women and the Subversion of the Community*.
45. The Frankfurt Institute for Social Research: *Aspects of Sociology* (Boston: Beacon Press, 1972); Max Horkheimer, "Authority and the Family" in *Critical Theory*; Talcott Parsons: *Social Structure and Personality*; Parsons and Bales: *Family, Socialization and Interaction Process*.

Chapter 4
Barriers to Women's Participation in the Labour Market and their Unionization: A Historical Perspective

IN THE PREVIOUS CHAPTER, we have analysed the evolution of family, patriarchy and sex-role ideology in historical terms. We have seen how the dichotomy between the public sphere and the private sphere emerged with the rise of private property and the state and how women were excluded from the sphere of social production until the rise of capitalism between the sixteenth and the eighteenth centuries. We pointed out that at the early phase of capitalist development women began to be drawn out of their confinement in the home and into the capitalist workplace. Then a second phase opened during which single women were more or less sent back to the domestic sector to raise a family. A third phase then emerged and continues till now with ever-increasing participation of married women in a segmented market.

As Engels noted in his *Origin*, the North-American tribes were in the upper stage of barbarism with its gentile society and communistic household at the time the continent was conquered by the Europeans. The natives were pushed to the background in "reservations" and the continent was settled by the European immigrants. It was possible for the immigrants of the toiling classes to acquire land and work for themselves. They evolved among themselves a society of small landowners living in isolated settlements. The arrival of the immigrants must then be the point of departure for any study of women's work in the New World.

In this chapter, we study this historical process, beginning from the immigrant settlement of the 1920's, and identify the barriers women have faced in entering the labour market and organizing themselves in established unions or in creating separate unions for themselves. Both patriarchal ideology and the economic interests of male workers and capitalists will be seen to have raised an interlocking system of labour-market (structural) and institutional (superstructural) barriers to women. This historical perception will be helpful in our subsequent conceptualization of these barriers in the contemporary period dating from around the 1930's.

Our primary focus is Canadian women and their experience in the historical development of Canadian capitalism, but this development is inseparably linked with the development of capitalism in Britain and the United States. Canada was not only "opened up" by British capitalism but also "settled in" by a British population with capitalist experience from back home. The Canadian economy is a branch-plant economy—a satellite of the United States economy and the Canadian "industrial unions" are the "locals" of the parent unions headquartered in the United States. We, therefore, examine below the history of women's participation in the British,* United States* and Canadian economies in turn.

England

The emergence of capitalism in the fifteenth to eighteenth centuries threatened patriarchal control based on institutional authority as it destroyed many old (feudal) institutions and created new ones such as the labour market in which labour power could be sold freely. It threatened to bring all women and children into the labour force and hence to destroy the family and, thus, the basis of the division of power between men and women. Pure competition in the free market without extra-economic coercion was expected to eradicate all arbitrary differences of status among labourers, including, in particular, the inferior position of women. Yet, contrary to the Engels expectation, as discussed in Chapter 3, that has not happened.

*The discussion on the U.K. and the U.S.A. is heavily drawn from Heidi Hartman: "Capitalism, Patriarchy, and Job Segregation by Sex" in Zillah R. Eisenstein's *Capitalist Patriarchy: The Case for Socialist Feminism*, New York: Monthly Review Press, 1979.

All family members, male and female, young and old, were now gradually drawn into the market as all production was moved out of the household and into the capitalist factory. With the development of capitalism, the needs of the economy changed; total wealth increased so substantially that male workers could demand and win a family wage. By the end of the nineteenth century, the ideal of the modern housewife in a nuclear family emerged. Women were expected to stop working upon marriage and return home to raise children and produce that "peculiar commodity", labour power, which capital could not yet produce capitalistically. Later on, as discussed in the next chapter, with the rise of corporate capitalism and its ever-expanding tertiary sector, married women would again come back to the marketplace and participate in ever-increasing numbers in what would become a segmented labour market with lower wages for women than for men. Before attempting to understand why this happened, let us look at women's role in production as the capitalist mode of production unfolded in England.

In the pre-capitalist society in England, the motherland of capitalism, agriculture, woollen textiles (a by-industry of agriculture), and the various crafts and trades in the towns were the major sources of livelihood. In the rural areas men worked in the fields on small farms which they owned or rented and women tended the household plots, small gardens and orchards, animals and dairies. The women also spun and wove. A portion of the products was sold in small markets to supply villages, towns and cities and in this way women supplied a considerable portion of their families' cash income, as well as their subsistence in kind. In addition to the tenants and farmers, there was a small wage-earning class of men and women who worked on the larger farms. Occasionally tenants and their wives worked for wages as well, the men more often than the women.[1] As small farmers and cottagers were displaced by larger farmers in the seventeenth and eighteenth centuries, their wives lost their main sources of support, while the men were able to continue as wage labourers to some extent. Thus women, deprived of these essential household plots, suffered relatively greater unemployment, and the families as a whole were deprived of a large part of their subsistence.[2]

In the 1700's the demand for cotton textiles grew, and English merchants found they could utilize the labour of the agricultural population, who were already familiar with the arts of spinning and weaving. The merchants distributed materials to be spun and woven, creating a domestic industrial system which occupied many displaced farm families. However, this putting-out system proved inadequate. The complexities of distribution and collection and, perhaps more importantly, the control the workers had over the production process (they could take time off, work intermittently, steal materials) prevented an increase in the supply of textiles sufficient to meet the merchants' needs. To solve these problems, first spinning, in the late 1700's, and then weaving, in the early 1800's, were organized into factories. At first, these were located in the rural areas, in order both to take advantage of the labour of children and women, by escaping the restrictions of the guilds in the cities, and to utilize waterpower. When spinning was industrialized, women spinners at home suffered greater unemployment, while the demand for male handloom weavers increased. When weaving was mechanized, the need for handloom weavers fell off as well.[3]

In this way, domestic industry, created by emerging capitalism, was later superseded and destroyed by the progress of capitalist industrialization. In the process, women, children, and men in the rural areas, all suffered dislocation and disruption, but they experienced this in different ways. Women, forced into unemployment by the capitalization of agriculture more frequently than men, were more widely available to labour both in the domestic putting-out system and in the early factories. It is often argued that men resisted going into the factories because they did not want to lose their independence and that women and children were more docile and malleable. If this was in fact the case, it would mean that these "character traits" of women and men were already established before the advent of the capitalistic organization of industry, and that they would have grown out of the authority structure prevailing in the previous period of small-scale family agriculture. Many historians suggest that within the family men were the heads of households, and women, even though they contributed a large part of their families' subsistence, were subordinate.[4]

We cannot of course be certain about the authority structure in the pre-capitalist family since much of what we gather about it is from prescriptive and class-biased literature. Nevertheless, the evidence on family life and on relative wages and levels of living suggest that women were, indeed, subordinate within the family. This conclusion is consonant with the anthropological literature which describes the emergence of patriarchal social relations along with early social stratification. Moreover, the history of the early factories suggests that capitalists took advantage of this authority structure, finding women and children more vulnerable because of familial relations and the changes in agriculture which had left them unemployed.

The transition to capitalism in the cities and towns was experienced somewhat differently than in the rural areas, but it tends to substantiate this line of argument; basically, that men and women had different places in the familial authority structure, and that capitalism proceeded in a way that built on that authority structure. In the towns and cities, before the transition to capitalism, a system of family industry prevailed—a family of artisans worked together at home to produce goods for exchange. Adults were organized in guilds, which had social and religious as well as industrial functions. Women and men generally performed different tasks, the men working at what were considered more skilled tasks, the women at processing the raw materials or finishing the end product. Men, usually the heads of the production units, had the status of master artisans. Women usually belonged to their husbands' guilds, but they did so as appendages; girls were rarely apprenticed to a trade and thus rarely became "journeymen" or "masters". Married women participated in the production process and probably acquired important skills, but they usually controlled the production process only if they were widowed (when guilds often gave them the right to hire apprentices and journeymen). Young men might have married within their guilds, that is, to the daughters of artisans in the same trade. In fact, young women and girls had a unique and very important role as extra or casual labourers in a system where the guilds prohibited hiring additional workers from outside the family; undoubtedly, they learned skills which were useful when they married.[5] Nevertheless, girls do not appear to have been trained as carefully as boys were, and, as adults, did not attain the same status in the guilds.

In most trades, men were the central workers and women the assistants. These were family trades. But some trades were organized on sex, rather than family, lines.[6] For example, carpentry was organized by male master craftsmen and millinery by female master craftswomen. Both hired apprentices and assistants. As Alice Clark points out, while some women's trades, such as millinery, were highly skilled and organized in guilds, there were many that could not be organized in guilds because the skills involved were such that all women could carry them on as part of their domestic work. For example, textile manufacturing, sewing, food processing and, to some extent, trading were women's domestic work; they are in every woman's hands. Every woman could acquire the skills for these trades as part of family socialization.[7]

In the seventeenth and eighteenth centuries the family industry system and the guilds began to break down in the face of the demand for larger output. Capitalists began to organize production on a large scale, and production became separated from the home. Women were excluded from participation in industry as it could no longer be pursued at home, where married women apparently tended to remain to carry on their domestic work. Yet many women out of necessity sought work in capitalistically organized industry as wage labourers. When women entered the ranks of wage-labour, they appear to have been at a disadvantage relative to men. First, as in agriculture, there was already a tradition of lower wages for women (in the previously limited area of wage work). Second, women appear to have been less well trained than men and obtained less desirable jobs. And third, they appear to have been less well organized.

Let us illustrate. First, we have the guilds themselves which were better organized among men's trades than women's, and in which, in joint trades, men held superior positions—women being seldom admitted to the hierarchical ladder of progression. Second, there was the rise of male professions and the elimination of female ones during the sixteenth and seventeenth centuries. For example, the medical profession, male from the beginning, established itself through hierarchical organization, the monopolization of new, scientific skills, and the assistance of the state. On the other hand, midwifing was virtually wiped out by men. Then, there were the breweries. Male brewers organized a fellowship, petitioned the King for monopoly rights, in exchange for a tax on every quart they brewed, and succeeded in forcing the numerous small-scale brewers to buy from them.[8] Third, throughout the formative period of industrial capitalism, men appear to have been better able to organize themselves as wage workers and, as shown later, when factory production became established men used their labour organizations to limit women's place in the labour market.

Men established supremacy over women in the household after the overthrow of mother-right. They were already heads of households and domestic production units. This facilitated their ascendance in the emerging market economy. With this superior position, vis-a-vis women, they could also establish superior organizations.

This historically observed superiority of men's organizations does not, of course, lend either eminence or natural monopoly of this quality to men. The causal explanation is not biological, it is social-historical. In explaining why men might have had superior organizational ability during this transitional period, we must consider the development of patriarchal social relations in the nuclear family, as reinforced by the state and religion. Since men acted in the political arena as heads of households and in the households as heads of production units, it seems likely that they would develop more organization structures beyond their households. Women, in an inferior position at home and without the support of the state, would be less able to do this. Men's organizational knowledge, then, grew out of their positions in the family and in the division of labour.

Thus, the capitalistic organization of industry, in removing work from the homes, served to increase the subordination of women, since it increased the relative importance of the area of men's domination. But it is important to remember that this domination was already established and that it clearly influenced the direction and shape that capitalist development took. As Clark has argued, with the separation of work from the home, men became less dependent on women for industrial production, while women became more dependent on men economically. English married women, who had supported themselves and their children, became the domestic servants of their husbands. Men increased this control over technology, production, and marketing, as they excluded women from industry, education, and political organization.[9]

When women participated in the wage-labour market, they did so in a position as clearly limited by patriarchy as it was by capitalism. Men's control over women's labour was altered by the wage-labour system, in the sense that it appeared more anonymous, but it was not eliminated. In the labour market the dominant position of men was maintained by sex-ordered job segregation. Women's jobs were lower paid, considered less skilled, and often involved less exercise of authority or control. Men acted to enforce job segregation in the labour market; they utilized trade union associations and strengthened the domestic division of labour, which required women to do housework, child care, and related chores. Women's subordinate position in the labour market reinforced their subordinate position in the family and that, in turn, reinforced their labour-market position.

The process of industrialization and the establishment of the factory system, particularly in the textile industry, illustrate the role played by men's trade union associations. Textile factories initially employed children, but as they expanded they began to utilize the labour of adult women and of whole families. While the number of married women working has been greatly exaggerated,[10] apparently enough married women had followed their work into the factories to cause both their husbands and the upper classes concern about home life and the care of children. Neil Smelser has argued that in the early factories the family industry system and male control could often be maintained. For example, adult male spinners often hired their own or related children as helpers, and whole families were often employed by the same factory for the same length of working day.[11] Technological change, however, made this increasingly difficult, and factory legislation which limited hours of work for children, but not for adults, further exacerbated the difficulties of the "family factory system".

The demands of factory labourers in the 1820's and 1830's were aimed at maintaining the family factory system,[12] but by 1840 male factory operatives were calling for legislation limiting hours of work a day for children between nine and thirteen to eight, and forbidding the employment of younger children. According to Smelser this caused difficulties for parents in training and supervising their children, and to remedy the situation male workers and the middle and upper classes began to recommend that women, too, be removed from the factories.

The upper classes of the Victorian Age, the age that elevated women to pedestals, were ostensibly motivated by moral outrage and concern for the future of the English race (and for the reproduction of the working class): "In the male", said Lord Shaftesbury, "the moral effects of the system are very sad, but in the female they are infinitely worse, not alone upon themselves, but upon their families, upon society and, I may add, upon the country itself. It is bad enough if you corrupt the man, but if you corrupt the woman, you poison the waters of life at the very fountain."[13] Note here Shaftesbury's paternalism: implying that it is acceptable to corrupt a man; it's just "bad enough", but excusable.

Engels, too, appears to have been outraged for similar reasons: "We find here precisely the same features reappearing which the Factories' Report presented,—the work of women up to the hour of confinement, incapacity as housekeepers, neglect of home and children, indifference, actual dislike to family life, and demoralization; further the crowding out of men from employment, the constant improvement of machinery, early emancipation of children, husbands supported by their wives and children, etc., etc."[14] Here, Engels touches upon the reasons for the opposition of male workers to the situation. Engels is apparently ambivalent about whose side he is on, for, while he often seems to share the attitudes of the men and of the upper classes, he also refers to the trade unions as elite organizations of grown-up men who achieve benefits for themselves but not for the unskilled women or children.

That male workers viewed the employment of women as a threat to their jobs is not surprising, given an economic system where competition among workers was characteristic. That women were paid lower wages exacerbated the threat. Hartman[15] says that the male workers' attempt to exclude women rather than to organize them is explained not by capitalism, but by patriarchal relations between men and women; men wanting to be sure that women would continue to perform the appropriate tasks at home. As we argue in the last section of this chapter, Hartman is taking a one-sided view here. Patriarchy is not the full explanation; competition from women must be given due importance.

Hostility to the competition of young females, less well trained and lower paid, was common. But, if anything, the wage work of married women was thought even less excusable. Engels illustrates this point by an incident which probably occurred in the 1830's. Male Glasgow spinners had formed a secret union: "The Committee put a price on the heads of all blacklegs [strike-breakers] and deliberately organized arson in factories. One factory to be set on fire had women blacklegs on the premises who had taken the places of men at the spinning machines. A certain Mrs MacPherson, the mother of one of these girls, was murdered and those responsible were shipped off to America at the expense of the Union."[16]

In 1846, the *Ten Hours' Advocate* suggested that attempts to improve the morals and physical condition of female factory workers would be abortive unless their working hours were substantially reduced. Furthermore, married females would be better occupied in the household than following the motion of machinery. The *Advocate* therefore hoped that the day was not far when the husband would "be able to provide for his wife and family, without sending the former to endure the drudgery of a cotton mill."[17]

Some British historians and economists accepted the logic of the male unions that women belonged at home and men's wages should be increased to make this possible, that is, they should be given a "family wage". Ivy Pinchbeck, for example, stated: "the industrial revolution marked a real advance, since it led to the assumption that men's wages should be paid on a family basis, and prepared the way for the more modern conception that in the rearing of children and in homemaking, the married woman makes an adequate economic contribution."[18]

Sidney Webb offered, as a justification for the lower wages women received, the explanation that they rarely did the same grade of work, even when engaged in the same occupation or industry. He cited cigar making, where men made fancy cigars and women made cheap ones requiring less skill.[19] Yet he also acknowledged the role male unions played in preventing women from gaining skills and admitted the possibility that, even for equal work, women received lower wages.

Millicent Fawcett argued in 1892 that equal pay for equal work was a fraud since women had been kept from obtaining equal skills and their work at the same jobs was, in fact, not equal.[20] The essence of trade union policy, she felt, was to exclude women if they were less efficient and, furthermore, to keep them less efficient. Eleanor Rathbone wrote in 1917 that male union leaders would support equal pay as "an effective way of maintaining the exclusion of women while appearing as the champions of equality between the sexes". She wrote:

> the line of argument I have been following usually either irritates or depresses all women who have the interests of their own sex at heart, because it seems to point to an impasse. If the wages of men and women are really based upon fundamentally different conditions, and if these conditions cannot be changed, then it would seem...that women are the eternal blacklegs, doomed despite themselves to injure the prospects of men whenever they are brought into competition with them.... If that were really so, then it would seem as if men were justified in treating women, as in practice they have treated them, as a kind of industrial leper, segregated in trades which men have agreed to abandon to them, permitted to occupy themselves in making clothes or in doing domestic services for each other, and in performing those subsidiary processes in the big staple trades, which are so monotonous or unskilled that men do not care to claim them.[21]

The arguments of these authors are powerful. As long as women are condemned to job-ghettos, there is no scope for the competitive process to equalize wages in equal jobs. Women are barred from the men's sanctuary.

World War I, however, raised women's expectations, and women were not likely to go back to their place willingly— even though the male unions had been promised that the women's jobs were only temporary, especially since, in addition to their wages, married women whose husbands were at war received government allowances according to family size. Rathbone[22] pointed out that any solution to the problem would be both difficult and doubtful of success and would open up class and sex antagonisms. For "women especially", she wrote, "it seems to offer a choice between being exploited by capitalists or dragooned and oppressed by trade unionists.' Describing both these alternatives as dismal, she recommended the continuation of family allowances after the war because they would insure that families would not have to rely on men's wages, that women who stayed at home would be paid for their work, and that women in the labour market could compete equally with men since their "required" wages would not be different. By 1918, Fawcett also considered equal pay for equal work a realizable goal. Advancement in the labour market required equal pay in order not to undercut men's wages. The main obstacles, she argued, were the male unions and social customs; both led to overcrowding in women's jobs.[23]

In 1922, F.Y. Edgeworth formalized Fawcett's job segregation and overcrowding model. According to him, job segregation by sex causes overcrowding in female sectors, which allows men's wages to be higher and forces women's wages to be lower than they would be otherwise. He agreed that male unions were the main cause of overcrowding,[24] and claimed that men should have an advantage in wages because of their family responsibilities. There was also the corollary that, since women did not have the same family responsibilities as men, and might even be subsidized by men, their participation would tend to pull wages down. And he seemed to suggest that equal competition in the job market would result in lower wages even for single women vis-a-vis single men, because women required 20 percent less food for top efficiency. In this last point, Edgeworth was simply taking seriously what many had remarked upon—that women had a lower standard of living than men and were willing to work for less.

That women indeed had a lower standard of living was borne out by facts. Laura Oren[25] found that within the English working class family women had less food, less leisure and less pocket money during the period 1860–1950. Therefore, the reproduction cost of female labour power was less than that of male labour power and hence, by the Labour Theory of Value, Edgeworth's neoclassically argued conclusion that lower wages for women were justified receives alternative Marxian justification. The point, however, is that the standard of living women had might not be the one they wanted to have, for in Marxian thinking "reproduction cost" is not only the physical subsistence, it has a "moral" element too.

To summarize, the main explanation the economic literature offers for lower wages for women is job segregation by sex; and to account for both lower wages and job segregation, it suggests several interdependent factors: (1) the exclusionary policies of male unions, (2) the financial responsibilities of men for their families, (3) the willingness of women to work for less, and their inability to get more, because of subsidies or a lower standard of living, and (4) women's lack of training and skills. According to Hartman,[26] the English historical literature strongly suggests that job segregation by sex is patriarchal in origin, rather longstanding, and difficult to eradicate. Men's ability to organize in labour unions—stemming perhaps from a greater knowledge of the technique of hierarchical organization—enables them to maintain job segregation and the domestic division of labour.

Here again, Hartman puts her characteristic bias into operation though somewhat contradictorily. As we saw in Chapter 3, men's ability to organize better than women had its origin not in patriarchy but in men's original advantage in the natural division of labour during barbarism, which allowed men to impose patriarchy, which changed in form through the epochs. The English literature, if anything, explains discriminatory wages rather than the political economy of discrimination, that is to say, it gives a neoclassical rationalization for wage differentials but shies away from a structural-institutional dissection of discrimination itself as a social phenomenon.

United States of America

The United States experience provides an opportunity to explore shifts in the sex composition of jobs and to consider further the role of unions, particularly in establishing protective legislation. The American literature, especially the works of Edith Abbott and Elizabeth Baker,[27] emphasizes sex shifts in jobs and, in contrast to the English literature, relies heavily on technology as an explanatory variable.

Conditions in the United States differed from those in England. First, the division of labour within colonial farm families was probably more rigid, with men in the fields and women producing manufactured articles at home. Secondly, the early textile factories employed young single women from the farms of New England: a conscious effort was made, probably out of necessity, to avoid the creation of a family labour system and to preserve the labour of men for agriculture.[28] However, this changed with the eventual dominance of manufacture over agriculture as the leading sector in the economy and with immigration. Thirdly, the shortage of labour and dire necessity in colonial and frontier America perhaps created more opportunities for women in non-traditional pursuits outside the family and colonial women were engaged in a wide variety of occupations.[29] Fourthly, shortages of labour continued to operate in women's favour at various points throughout the nineteenth and twentieth centuries. Fifthly, the constant arrival of new groups of immigrants created an extremely heterogeneous labour force, with varying skill levels and organizational development and rampant antagonisms.[30]

Major shifts in the sex composition of employment occurred in boot and shoe manufacture, textile manufacture, teaching, cigar making and clerical work.[31] In all of these, except textiles, the shift was toward the employment of more women. New occupations opened up for both men and women, but men seemed to dominate in most of them. There were exceptions;

telephone operating and typing, for example, became women's jobs.

In all cases of increase in female employment, the increases were partially stimulated by a sharp rise in the demand for the good or service. During the late 1700's and early 1800's, domestic demand for ready-made boots went up because of the Civil War, a greater number of slaves, general population expansion, and the settling of the frontier. The demand for cheap machine-made cigars grew rapidly at the end of the nineteenth century. The demand for teachers increased rapidly before, during, and after the Civil War as public education spread. The upward shift in the number of clerical workers came between 1890 and 1930, when businesses grew larger and became more centralized, requiring more administration, distribution, transportation, marketing and communication personnel.

In several cases, the shift to the employment of women was accompanied by technical innovations which allowed increased output and sometimes reduced the skill required of the worker. By 1800, bootmakers and shoemakers had devised a division of labour which allowed women to work on sewing the uppers at home. In the 1850's, sewing machines were applied to boots and shoes in factories. In the 1870's, the use of wooden moulds, rather than hard punching, simplified cigar making, and in the 1880's, machinery was brought in. And in clerical work, the typewriter, of course, greatly increased the productivity of clerical labour. The machinery introduced in textiles—mule spinners—was traditionally operated by males. In printing, where male unions were successful in excluding women, the unions insisted on staffing the new Linotypes.[32]

The central purposes of subdividing the labour process, simplifying tasks, and introducing machines were to raise production, cheapen it and increase management's control over the labour process. Subdivision of the labour process ordinarily allowed the use of less skilled labour in one or more sub-portions of the task. *Cheapening* of labour power and more control over labour were the motive forces behind scientific management of earlier efforts to reorganize labour.[33]

Machinery was an aid in the process, not a motive force. Machinery, unskilled labour and women workers often went together. In other words, technical progress embodied in machinery meant the routinization of jobs which now became less demanding of skill. Women, unskilled as they were, could therefore now be employed in larger numbers than before.

In addition to greater demand and technical change, often a shortage of the usual supply of labour contributed to a change in the labour force and "sex-typing" of jobs. In textiles, for example, in the 1840's the young New England farm women were attracted to new job opportunities, such as teaching for middle-class women. Their places in the mills were taken by immigrants. In boots and shoes, the increased demand could not be met by the available trained shoemakers, and in clerical work, the supply of high-school educated males was not equal to the demand. Moreover, in clerical work in particular, the changes that occurred in the job structure reduced its attractiveness to men. With expansion, the jobs became dead-ends for men while for women the opportunities compared favourably with their opportunities elsewhere.[34]

Male unionists opposed women's participation in wage labour in general, contributed to job segregation and helped establish protective legislation for women rather than their organization. Cigar making is a case in point. It was a home industry before 1800, when women on farms in Connecticut and elsewhere made rather rough cigars and traded them at village stores. Early factories employed women, but they were soon replaced by skilled male immigrants whose products could compete with fancy European cigars. By 1860, women were only 9 percent of those employed in cigar making. This switch to men was followed by one back to women, but not without opposition from the men. In 1869, the wooden mould was introduced, and so were Bohemian immigrant women who had been skilled workers in cigar factories in Austria-Hungary.[35] The Bohemian women, established in tenements by tobacco companies, perfected a division of labour in which young girls (and later their husbands)[36] could use the moulds.

Beginning in 1873 the Cigarmakers International Union agitated vociferously against homework, which was eventually restricted (for example, in New York in 1894). In the late 1880's machinery was introduced into the factories, and women were used as strike-breakers. The union turned to protective legislation.

The attitude of the Cigarmakers International Union toward women was ambivalent at best. It excluded women in 1864 but admitted them in 1867. In 1875 it prohibited locals from excluding women but apparently never imposed sanctions on offending locals.[37]

Male unions denied women skills while they imparted them to young boys. As Abbott and Baker showed, this was clearly illustrated in the case of printing.[38] Women had been engaged as typesetters in printing from colonial times. It was a skilled trade but required no heavy work; it suited women. In any case, male printers' unions seem to have been hostile to the employment of women from the beginning. In 1854 the National Typographical Union resolved not to encourage the employment of female compositors.[39] Baker suggests that since the unions discouraged girls from learning the trade, women learned what they could of it in non-union shops or as strike-breakers.[40] In 1869, at the annual convention of the National Labor Union, of which the National Typographical Union was a member, a struggle occurred over the seating of Susan B. Anthony, because she had allegedly used women compositors as strike-breakers. She had, she admitted, because they could learn the trade no other way.[41] In 1870 the Typographical Union chartered a women's local in New York City but the latter eventually folded in 1878 due to men's lack of support.

Apparently, the general lack of support was successful from the men's point of view, for, in 1910, Abbott claimed: "Officers of other trade unions frequently refer to the policy of the printers as an example of the way in which trade union control may be successful in checking or preventing the employment of women."[42] The Typographical Union strongly backed equal pay for equal work as a way to protect the men's wage scale, not to encourage women. Women who had fewer skills could not demand, and expect to receive, equal wages.[43]

Unions excluded women in various ways, not the least among them being protective legislation. Falk noted that unions used several devices such as constitutional exclusion, exclusion from apprenticeship, limitation of women to helper categories or non-ladder apprenticeships, limitation of the proportion of union members who could be women, i.e., quotas and excessively high fees. Moreover, the craft unions of this period, pre-1930, had a general hostility toward organizing the unskilled, even those attached to their crafts.[44] In this exclusionary policy, the unions were aided by the prevailing social sentiment about work for women, especially married women, and by a strong concern on the part of feminists and others that women workers were being severely exploited because they were unorganized.[45]

The social feminists did not intend to exclude women from desirable occupations, but their strategy paved the way for this exclusion, because to get protection for working women they argued that women, as a sex, were weaker than men and more in need of protection.[46] Their strategy was successful in 1908 when, in Muller vs. Oregon, the Supreme Court upheld maximum-hours laws for women, saying:

> The two sexes differ in structure of body, in the capacity for long-continued labour particularly when done standing, the influence of vigorous health upon the future well-being of the race, the self-reliance which enables one to assert full rights, and in the capacity to maintain the struggle for subsistence. This difference justifies a difference in legislation and upholds that which is designed to compensate for some of the burdens which rest upon her.[47]

In general, unions did not support protective legislation for men, although they continued to do so for women. Protective legislation, rather than organization, was the preferred strategy only for women.[48] The effect of the laws was limited by their narrow coverage and inadequate enforcement; but despite their limitations, in those occupations, such as printing, where night work or long hours were essential, women were effectively excluded.[49] While the laws may have protected women in the "sweated" trades, women who were beginning to get established in "men's jobs" were turned back.[50] Some of these women fought back successfully, but the struggle is still being waged today along many of the same battle lines. As Ann C. Hill argued, the effect of these laws, psychologically and socially, has been devastating. They confirmed women's "alien" status as worker.

Canada

There is a major difficulty in studying women's work in Canada from a historical perspective for the simple reason that very little has been written on the subject. Canadian researchers have not produced anything comparable to the work of Alice Clark and Ivy Pinchbeck on England or Edith Abbott and Elizabeth Baker on the United States. The only historical work seems to be the recent collection of essays, *Women at Work: 1850–1930,* edited by Janice Acton *et al.*[51] We shall draw on this source and supplement it by the historical statistics presented in this chapter and in Chapter 2.

Leo Johnson's[52] essay in *Women at Work* is the only work of historiography on the subject but is confined to Ontario society. According to him, society in nineteenth century Ontario can be divided into three phases: the "Toiler Society", the "Independent Commodity-producer Society" and the "Industrial Capitalist Society".

Toiler Society

By 1820, "The great majority of Upper Canadian Society" was composed, according to Johnson, of independent smallholders. In this "toiler society", the basic economic unit was the family engaged in production, by and large, for the family.

A minuscule commodity circulation took place for acquiring commodities such as ironware, tinware, books, clothing, tobacco, tea and alcohol. In this economic unit, the division of labour was the usual sexual one: men in the field or woods, women assisted by children in the home, the garden and the outbuildings.

The ruling class until 1850 consisted of the aristocracy and its bureaucrats. The basis of power of this elite clan lay in the possession of land and its legal-social ability to pass it on to future generations. So the ancient "paternity—rightful heir—based arguments" required monogamous marriage for the aristocratic women with their "charm", "chastity", "emotion", "passivity", "timidity", "tenderness", "compliance", and a host of other feministic virtues. Girls were socialized to possess these "virtues" while boys were socialized to be intellectual, aggressive, courageous, hardy, competitive and so on. Aristocratic women were in charge of this socialization process and also the welfare system via private charity.

The bureaucratic stratum of the ruling class aped the norms of the aristocracy in whose hands lay the gift of land, office and promotion.

A major social class, the servants, was integral to the aristocratic-bureaucratic household. Much of Canadian immigration policy in the nineteenth century concerned bringing in and maintaining a steady supply of servants for the upper class. Though not slave, this class remained subservient. Children of the servant class became servants at an early age and could expect to remain servants for life. Pay was low and work demanding. Life was particularly difficult for the female servant. When thrown out of work, she was faced with finding another servant job or ending up on the street as a beggar, thief or prostitute. There was one avenue of escape, however. Women were scarce on the frontier. Sometimes the girl servants would marry the toiler farmers and thereby escape from servitude to the aristocracy but plunge into another life of toil.

A bourgeoisie was growing between the two principal social classes—the aristocrats and the toilers. These were the merchants, millowners, moneylenders and so on. The socialization process of this class resembled that of the aristocracy and their attitude to sexual behaviour and moral rules were similar. Johnson traces this similarity to private property which is the common denominator of the two classes. Historically, in the formative stages of the bourgeoisie, this emerging class tries to imitate the culture of the aristocracy. It takes a while for it to invent values appropriate to its own mode of production.

There was one important issue which highlighted the contradictions among the social classes. This was education. The toilers wanted no more education than the Three R's so that the children's labour power could be harnessed for the benefit of the family as early as possible. The aristocracy wanted their children trained in cultural artifacts and moral attitudes to facilitate their future political leadership roles. Their girls were generally taught at home by tutors and governesses, and the boys in private schools and government-financed grammar schools. The bourgeois class wanted an education that would be conducive to their business. This required training their own children, as also the children of the lower classes who would serve them in future as clerks and managers, in more useful subjects like grammar, composition, mathematics, logic, and other subjects that impart a practical problem-solving orientation. Therefore, they campaigned for a public, compulsory, state-financed, non-sectarian education system in Ontario. Since women were in charge of the socialization and enculturation of children, they were deeply drawn into the education controversy and played some role in the future stages of social development.

Independent Commodity-producer Society

The period 1850–1880 saw the transition to industrial capitalism. In the mother country, England, the triumph of the capitalist class over the aristocracy called for a shift in Britain's interests in the white colonies. England's need for cheap food to feed its proletariat created a shift away from Canadian grain to that from Central European sources. Aristocracy was thus on the wane economically. It also lost political power to the capitalists with the creation of reciprocity between Canada and the United States in 1851 and, more generally, with the establishment of the Confederacy in 1867.

Along with the triumph of the capitalist class, the toiler society began changing from a subsistence family economy to a market-oriented cash economy. Among the toilers, capital accumulation in the form of cleared land, buildings, livestock and agricultural machinery took place. This facilitated the introduction of capitalistic lines of production in agriculture with increasing specialization and production for the market.

The capitalist British government in 1826, by ending the free land-grant policy to immigrants, while simultaneously encouraging immigration, was creating a Canadian proletariat to meet the labour needs of the indigenous bourgeoisie. By 1850, therefore, a growing scarcity of cheap land and a flood of immigrant Irish paupers created significant pools of proletarian labourers in cities such as Quebec, Montreal, Kingston, Toronto and Hamilton.

With the ascendancy of the bourgeoisie, a profound change took place in the lives of women. First, as far as agricultural women were concerned, they began losing their economic and social status established in the earlier toiler society. With the increasing employment of farm machinery, family labour became over-abundant. The capitalists' school programme triumphed in the class battle on education referred to earlier. Children were now removed from the mother-led home-production team because of the compulsory education programme that had meanwhile been established. Because of specialization, many products began to be purchased as commodities rather than being manufactured by the mother-child team. The farm woman found herself increasingly cut off from economic production and more and more relegated to the routine tasks of housekeeping. Her position began to be changed from that of a productive worker parallel to her husband to that of a domestic servant catering to her husband's and children's needs, as in the case of the hired domestics in aristocratic homes. She was becoming a reproductive machine like the women of the propertied classes. Her role would now be to produce good, obedient workers with the proper attitude for exploitation by capitalism.

Yet the agricultural family as a whole was not better off economically with capital accumulation on the farm and employment of farm children by urban industry. The agriculturists as a class were bitter about the greed of the exploitive capitalists but found themselves caught in a new dilemma posed by the newly created proletarian class. To this class, private property was not only no longer sacred but was also the main cause of its misery. Thus, when working-class women rose against their oppression and exploitation and began to organize, farm women remained aloof because of their objective class interests.

Now, even though their husbands triumphed against the aristocracy, socially bourgeois women found themselves similarly situated as the aristocratic women of the earlier stage. They would now have to undertake the safe transmission of their husbands' property to the inheriting male children. So their personal parity became a central issue as in the aristocratic class. The duties of organizing charity and leading the battle for social "morality" were now inherited by these bourgeois women from their earlier aristocratic sisters. They, however, needed to have higher levels of education and a greater degree of worldly knowledge than the aristocratic women. The objective conditions of capitalist development with its ever-increasing complexity demanded this. This, however, backfired against capitalist men. With their better education, bourgeois women began to be conscious of their social subordination. Here then could lie the genesis of liberal feminism in Canada, of which more will be said later.

Side by side with the developments narrated above among the agricultural and capitalist classes, by the mid-nineteenth century a large proletariat came into being with a profound internal contradiction. Industrial production in the toiler society took place in small workshops owned by independent highly skilled master-craftsmen who hired skilled journeymen who in turn attached to themselves apprentices learning the trade. The journeymen were well-paid and constituted the elite of the working class. Now, although by 1870 many larger establishments arose, sometimes employing as many as five hundred men, as a consequence of a market created by Canada's growing population and improved communication networks, the essential change was the replacement of workshops by manufactories based on craft production rather than factories based on machinery and unskilled labour.

The labour process lay in the hands of journeymen (mechanics, as they were called) while unskilled manual labourers were employed as helpers to the journeyman-apprentice teams. The skilled mechanics received higher wages and often owned their own homes. The unskilled labourers were ill-paid and normally lived in tenements or squalid rented cottages on or close to the manufactory grounds. The capitalists, owners of the manufactories, frequently tried to cut production costs by replacing the mechanics by semi-skilled labour while the mechanics organized into "craft unions" in order to defend their status against such encroachments. This was one of the early barriers against women's unionization because women were unskilled and the then unions were organized by skilled journeymen (mechanics) against all unskilled and semi-skilled workers.

This division into skilled and unskilled labour prompted a corresponding division in the working-class household. The wife of a skilled worker looked up to the wife and family of her husband's employer and struggled to approximate the latter's life-style by herself constantly cleaning, cooking, sewing and stretching the wage as frugally as she could. The unskilled labourer's wife, although doing back-breaking toil, could not approximate, due to her husband's poor wages, even the style of the mechanic's wife. For both kinds of working wives, however, the essential task was to do housework in order to keep the faculties of their husbands in working order for a sixty to seventy-two hour working week.

Industrial Capitalist Society

In the last quarter of the nineteenth century, the Canadian economy became increasingly dependent upon the United States economy and her manufactories succumbed to the factory system. A protected Canadian market was created in consequence of John A. MacDonald's national policy; huge amounts of foreign capital were attracted to the country. Overnight, an industrial revolution occurred in Canada.

Mass production techniques involved replacement of muscle power by machine power, skilled labour by unskilled labour. Complex skills that any simple worker had to learn earlier were now broken down into a series of repetitive monotonous tasks that required only a rudimentary mechanical knowledge and could be done by the cheapest available unskilled labour. This job could also be done by women in direct competition with the men.

The skilled labourers, the mechanics, were hit directly. Industrialists took the fullest advantage of cheap unskilled labour. The Blacks, Chinese, Irish, women and children, were drawn into the factory by the industrialist. The craft workers (mechanics) raised a hue and cry against these inroads into their preserves.Their initial reaction was to oppose equal wages for women and children. Women, they held, were by nature unequal to them and it was unjust and demeaning to men to pay women at men's level. Women took up the fight for equal pay. Finally, the male skilled workers found a loophole in their own arguments. To demand lower wages for women and children would automatically invite competition from the latter. To demand, instead, equal wages for them would mean that the employers would automatically exclude women and children who were unskilled and could not do men's jobs. This latter view was not necessarily correct because, as we saw earlier, the factory system, due to the division of complex jobs into monotonous routine tasks, did not need sophisticated skill. Besides, as we shall see later, women did "men's jobs" in munitions and in other plants during World War I.

To the other classes, employment of women was undesirable for the usual reasons given in similar situations of capitalist development in England and America. Female workers were pictured to be physically weaker and morally more corruptible than male workers. Mixing of the sexes would cause moral and spiritual breakdown among female workers due, for instance, to sexual harassment or "fooling around".

Men in the capitalist and agricultural classes turned out to be ready allies of the proletarian men. The solution discovered by the capitalist was ingenious indeed. Although the appeals against the employment of women failed because capitalists found their labour cheap, the separation of sexes was achieved. Within the factory and office, an apartheid[53] system was developed in which certain tasks were designated as "women's work", and paid for with low wages. As a result, both male goals were achieved. For the capitalists, women still provided a source of cheap industrial labour, while for working class men, there was a reduction of direct job competition from cheap female labour. Liberal middle-class men seemed to have been satisfied with this arrangement but those it concerned directly, the female workers, were not, as we shall see later on.

It is to be noticed here that it is not male chauvinism and patriarchy as such that turned "the men" against women. The male worker was objectively in competition for a job with all workers, including male co-workers. The women worker appeared as a new threat, an extra nuisance. His consciousness was not class consciousness—the rational application of the collective labour power of all workers, male and female, in a workers' state was beyond his understanding. To this overriding economic fact, we may add the prevailing superstition of male dominance that had infected him also.

To the female worker, capitalism seemed to offer an escape route from domestic slavery whether under husband or master. As we shall see, this prospect turned out to be rather limited as industrial capitalism unfolded over the next century.

Upper-class women would find in education an escape route from domestic oppression by their husbands. Female stereotype jobs, such as nursing and teaching, would provide an outlet for them, albeit at a lower pay than that of their male counterparts.

Canadian Women During World War I[54]

By the turn of the century a trend in increased female employment in industry began. The war accelerated this trend. The market economy was developing gradually, removing production from home to organized industry. The family's role in production diminished and the daughter's domestic labour became redundant. This also meant that their outside wage-income was not necessary to buy substitutes for the goods that they previously produced at home. The population shift from the rural areas to the cities and the influx of impoverished immigrants stimulated the development of labour-intensive industry, thereby creating new markets for women's labour power in manufacturing such as in the garment industry and clerical, sales and other white collar jobs. This increased female participation in the labour market did bring about occupational and attitudinal changes.

By the first decade of the twentieth century, the Canadian economy had undergone rapid changes. Though the primary sector was still predominant, manufacturing and trade were making rapid strides. Between 1901 and 1911, the proportion of women in the labour force increased sharply due, on the supply side, to a 52.8 percent jump in the labour force caused by immigration and, on the demand side, development of new jobs by industrial capitalism. Because of the availability of cheap labour from both immigration and rural-to-urban migration, industry opted for labour-intensive technology; thus exploiting women, children and immigrants as sources of cheap labour while simultaneously eliminating craft production. The garment and textile industries used to be largely served by female labour under craft production. Now, with the elimination of the latter, these women were transferred from household production to the factory. The expansion of the economy necessitated the development of service industries. By 1900, banks and Eastern chain stores were set up and British finance capital was employed for developing transportation, public utilities and the finance sector. Opportunities thus opened up for women during this period not only in manufacturing but also in white collar jobs—clerical, sales, banking, railways, public utilities and retailing.

However, it was not until the first decade of the twentieth century that there were a significant number of women in the paid work-force. Before this period, almost all the paid work of women was in areas closely associated with household tasks. The 1891 census has listed the following ten leading occupations of women: servants, dressmakers, teachers, seamstresses, tailoresses, housekeepers, laundresses, milliners and saleswomen. Table 4.1 brings this out clearly. This picture remains about the same in the 1901 census, as Table 4.2 shows. However, the female percentage in the labour force systematically increased from 1911 onwards (see Table 2.4, Chapter 2).

Table 4.1: LEADING OCCUPATION OF PAID WOMEN WORKERS, CANADA, 1891, 1901, 1911, 1921

	1891	1901	1911	1921
Farmers	11,638	8,421	15,094	16,315
Servants	79,473	81,493	98,128	78,118
Housekeepers	4,035	7,572	6,762	23,167
Other domestic service	1,609	8,844	19,170	-
Charworkers and Cleaners	-	-	-	6,251
Hotel and restaurant and boarding housekeepers	2,344	594	4,311	6,028
Waitresses	-	-	-	6,372
Boot and shoe makers	-	-	-	3,276
Dressmakers and seamstresses	32,975	22,063	20,357	16,612
Milliners	3,777	-	-	3,029
Clothing factories	1,740	1,017	5,269	14,470
Textile factory operatives	-	-	-	15,193
Municipal Public Administration officials and clerks	767	892	-	12,000
Clerical operations	-	-	-	78,342
Stenos and typists	-	-	-	-
Bookkeepers and cashiers	-	-	-	-
Telephone operators	-	-	-	12,827
Saleswomen in stores	-	-	-	35,474
Teachers	-	-	-	49,795
Nurses	-	-	-	21,162

SOURCE: Ceta Ramkhalawansingh, "Women during the Great War" in Amy Curthoys *et al.* eds., *Women at Work:* Table B, p. 267.

Table **4.2: OCCUPATIONS IN WHICH 70 PERCENT OR MORE OF THE WORKERS WERE WOMEN, CANADA, 1901**

Occupation	Percentage of Female Work-force in Occupation	Females as a Percentage of Total Work-force in Occupation
Dressmakers and seamstresses	13.5	100.0
Servants	34.2	83.7
Housekeepers	3.2	87.0
Teachers	13.0	78.0
Milliners	1.8	99.4
Paperbox and bag makers	0.1	70.8
Nurses	0.1	100.0
Office employees not elsewhere classified	3.7	79.6

SOURCE: Census of Canada, 1921, Table 1.

The major source of employment for women in the earlier periods used to be the domestic service industry. As industrialization began, this source began to decline in importance, as is evident from Table 4.3, but still remained consequential until the mid-twentieth century. The shift from the primary to the secondary sector in Canada's development opened up some opportunities for women in the manufacturing sector, mainly in textiles, clothing and food industries. As we shall see later, the greatest employment opportunity for women turned out to be the service sector which came in the wake of the secondary (manufacturing) sector. Service industries duplicated many of the jobs women did earlier as family members and domestic servants.

Capitalism created a need for services not only directly related to the needs of manufacturing but also for services directly supplied to people. In pre-industrial Canada, women provided most of the social services such as teaching and nursing. This no longer was adequate for the needs of capitalism, i.e., the needs for literate and healthy workers dictated by the large-scale operation of capitalist industry.

Table **4.3: FEMALE LABOUR FORCE IN SELECTED OCCUPATIONS, CANADA, 1901–71**

	Number of Females in Occupation (1)	Percentage of Female Labour Force in Occupation (2)	Females as a Percentage of Total in Occupation (3)
(a) *Dressmakers and Seamstresses*			
1901	32,065	13.5	100.0
1911	29,567	8.1	99.8
1921	17,933	3.7	100.0
1931	10,411	1.6	100.0
1941	20,885	1.3	100.0
1951	14,237	1.2	98.3
1961	15,516	0.9	95.8
1971	16,555	0.6	73.0
(b) *Servants/Maids and Related Workers*			
1901	81,493	34.3	83.7
1911	98,128	26.9	78.1
1921	88,825	18.1	77.7
1931	143,043	20.2	94.0
1941	148,999	17.9	95.2
1951	88,775	7.6	89.1
1961	120,392	6.8	88.0
1971	89,290	3.0	93.5
(c) *Nurses, Graduates and in Training*			
1901	280	0.1	100.0
1911	5,475	1.5	97.8
1921	21,162	4.3	99.0
1931	31,898	4.8	100.0
1941	38,283	4.6	99.4
1951	49,780	4.2	98.1
1961	81,868	4.7	96.7
1971	113,780	3.8	96.0
(d) *Teachers, Elementary and Secondary*			
1901	30,863	13.0	78.0
1911	34,063	9.3	80.6
1921	49,795	10.2	81.9
1931	64,709	9.7	78.0

	(1)	(2)	(3)
1941	64,465	7.7	74.6
1951	74,319	6.4	71.7
1961	118,594	6.7	70.7
1971	180,515	6.1	66.4

(e) *Office Employees, Clerical Workers*

	(1)	(2)	(3)
1901	8,749	3.7	22.8
1911	30,625	8.4	39.4
1921	78,824	16.1	43.4
1931	116,927	17.6	45.1
1941	152,216	18.6	50.1
1951	321,809	27.7	56.7
1961	508,021	28.9	61.7
1971	940,180	31.8	68.5

(f) *Saleswomen/Salesclerks*

	(1)	(2)	(3)
1901	2,729	1.2	15.4
1911	24,321	6.7	21.4
1921	36,189	7.4	16.4
1931	56,413	6.8	30.9
1941	68,456	6.8	41.1
1951	95,670	8.2	52.9
1961	133,773	7.6	53.6
1971	169,250	5.4	66.0

SOURCE: *Census of Canada,* 1921, Table 1.

Teaching and nursing now become institutionalized and commoditized; schools and hospitals now start selling these services.

Table 4.4 shows the changes in the occupational structure. The proportion of the labour force as well as the number of workers in primary occupations in general steadily declined from 1901. Within manual occupations, the category "Labourers", meaning unskilled labour, becomes less important relative to the skilled labourers as industrialization advanced. Service occupations declined until 1921 and thereafter showed modest growth. The greatest growth occurred in white collar occupations—the most dynamic being clerical work.

Table 4.4: PERCENTAGE OF THE TOTAL LABOUR FORCE IN MAJOR OCCUPATIONAL GROUPS, CANADA, 1901–71

Occupation	1901	1911	1921	1931	1941	1951	1961	1971
WHITE COLLAR	15.2	16.8	25.1	24.5	25.2	32.4	38.6	42.5
(a) Proprietary and Managerial	4.3	4.6	7.2	5.6	5.4	7.5	7.9	4.3
(b) Professional	4.6	3.7	5.5	6.1	6.7	7.4	10.0	12.7
(c) Clerical	3.2	3.8	6.8	6.7	7.2	10.8	12.9	16.0
(d) Commercial and Financial	3.1	4.7	5.6	6.1	5.9	6.6	7.8	9.5
MANUAL	32.2	36.1	31.3	33.8	33.4	37.7	34.9	29.2
(a) Manufacturing and Mechanical	15.9	13.7	11.4	11.5	16.0	17.4	16.4	13.7
(b) Construction	4.7	4.7	4.7	4.7	4.7	5.6	5.3	5.6
(c) Labourers	7.2	12.0	9.7	11.3	6.3	6.8	5.4	3.2
(d) Transportation and communication	4.4	5.7	5.5	6.3	6.4	7.9	7.9	6.7
SERVICE	8.2	7.7	7.1	9.2	10.5	8.6	10.8	11.2
(a) Personal	7.8	7.5	8.3	9.3	7.4	9.3	8.9	
(b) Protective and Other	0.4	0.2	1.3	0.9	1.2	1.2	1.5	2.3

PRIMARY	44.4	39.4	36.3	32.5	30.6	20.1	13.1	7.7
(a) Agriculture	40.3	34.3	32.7	28.8	25.8	15.9	10.2	5.9
(b) Fishing, Trapping	1.6	1.3	0.9	1.2	1.2	1.0	0.6	0.3
(c) Logging	0.9	1.5	1.2	1.1	1.9	1.9	1.2	0.8
(d) Mining, Quarrying	1.6	2.3	1.5	1.4	1.7	1.3	1.0	0.7
NOT STATED	-	-	0.2	-	0.3	1.2	2.6	8.5
NOT ELSEWHERE CLASSIFIED	-	-	-	-	-	-	-	0.9
ALL OCCUPATIONS Percent	100	100	100	100	100	100	100	100
Number (in thousands)	1782.8	2723.6	3164.3	3917.6	4196.0	5214.9	6342.3	8626.9

SOURCE: Patricia Connelly, *Last Hired First Fired*, Women's Press, 1978; Table 7.1, pp. 98–9.
NOTE: - means "none".

Tables 4.5 and 4.6 give trends in occupational growth for females and males, respectively. From 1901 onwards, white collar jobs increased relative to other occupations for both men and women. The percentage of women in manual occupations was on a declining path; the converse obtaining for men. Manual jobs in manufacturing and mechanical industry, construction, transportation and communication are "men's jobs" and women would be excluded from them. The percentage of women in service occupations declined while that of the men increased with the march of industrialization. In primary occupations, the percentage of women increased with the onset of industrialization but was on a declining trail from the twenties through the forties of the present century (Table 4.7). For the most part, since 1901 the majority of women has been employed in service and white collar occupations—the women's ghetto.

This trend in increasing women's paid work was accelerated by the First World War. This did not happen, however, until conscription began in June 1917. Jobs done by men who went to the war had to be filled by women now. Yet this social need met with opposition from the financial and business community. The banks, for instance, discouraged tellers (men) from volunteering for the army; the *Financial Post*[55] urged, through its editorials, the "conservation" of the business community. As war production began to increase, a shortage of labour arose with men gone to the front or relocated to the war industries. Economic necessity dictated the employment of women in jobs vacated by these men. The *Financial Post* begrudgingly began to approve women's employment which had already become a significant trend.

The need for mobilizing women to work in the munitions plants led the Imperial Munitions Board to react to the scepticism of the business community against female employment through the publication[56] of a report: *Women in the Production of Munitions in Canada*. It said:

Table 4.5: PERCENTAGE OF THE FEMALE LABOUR FORCE IN MAJOR OCCUPATIONAL GROUPS, CANADA, 1901–71

Occupation	1901	1911	1921	1931	1941	1951	1961	1971
White Collar	23.6	29.9	47.9	45.4	44.6	55.4	57.4	59.8
Manual	30.6	28.0	21.1	16.9	18.5	19.4	13.3	10.1
Service	42.0	37.6	27.0	34.0	34.4	21.3	22.5	15.2
Primary	3.8	4.5	3.7	3.7	2.3	2.8	4.3	3.7
Not Stated	-	-	0.3	-	0.2	1.1	2.5	10.8
Not Elsewhere Classified	-	-	-	-	-	-	-	0.4
All Occupations Percent	100	100	100	100	100	100	100	100
Number (in thousands)	237.9	364.8	489.1	665.3	832.8	1163.9	1760.5	1961.2

SOURCE: Patricia Connelly, ibid., Table 7.2a, pp. 100–01.
NOTE: - means "none".

Table 4.6: PERCENTAGE OF THE MALE LABOUR FORCE IN MAJOR OCCUPATIONAL GROUPS, CANADA, 1901–71

Occupation	1901	1911	1921	1931	1941	1951	1961	1971
White Collar	14.1	14.8	21.0	20.2	20.4	25.8	31.4	33.1
Manual	32.5	37.3	33.1	37.2	37.1	42.9	43.2	39.2
Service	2.9	3.1	3.4	4.1	4.6	4.9	6.3	9.2
Primary	50.5	44.8	42.3	38.5	37.6	25.1	16.4	9.9
Not Stated	-	-	0.2	-	0.3	1.3	2.7	7.4
Not Elsewhere Classified	-	-	-	-	-	-	-	1.2
All Occupations								
Percent	100.0	100.0	100.0	100.0	100.0	100.0	100.0	100.0
Number (in thousands)	1544.9	2358.8	2675.3	3252.3	3363.1	4051.0	4581.8	5665.7

SOURCE: Patricia Connelly, ibid., Table 7.2b, pp. 100–02.
NOTE: - means "none".

Table 4.7: FEMALES AS A PERCENT OF THE TOTAL LABOUR FORCE IN EACH MAJOR OCCUPATIONAL GROUP, CANADA, 1901–71

Occupation	1901	1911	1921	1931	1941	1951	1961	1971
White Collar	20.6	23.8	29.5	31.5	35.1	38.1	41.3	48.5
Manual	12.6	10.4	10.4	8.5	11.0	11.5	10.6	12.0
Service	68.7	65.3	58.9	63.0	65.1	55.4	57.8	46.2
Primary	1.1	1.5	1.6	1.9	1.5	3.1	9.2	16.4
Not Stated	-	-	23.0	18.0	15.1	20.5	25.8	43.3
Not Elsewhere Classified	-	-	-	-	-	-	-	13.6
All Occupations	13.3	13.4	15.5	17.0	19.8	22.3	27.8	34.3

SOURCE: Patricia Connelly, ibid., Table 7.3, pp. 103–04.
NOTE: - means "none".

When the Dilution of Labour became imperative, the manufacturer naturally thought that the heavier the shell the less adapted they were to female labour. The direct opposite has proved the case. The repetition in handling the smaller shell produced a physical strain that was not present in the slower and more deliberate moving about of the big projectile. In the smaller shell men can conveniently, without mechanical assistance, handle them, whereas in the larger shell, men were obliged to use assistance of machinery, and consequently men and women here became equal.

The report thus implied that an optimal allocation of labour would have men handle the smaller shells unless, of course, male labour were in extremely short supply. The report went on:

There are many operations in the Machine Shop which can safely be assigned to women.... The tool room represents every advantage for female labour, in spite of the fact that engineering history tells us that it is the department for highly trained mechanics, but it has been clearly demonstrated that women under the guidance of trained toolmakers, are efficient and useful. The grinding of milling caps, cutters, general cutting tools and other repetitive work is particularly suited for them. The making of jigs and dies is, and probably always will be, a highly skilled mechanic's task, but we look forward to the time when many more women will be admitted to this branch of engineering work. Especially have the women astonished engineers in their aptitude for the handling of milling machines.

Enid Price[57] studied the changes in women's occupations during the war in the Montreal area. She surveyed munitions plants, railway shops, wholesale houses, department stores, civil and municipal services, office buildings, banks and factories. She found that within industry women moved from light industrial work to a wide range of heavier work. By 1918, in Montreal, there were 2,315 women employed by railway, steel and cement companies in men's jobs. In the transportation sector, women took over the jobs of firemen, freight handlers and trackmen. At the munitions plants, there were at least 35,000 women employed in Ontario and Montreal. In the eight munitions plants surveyed by Price, there were 9,931 men and 5,460 women. To inspect the work of about 8,000 munitions workers, about 650 government inspectors were appointed. At the beginning, all inspectors were male but later on women constituted 33 and then 83 percent of the total.

Within factories that were not involved in war production,[58] there was not much change in the sex-composition of the labour force. In textile, clothing, leather, rubber, electrical appliances, confectionery and tobacco factories, at least 50 percent of the employees were women. No women were employed in flour mills, cement plants, iron and steel works, and machinery, tool and carriage shops, except in plants involved in war production. Price also found that in at least one-half of her surveyed industries, women had been employed for years in every capacity suitable to their skill and physique. Moreover, employers opined that in the tasks women were capable of doing, they did better than men and at lower wages.

The war undoubtedly helped change popular attitudes[59] towards single women's paid work outside the home. However, this was a slow realization and the basic societal attitude towards women as responsible for maintenance and reproduction of labour power remained unchanged.

The need for universal domestic education for all women was expressed by the 1916 Ontario Commission on Unemployment because "home occupations are the *ultimate* employment of all but a comparatively small percentage of women". The Commission felt that the only true natural place for women was in the household and that many of the women's occupations would be injurious to their physical and mental health if allowed to dominate their lives. The "positive hope" was that women would not remain in paid work too long. The Victorian ideology upon which such sentiments were based ensured that women employees would return home after marriage.

Capitalism, objectively, needed workers to fill the new occupations that it generated. The government therefore actively tried to promote a positive popular attitude towards *single* women working. In 1919, the Ministry of Education in Ontario published a book authored by Marjorie MacMurchy[60] entitled, *The Canadian Girl at Work*.

MacMurchy's objective was to assist women in finding satisfactory employment and to tell them what constituted a right attitude to work. She saw the life of an average woman as generally divided into two periods, that of paid employment and that of homemaking. As she saw it, any adequate scheme of training should equip girls with knowledge and skills for homemaking. This knowledge, according to her, would also be to their advantage in paid employment. Technical training and skill were no more helpful to a girl at work than "specialized knowledge in matters of food, clothing, health and family regimen". She went on to suggest that girls should learn how to stretch their meagre wages, an important skill which they would find handy later on in married life.

Most female occupations were thought to be preparations for married life and not ends in themselves. The Ontario Commission[61] recommended "that girls and women should be taught, so that they may realize that if a girl is an unsatisfactory, indifferent saleswoman, factory worker, teacher, nurse or other worker, the probability is that she will be an unsatisfactory wife and mother." MacMurchy[62] similarly advised women to be tranquil and well poised, to put themselves into the background and work harmoniously with their associates. The message is clear: good, obedient workers would be good, obedient wives and make good, obedient workers of their children.

With the rising need for clerical workers, shop girls and light manufacturing workers, societal attitudes towards employing single girls changed in favour of the latter but continue to oppose married women's participation in the labour market.

Destitute married women—separated, divorced, deserted, widowed, married to unemployed men—had to take whatever employment they found, often as domestic servants, housekeepers and charwomen. Some charitable nurseries were operated for these "unfortunates".

In sum, the purpose of education, both formal schooling and the years in paid work prior to marriage, was to make a girl a good, obedient wife/mother and not to prepare her for a competitive career in paid work demanding appropriate skill and professional training.

Women's work became significant though the women workers were transient. To the employer, the interesting thing about women's work was its cheapness. Comparison of wages for men and women in similar types of work are hard to make for the years before 1931 not only because data are hard to come by but also because men and women did dissimilar work. The annual, *Wages and Hours of Labour,* a Federal Department of Labour[63] report does, however, give some idea. In Toronto in 1914, a building labourer working a 44-hour week earned $13.20 a week and a bricklayer about $24.20 per week. These were men's jobs, though craft jobs. Factory wages were lower. In cotton textiles, a man would earn as little as $11.80 per week as a mule spinner in New Brunswick, or as much as $15.00 as a loom fixer in Ontario. On the other hand, women in the same plants earned just $6.90 per week as ringspinners and warpers in New Brunswick. The maximum rate the women got was $9.95 per week as warpers in Quebec. The Bell Telephone Company in Toronto paid operators from $6.60 to $9.00 per week. In laundries, the average was $9.00 per week. Female store clerks earned from $4.00 to $12.00 per week. Senior retail employees and stenographers earned as much as $14.50 per week; teachers and nurses earned less.

Domestic servants in Vancouver earned, in 1915, $12.00 per month on the average plus room and board. In 1913, domestics in Calgary made $25.00 to $30.00 per month.

During the war, women's wages were on the increase but always remaining significantly below men's wages. In shops that produced munitions, women's wages were 35 percent lower than those paid to men before the war, but by 1918 the deficit was reduced to 25 percent. Generally, women in munitions earned between 50 to 80 percent of men's wages. In wholesale houses and department stores, women's wages ranged from 20 to 60 percent of men's wages. Between 1914 and 1918, office clerks (women) earned from 10 to 60 percent of men's wages. Wage discrimination and job segregation along sex lines were the norm as Table 4.8 highlights.

Bargaining power of both men and women decreased during the war and employers were able to increase the length of the working day, using the war as an excuse. One munitions plant in Toronto increased the working day from thirteen to fourteen hours. At the Verdun Munitions Board plant, women worked upwards of 70 hours per week.

By the 1920's women were sustaining and, in some fields, improving upon their pattern of involvement in the labour market established before the war.[64] After the war, the women who had replaced men during the war stepped into new peacetime industrial jobs if they could get them or returned home if they could not. On the whole, the increase in the size of the female labour force corresponded to an increasing emphasis on education. This is indicated by the increase in the percentage of women under 25 who entered the work-force and the accompanying decline in employment among those aged 10 to 19 years. The largest rate of increase in women's participation in the labour market occurred in the 1920's among women aged 20 to 24 followed by those aged 25 to 34. This continuing involvement in education and employment was accompanied by a decrease in marriages among women under 25 and a substantial decrease among those aged 25 to 34. Women comprised about 25 percent of the enrolment in graduate and undergraduate studies by the end of the 1920's. The traditional role of women was changing. Contrary to MacMurchy's advice earlier, training and paid work would no longer constitute only a preparation for married life. Indeed,

Table 4.8: JOB SEGREGATION AND WAGE DIFFERENTIAL BY SEX, CANADA, 1914, 1917, 1918

Workplace		Number of Women (Men)	Average Range of Wages for Women	Percentage of Male Wages
MUNITIONS—8 PLANTS				
Manual Workers	1917:	5,460 (9,746)	$20.00 to $35.00/hr.	50 to 83%
	1918:	2,715 (10,050)	$25.00 to $45.00/hr.	60.8 to 81.8%
Clerical Workers	1918:	193 (527)	$12.00 to $20.50/wk.	46 to 93%
Government Inspectors of Munition Plants—6 plants	1918:	333 (901)	$1.89 to $2.75/day	25 to 70%
RAILWAY SHOPS—2 PLANTS				
Manual Workers	1914:	5 (7,428)	$16.00 to $17.00/hr.	61 to 68%
	1918:	280 (7,677)	$34.00 to $45.00/hr.	59 to 83%
Clerical Workers	1914:	2 (78)	$12.50/wk.	104%
	1918:	26 (59)	$20.26 to $20.50/wk.	77 to 93%
Clerical Staff One large office building	1914:	300 (1,420)	$42.50/mth.	60.7%
	1918:	457 (960)	$89.50/mth.	86%
BANKS—19 BRANCHES				
Clerks	1914:	195 (1,344)	$400 to $900/yr.	41 to 128%
	1918:	913 (1,281)	$408 to $802/yr.	41.8 to 82.3%

SOURCE: Ceta Ramkhalawansingh, ibid., Table E, p. 277.

married women would become a significant force in the labour market in the years ahead.

Barriers to Women's Unionization in Canada

The first trade unions were organized in Canada in the 1830's under the influence of British unions.[65] Large numbers of skilled tradesmen had already come to Canada from Britain and had brought with them the traditions of an established trade union movement. Before 1886, however, there were only a few unions operating in isolation and without any public attention to speak of. In 1886, the Trades and Labour Congress of Canada was formed, the first central body to which the isolated "local" unions federated. International unions, i.e., United States-based unions, were well established by this time and had already affiliated some of the Canadian unions and they continued to play a crucial role in the development of the trade union movement in Canada. By the 1920's, the British influence had completely disappeared.[66]

While the unions were growing in the industrial centres, Canada was still a predominantly agricultural country. As Julie White says, "In 1881, three-quarters of the population were rural, declining to just over half by 1921. In 1911 only 5 percent of the total labour force were union members, rising to just 10 percent by 1921."[67] Thus the unions involved only an insignificant minority of workers, male and female. Unions in this period were craft unions, the "industrial unions" would be a later phenomenon arising in the 1930's. Below we discuss some institutional and labour-market barriers to unionization of women workers in the pre-1930 period.

(a) Family Socialization
Women's role in the Canadian trade union movement prior to the 1930's was necessarily limited because the movement itself was in its infancy. But even in this formative phase, certain factors inhibiting women's unionization, nay, their labour-market participation itself, developed that continue to act as barriers to

women to this day. We have already seen the Victorian sex-role ideology that was imported to English Canada from Britain. The ideal of womanhood was domestically combined with religious piety and moral purity. In Quebec, these beliefs were held even more strongly. Working women were perceived by various upper- and middle-class women's organizations, reformers and factory inspectors to be the cause of a social crisis. Among these organizations were the National Council of Women, Saint Jean Baptiste Society and a number of Christian groups.

Factory inspectors insisted on cleanliness, male–female separation (for moral reasons), separate lavatories, and seats for shopgirls (so that they need not stand all day and thereby endanger their reproductive organs). Madame Provencher, a factory inspector in Quebec, recommended: "Every working girl caught using certain words or raising improper questions should be immediately discharged." The 1922 Annual Report[68] of the Quebec Department of Labour lamented:

> Woman's work, outside of her home, is one of the sad novelties of the modern world; it is a true social heresy.... Such singularities are due to a fleeting crisis, the social crisis of the present day...with regard to the work of single women, it would be wonderful if society could, some day or another, find an economic formula capable of doing away with it.

Beliefs and opinions such as these only reflect the transitional nature, in the early 1920's, of Canadian society. While the economic base of capitalism was being laid at a fast pace, social values still remained largely pre-capitalist so far as women's role in society was concerned. Objectively, capital needed women's cheap labour; subjectively, society at large lamented this need. The "sad novelties of the modern world" were, as we have seen, the economic needs of capitalism although they clashed with the conservative ideology inherited from the immediately preceding feudal past. Capital at this stage needed only "single girls"—its labour demand was not yet large enough to trespass on the "moral purity" of married women, with the exception of the "unfortunates". Patriarchal ideology would have to adjust itself again to the needs of capitalism in the ensuing decades when married women became a permanent factor in the labour market—the tertiary (ghetto) part of it, to be sure. Meanwhile, capital and patriarchy compromised on the division of a woman's life into two parts: paid work until marriage and domestic work thereafter. Educational planning, as we earlier saw, was, according to Marjorie MacMurchy, to facilitate this division. Paid work was an apprenticeship, a preparation, for better housework as much as formal schooling was.

Let us summarize this discussion by noting that family socialization presents a barrier to women's unionization. The socialization process in the family insofar as it prepares the girl to be passive, also prepares her not to be insubordinate in paid work. Since "insubordination" is part and parcel of unionization, family socialization is an institutional barrier to unionization.

Earlier, we hinted at the root of "feminism" in the educational system that the capitalist state introduced. We noted earlier that educated upper-class women were in charge of charity and the moral purity of society under the rule of capital, as they had been in the earlier epoch of aristocratic rule. During the war, the federal government turned to various women's organizations in charge of "charity" and "moral purity" for advice on agricultural production, commercial and industrial occupations, the compilation of the national register, conservation of food and the further development of the spirit of service among the Canadian people—thus the Women's War Conference[69] was held in Ottawa in February, 1918. By the time of the conference, the 35,000 women in the munitions plants had been reduced by 5,000. Several women in the conference expressed concern about this and women's employment in general. The conference recommended that women's increasing role in the labour market be maintained through protective measures, indicating thereby the middle-class women's growing concern at female unemployment.

During this period, women were also gaining political rights.[70] The feminists undertook many activities of which the struggle for the right to vote was the most protracted and publicized. The majority of the feminists accepted the view that women had a special maternal role to play and sought to extend this role beyond the family. They argued that only by participating in public life could they fulfil their mothering role and ensure the welfare of their children and their homes. It was not until 1916 that Manitoba women won the right to vote; other provinces followed suit within a few years. In Quebec, women had to wait until 1940.

At that time liberal feminists fundamentally believed in women's mothering and homemaking as their principal occupation. On this ground, liberal feminism reinforced the family socialization aspect of Victorian ideology—of patriarchy. Their progressive stance, expressed in their concern about women's employment and related problems, their supporting the demand for minimum wages and protective legislation for women had mixed effects. We shall return to this point when we deal with protective legislation.

(b) *Job Fragmentation*

Job fragmentation occurs when employees work either in total isolation or in the company of a handful of co-workers. As Table 4.1 shows, this was the case with women in the period 1891–1921. During this period, women's paid work had two principal characteristics: it was highly fragmented and it was generally unskilled. Both acted as significant labour-market barriers to unionization. This isolation and lack of collectivized work inhibited collective action, rendering it very difficult to organize. Domestic service was the leading female occupation in 1891. In 1921, it almost tied with clerical work as the two principal female occupations. The textile and clothing industries also became important employers of women.

Domestic service was the most fragmented occupation. Unlike the factory or office which brought workers together, revealed their common interests and provided a base for action, the private household separated the domestic servant from her sisters. As servants they lacked free time for meetings and had great difficulty in communicating with one another. They were not subject to the Factory Acts and were therefore not covered by whatever protection those Acts gave. This made them extremely vulnerable to victimization by employers. The only way out was quitting and seeking another job, frequently as a servant again. This high rate of turnover hindered union organization.

In the clothing and textile industry in the late nineteenth century and through the early twentieth century, contract labour and the sweat workshop was the norm. Firms such as Eaton's contracted out their work to the owners of small shops or subcontracted it out to women who would do the work in their own homes. According to the report, *Upon the Sweating System in Canada, 1896*,[71] in Toronto the proportion of work done by women in their own homes on subcontract was "greater" than work done in small shops on contract and "far surpassed" what was done in factories. The women were subject to extreme exploitation under this system which prevented even age comparison, not to mention unionization. Workers in the small shops, like workers in homes, were not covered by the Factory Acts. Wages were held down and unionization prevented by the employers.

These jobs needed little skill. The ranks of the unskilled women workers were swelled by immigration and rural-to-urban migration. This presented great risks in union organization. The employer could fire a dissatisfied woman worker and immediately replace her at no loss of business. Excess supply of female labour held wages down to such a low level that the Factory Acts did not affect an insolent employer too adversely. Wayne Roberts[72] reports a case in a Toronto laundry where women complained about violations of factory legislation to an inspector. The employer fired them and was "let off with a two dollar fine".

This lack of bargaining power in a closely regimented workplace and without any control over their labour process did not give any inducement to women to job commitment. On the contrary it led to high turnover as in domestic service.

(c) *Domestic Mode of Production of Labour Power*

A third barrier to women's unionization in Canada was the domestic mode of production of labour power. As Table 2A appended to Chapter 2 shows, women constituted 13.4 percent of the labour force in 1911 and increased only to 15.4 percent in 1921. Women constituted an insignificant portion of the labour force. Although on the rise steadily, women's participation in the labour market would not be a major factor until the middle of the century. We have also seen that throughout the twenties, women workers were single but for a few "unfortunates". Women had to stay in the home after marriage. A good deal of the explanatory burden of this phenomenon has been laid on the back of the sex-role ideology. But ideology does not hang in the air, disconnected from the economic base. It cannot be totally separated from the dominant mode of production—capitalism.

While generalized commodity production was the rule, rather than the exception, during the twenties in Canada, labour power, called the "peculiar commodity" by Marx, was not then, and not even today, produced capitalistically, i.e., under the capitalist mode of production. The production of this commodity was the responsibility of the household, the domestic sphere. The ideology of male dominance, patriarchy, may explain this up to a point, but only to a point. We shall argue, in the sequel, that the dialectic of capital is largely responsible for this.

In any case, during this early phase of Canadian capitalism, labour power was produced more or less under the auspices of the household. Public involvement through the social sectors, education, health, welfare, etc., were of a rudimentary nature at that time. The housewife/mother, with primitive birth control methods and domestic technology, had to shoulder an enormous responsibility in the survival of an ever-growing family. She did not have the time available to combine paid labour with domestic labour at this stage of development of capitalism.

Female labour thus changed every few years as new generations of women assumed family responsibilities and got "hidden in the household". This constant turnover of women workers was a barrier to unionization. A constantly changing work-force has an extremely hard time maintaining a union. With only a few years in the labour force, women were denied the opportunity of building up a collective ethos, passing on experience and knowledge of labour relations to the next generation and thereby developing a history of action by labour. Wayne Roberts[73] commented:

Unlike working women of today who can evaluate their experiences in terms of widespread public discussion on the status of women and who can draw inspiration, clarity and legitimacy from a generalized movement, working women before 1916 operated in an ideological vacuum.... They were a small detachment who could not share in the process of reevaluating sexual standards with any substantial core of the population.

(d) Cultural-linguistic Barriers

Due to the unskilled nature of the female work-force, it continually attracted immigrants and rural migrants to the city. There were, as a result, cultural, linguistic and ethnic diversities that acted as a hindrance to collective action. In 1911, 24 percent of the women in gainful occupations in Canada and 58 percent of the domestics in Toronto were immigrants.[74] Far from pushing towards solidarity, this imported competition in the face of an already abysmally low wage turned the Canadian-born women against the immigrants and the earlier immigrants against the later ones. Thus, the ethnic-cultural-linguistic heterogeneity served as institutional barriers to unionization.

(e) *Employer Opposition*

Capitalists were interested in cheap supplies of labour power and, as such, opposed unionization of any kind, male or female. In the early phase of accumulation with labour-intensive technologies, capitalists fought unionization tooth and nail. Anti-union techniques included firing pro-union workers, blacklisting workers so that they could not get jobs anywhere, lockouts and hiring workers signing a "yellow-dog contract"—agreeing not to join unions.[75] Such methods were supported by courts and enforced by the police.

In this discouraging climate for unionization, women workers were more closely regimented than men. They were constantly supervised and penalized for small infractions. They were constantly reminded by these measures of their vulnerability and powerlessness. Roberts[76] says:

> Although employers found this punishment impossible to impose on men, the practice of fining women workers for laughing, talking, using toilet-paper, hair-curlers, or damaging work was common, especially in the early years of industrialism.

Roberts[77] records an incident in 1905 of an employer intending to install a clock timed to the half-second, by which the women workers would lose a half-hour's pay for being one minute late.

Such harassment was not confined to factory workers; female teachers were equally subject to surveillance of their morals, religion, dress and personal habits. In 1895, the Toronto School Board "dutifully" met to discuss the case of a woman teacher who was found wearing bloomers while riding a bicycle and decided not to hire women who chewed gum.[78]

Such methods of suppressing "insubordination" acted as major labour-market barriers to female unionization. Regardless of the patriarchal values of the capitalists, economic self-interest must have been their primary motivation in opposing unionization. Capitalists did their best to control the labour process so that their profit and their rule could be ensured. Division in the ranks of the proletariat through a hierarchical system of division of labour was the weapon they discovered for this purpose. This system achieved two goals for capital at one stroke. On the one hand, it stood in the way of workers cementing bonds of solidarity; on the other, it raised the productivity of each worker who now specialized in one job unlike under the craft system where he produced the entire product. In this job division, women were placed at the bottom. In the department stores, for example, work was finely divided and women were assigned the jobs considered least skilled and hence least paid. In the second half of the nineteenth century, education was expanded by introducing the "grading system". Teaching of lower grades required lower skills and hence commanded lower pay,[79] and women were assigned to these lower grades.

This "caste system" in teaching and retail trade worked against creation of bonds of solidarity both among the ranks of the teachers and among the retail workers. Similarly, in the garment industry, the women were divided into dressmakers, seamstresses, tailoresses and milliners, each category insulated from the other and hence hard to organize and easy to exploit.

(f) Trade Union Discrimination

Yet another institutional barrier was trade union discrimination. Trade unions from the last quarter of the nineteenth century through the 1930's were on the one hand craft unions and, on the other, international unions based in the United States. These two characteristics of the union movement profoundly affected women workers. The craft unions were organized by the skilled labour (mechanics) before the introduction of the factory system employing cheap unskilled labour. The very basis of the bargaining power of these workers was that they could not be easily replaced. Restricting access to such crafts was consequently an integral part of the strategy of maintaining this bargaining power and was a central tenet of craft unionism. Admitting unskilled workers, hence women, into those unions was for the craftsmen a self-defeating proposition.

We have seen in our discussion of the United States situation how the National Typographical Union opposed in 1854 the apprenticeship of women. In 1865, this very union issued charters to Canadian typographical unions[80] and the International Typographical Union arose. Although we have no direct evidence of how this international union treated the Canadian women workers in printing, it is highly unlikely that they were treated differently from their sisters south of the border. At the Trades and Labour Congress of Canada[81] in 1902, an amendment to the constitution was adopted which stated that no national union would be recognized where an international existed. This amendment effectively undermined the development of a national labour movement. White[82] says that, in 1912, 85 percent of Canadian unionists belonged to the international unions; the figure dropped to 71 percent in 1921. All these internationals were affiliated to the American Federation of Labour (AFL) and, as Alice Kessler-Harris[83] documented, the AFL failed to support and organize women workers in America. Hence, as a corollary, they failed to do so in Canada.

The unions were torn between the prevailing sex-role ideology and their role of defending worker interests against employers. This led them to an ambivalent position consisting of two lines of action:

(a) oppose inclusion of new women in the work-force, and
(b) defend those women who are already in it.

According to the first line, women were encouraged to contribute to the union movement either through the *label campaign* or *women's auxiliaries*. The label campaign promoted the purchase of goods with a union label indicating that the goods were made by unionized workers; it was intended to pressure employers to permit unionization while penalizing non-union enterprises. Auxiliaries supported men's unions and organized social activities.

The unions openly advocated the exclusion of women. The Trades and Labour Congress of Canada[84] in 1898 called for the "abolition of child labour by children under 14 years of age and of female labour in all branches of industrial life, such as mines, workshops, factories, etc." The AFL, to which most Canadian Unions were affiliated, took the same position. In 1905, its treasurer[85] said: "The great principle for which we fight is opposed to taking ... the women from their homes to put them in the factory and the sweatshop." AFL president Samuel Gompers[86] explained the economic reasons for this exclusion: "It is the so-called competition of the unorganized defenseless woman worker, the girl and the wife, that often tends to reduce the wages of the father and the husband."

This competition from women was real. With industrialization, cheap unskilled female labour became the basis of the employer's profit. Since skill *per se* was not as important in the factory system as it was in the small workshop or the manufactory, unskilled women became competitive with the skilled mechanics and thereby lowered the latter's wages. Men could not support their families with the wages they got, so they succumbed to the competition of the single women, who supported themselves at lower wages. A member[87] of the United Garment Workers wrote in the "Weekly Bulletin of the Clothing Trades" in June 1905:

It is the men who suffer through the women who are employed in the manufacture of clothing. While the men through long years of struggle have succeeded in eliminating the contracting evil and the rotten system of piece work, the girls are now trying to deprive the older members of the Garment Workers of the benefits because [they]...can afford to work for small wages and care nothing about the condition of the trade.

The "contracting evil" here refers to work in the small-shop on contract and "piece-work" to women's work at home under subcontract. The paternalistic statement about "the condition of the trade" has no explicit suggestion for the maintenance of the single woman "liberated" from the contracting evil and the rotten system of piece-work. Its logical implication, however, is a "family wage" because the implied way in which women can "care" about the "condition of the trade" is by withdrawing from the market and cancelling their competition with men. Women's support has to come, therefore, from a family wage.

The threat to men's jobs and wages came from women during the war, as we have seen. Women could do men's work, sometimes better, and at lower wages. Alarmed by this threat, the *B.C. Federationist*,[88] the journal of the British Columbia Federation of Labour stated:

Women have worked for less than men ... and women will continue to work for less than men. Employers have had a taste of cheap labour and will be loath to part with their feminine employees at the close of the war.... The "heroes" will have to accept employment at such work and wages as the employers see fit to give. The work of the trade unions will have to [be] done all over again.

This "work of the trade union" was "done all over again" by advocating exclusion of women from the labour force; the lip service to the prevailing ideology of women's place at home came, hereby, to combat competition from women. While advocating exclusion of women from the labour force in male self-interest, the trade unionists had also to discharge their historical duty of defending workers' interest against the employers. So the women workers already in the labour force and without any intention of leaving it had to be given some support, however half-heartedly and even before the war. The women's column of the *Tribune*,[89] a Toronto labour paper, said in 1905:

Ideas, like conditions, are changing and the old idea that woman must confine her attention entirely to the home and the raising of children is fast becoming a thing of the past.

The 1902 constitution of the Toronto and District Labour Council[90] included in its programme "equal pay, civil and political rights for men and women, and the abolition of all law discrimination against women." In 1914, the Trades and Labour Congress of Canada[91] replaced its call for the exclusion of women from the work-force with "equal pay for equal work for men and women". In specific instances, the union movement, local unions or groups of male unionists did support women workers. For instance, in an organizing meeting in 1897, the journeymen tailors made a reference to organizing women.[92] In 1907, during the Toronto Bell Telephone strike, bell-boys at a local hotel refused to work when strike-breakers stayed there and forced the scabs to move elsewhere. In 1912, a strike by women boot and shoe workers over pay reduction was supported by the union. As women were replacing men during the war, the Canadian Trades and Labour Congress[93] stated:

Equal pay for women employed in work usually done by men, as men are or were receiving for the same work, will be insisted upon.

While policy statements like those mentioned above might have favoured equal pay, unions in fact bargained lower increases for the already ill-paid female workers. In 1907, male bookbinders were to earn from $13.50 to $14.50 a week, while for 400 female bookbinders a scale of $5.00 per week for 1907, $5.25 per week for the second year and $5.50 for the third year was adopted. In Vancouver in 1918, the Hotel and Restaurant Employees' Union obtained a scale of $15.00 to $18.00 per week for male waiters only, an increase of 17 cents per day over the old wage.[94] Unions not only felt that women, as single workers, did not need the same wage as men, but that ultimately women should be supported by men. The *Tribune*[95] stated in 1913:

Give the male workers a decent living wage and a minimum wage for women will be unnecessary.

Now let us put this unionists' defense of women workers in perspective. Women were excluded from men's work in the secondary sector and condemned to the tertiary sector ghetto. Where men and women worked side by side in the same or roughly the same jobs, unions bargained for lower increases for women than for men as the bookbinding and restaurant examples above show, not to speak of the International Unionists' exclusionary policies reviewed in the US case earlier. Finally, a further argument is that male unionists, abandoning the feeble attempts at organizing women, turned to protective legislation for women and not for men.

(g) *Protective Legislation*

One of the results of the war was protective legislation. The war had brought women's participation in the labour market into the open. This raised considerable public concern about the treatment of working women. The National Council of Women (NCW),[96] an organization of influential and wealthy women concerned with social issues, early espoused the cause of the working girl. This espousal was consistent with its members' self-definition as Canada's "national mother", a role that suited their assumption of the responsibility for guardianship of all those who, in their eyes, need protection. They attached the issue of female workers to the broad moral and social concerns of their age. Befitting the role of guardians, they clung avowedly to the notion of the working girl's helplessness in the web of amoral forces of the then society.

In keeping with their patronizing attitudes, one important aspect of their work was the promotion of protective legislation. Their major focus was the future mother in the working girl, the sacrifice of whose health would degrade the community. As defenders of purity, morality and other qualities of wifely and motherly virtue, they were obsessed with the need for separate lavatories—one of the key goals of factory inspection. Similarly, concerned with the preservation of reproductive organs, they demanded seats for shopgirls so that they would not have to stand all day. In fairness to these ladies, they were making use of the physiological knowledge then current. As middle-class liberals, their emphasis was national morality rather than working women's economic emancipation.

The male unionists in their capacity as "defenders" of the working women found in these middle- and upper-class women's organizations an escape route from going full steam with women workers' unionization. Thus, D.J. Donahue,[97] a labour representative in Toronto, expressed to the NCW the need of some women of leisure and education to assist women workers to form benefit societies and other organizations for their help and improvement.

In British Columbia, the Royal Commission on Labour Conditions[98] invited the Vancouver Trades and Labour Council to provide suggestions on legislation for women shop and office workers. This union organization turned to the local Council of Women to form a committee. The Council recommended a minimum wage for women of only $5.00 per week although the union representative suggested $16.50. The committee also recommended seats for women workers, a female inspector and the separation of Caucasian women from Asiatics—on grounds of morality.

The protective legislation passed during the 1920's[99] included laws prohibiting for women night work, the cleaning of certain machinery and eating in the same room as that in which the manufacturing process was taking place. British Columbia was the only province that enacted a maternity protection law in 1921 which granted women six weeks of maternity leave before and after a childbirth. Women were protected from working between midnight and 6:00 a.m. and from employment in mines.

The minimum wage laws were enacted in the 1920's and boards were set up in every province to examine the existing wage rates and to recommend minimum rates for women working full time. The minimum wage was defined to be "the least sum upon which a working woman can be expected to support herself".[100]

The legislation contained, however, enough loopholes for employers to evade, and often violate, the legal provisions, as complained by the Royal Commission on Price Spreads in 1935, a decade after minimum wage legislation had been enacted in most provinces. Besides, protective legislation did not apply to farm workers, domestic servants and sweatshops—the very areas where there was a high concentration of women workers.

The issue of protective legislation was hotly debated by women in the suffrage groups and labour organizations. The suffragettes argued that protective legislation would simply segregate female labour and withhold them from certain types of work. As a matter of fact this segregation, this apartheid, already existed; protective legislation would simply legalize it. Women would not be working in equal jobs, i.e. in men's jobs, and hence would not be earning equal pay. The women in labour organizations seem to have understood this. Thus the Federation of Women's Labour Leagues, formed in 1924, favoured protective legislation, arguing that any protection against arduous working conditions was desirable.

Insofar as protective legislation provided for minimum wages for women, it was responsible for wage discrimination between male and female workers in segregated jobs. It was a legal recognition of their weakness, powerlessness, passivity, vulnerability and low bargaining power; the minimum wage was protective but did not eliminate the gap between men's and women's wages and hence tacitly gave social and legal recognition to the gap.

Before protective legislation, women were considered inherently weaker than men and hence undeserving of equal wages with men in similar jobs. This sex-role ideology was a psychological deterrent to women's militancy and organization. Protective legislation, as a legal recognition of this passivity and weakness of women, reinforced that ideology in discouraging women from unionization. It served as an added legal–institutional barrier to the already existing labour-market segregation barrier.

Protective legislation effectively excluded women from certain jobs by limiting hours: they were "protected" from working between midnight and 6:00 a.m. They were formally excluded from certain men's jobs such as mining. This, therefore, reinforced the craft union's exclusionary policy and contributed towards condemning women to non-competing job segments—the women's ghettos in the tertiary sector. Again, as an institutional barrier, protective legislation reinforces a labour-market barrier, viz. segmentation. In a word, protective legislation might have been protective of women physically and morally but certainly not economically.

(h) *Labour-Market Segmentation*

A labour market is segmented when it is divided into non-competing groups. Insofar as women have been confined to white collar tertiary sector jobs, they do not compete with men for blue collar production (manufacturing, mining, transportation, etc.) jobs. The tertiary sector jobs were new, demanding no previous union experience; besides, women workers in the pre-1930 period were a transient labour force expected to be in the labour market only until marriage and as a preparation for the ensuing family life. As such, they could not develop a job commitment and were more or less passive as far as the job was concerned. This naturally created a barrier to unionization within this newly created white collar sector.

Having presented, in a historical perspective, eight major barriers to women's participation in the labour market that hindered their unionization, we turn in the next chapter to post World War II developments in the framework of the political economy of monopoly capitalism.

REFERENCES

1. Alice Clark, *The Working Life of Women in the Seventeenth Century.*
2. Ivy Pinchbeck, *Women Workers and the Industrial Revolution.*
3. Stephen Marglin, "What Do Bosses Do? The Origins and Functions of Hierarchy in Capitalist Production", *Review of Radical Political Economics,* Vol. 6, No. 2, Summer 1974, pp. 60–112.

4. E.P. Thompson, *The Making of the English Working Class; Alice Clark*, op. cit.; Ivy Pinchbeck, op. cit.
5. B.L. Hutchins, *Women in Modern Industry*, p. 16; Olive J. Jocelyn, *English Apprenticeship and Child Labour*, pp. 149–50; Alice Clark, op. cit., Chapter 5.
6. Heidi Hartman, "Capitalism, Patriarchy, and Job Segregation" in Zillah R. Eisenstein's *Capitalist Patriarchy: The Case For Socialist Feminism*.
7. Alice Clark, op. cit.
8. Ibid., pp. 221–31.
9. Ibid., Ch. 7.
10. Pinchbeck, op. cit., p. 198; Margaret Hewitt, *Wives and Mothers in Victorian Industry*, pp. 14–ff.
11. Neil Smelser, *Social Change and the Industrial Revolution*, Chs. 9–11.
12. Ibid., p. 265.
13. Hartman, op. cit., p. 218.
14. Friedrich Engels, *The Conditions of the Working Class in England*.
15. Hartman, op. cit., p. 219.
16. Engels, op. cit., p. 251.
17. Smelser, op. cit., p. 301.
18. Pinchbeck, op. cit., pp. 312–13.
19. Sidney Webb, "The Alleged Differences in the Wages Paid on Women's Work", *Economic Journal*, Vol. 2, No. 1, March 1892, pp. 172–76.
20. Millicent G. Fawcett, "Mr. Sidney Webb's Article on Women's Wages", *Economic Journal*.
21. Eleanor F. Rathbone, "The Remuneration of Women's Services", *Economic Journal*, Vol. 27, No. 1, March 1917, p. 58.
22. Ibid., p. 64.
23. Millicent G. Fawcett, "Equal Pay for Equal Work", *Economic Journal*, Vol. 28, No. 1, March 1918, pp. 1–6.
24. F.Y. Edgeworth, "Equal Pay to Men and Women for Equal Work", *Economic Journal*, Vol., 32, No. 4, December 1922, p. 439.
25. Laura Oren, "The Welfare of Women in Labouring Families: England 1860–1950", *Feminist Studies*, Vol. 1, No. 3–4, Winter–Spring, 1973, pp. 107–25.
26. Hartman, op. cit., p. 223.
27. Edith Abbott, *Women in Industry*; Elizabeth F. Baker, *Technology and Women's Work*.
28. Ibid., Ch. 4.
29. Ibid., Ch. 2.
30. Ibid., p. 207.
31. Ibid.
32. Ibid., p. 92.
33. Harry Braverman, *Labor and Monopoly Capital*, Ch. 3–5.
34. Margery Davies, "Women's Place Is at the Typewriter" in Richard Edwards *et al.*, eds. *Labour Market Segmentation*.
35. Abbott, op. cit., p. 197.
36. Ibid., p. 199.

37. Ibid., p. 207.
38. Ibid.; Baker, op. cit.; Gail Falk, "Women's Rights." *Law Reporter*, Vol. 1, Spring 1973, pp. 54–66.
39. Abbott, op. cit., pp. 252–53.
40. Baker, op. cit., pp. 39–40.
41. Falk, op. cit.
42. Abbott, op. cit.
43. Baker, op. cit., p. 419.
44. Falk, op. cit.
45. William O'Neill, *Everyone Was Brave*, Ch. 3; William H. Chafe, *The American Woman*.
46. Barbara A. Babcock, Ann F. Friedman, Eleanor H. Norton and Susan C. Ross, *Sex Discrimination and the Law*.
47. Ibid., p. 32.
48. Ann C. Hill, "Protective Labor Legislation for Women" in Babcock *et al.*, op. cit.
49. Ibid.
50. Ibid.
51. Janice Acton, Penny Goldsmith and Bonnie Shepard eds., *Women at Work: Ontario 1850–1930*.
52. Leo Johnson, "The Political Economy of Ontario Women in the Nineteenth Century" in Amy Curthoys' *Women at Work*, pp. 13–31.
53. Ibid., p. 29.
54. This section draws on the data given in: Ceta Ramkhalawansingh, "Women during the Great War" in Amy Curthoys' *Women at Work*, op. cit., pp. 261–307; and Patricia Connelly, *Last Hired First Fired: Women and the Canadian Labour Force*.
55. Ramkhalawansingh, Ibid., p. 272.
56. Ibid. pp. 274–75.
57. Enid M. Price, *Changes in the Industrial Occupations of Women in the Environment of Montreal during the Period of the War, 1914–1918*.
58. Ramkhalawansingh, op. cit., p. 278.
59. Ibid., pp. 288–90.
60. Marjorie MacMurchy, *The Canadian Girl at Work*.
61. *Report of the Ontario Commission on Unemployment*, 1916, p. 59.
62. MacMurchy, op. cit., p. 47.
63. *Wages and Hours of Labour*, Department of Labour, Canada, 1914, p. 27; Ramkhalawansingh, op. cit., pp. 267–69, 279.
64. Ibid., pp. 293, 302.
65. Jack Williams, *Unions in Canada*, London: pp. 2–3.
66. Julie White, *Women and Unions*, p. 1.
67. Ibid., p. 1.
68. Quoted in Julie White, ibid., p. 3.
69. Ramkhalawansingh, op. cit., pp. 285–86.
70. White, op. cit., p. 4.
71. Ibid., p. 6.
72. Wayne Roberts, *Honest Womanhood*, p. 17.

73. Ibid., pp. 10–11.
74. White, op. cit., p. 9.
75. Ibid., p. 10.
76. Roberts, op. cit., p. 49.
77. Ibid., p. 40.
78. White, op. cit., p. 10.
79. Ibid., p. 11.
80. Williams, op. cit., p. 11.
81. White, op. cit., p. 14.
82. Ibid.
83. Alice Kessler-Harris, "Where are the Organized Women Workers?" *Feminist Studies*, Vol. 3, Nos. 1–2, Fall 1975.
84. White, op. cit., p. 15.
85. Kessler-Harris, op. cit., p. 97.
86. Ibid., p. 96.
87. Quoted in White, op. cit., p. 16.
88. Quoted in White, Ibid., p. 16.
89. Cited in White, Ibid., p. 18.
90. Ibid., p. 18.
91. Ibid.
92. Ibid.
93. Ibid., p. 19.
94. Ibid.
95. Ibid.
96. Alice Klein and Wayne Roberts, "Besieged Innocence: The 'Problem' and Problems of Working Women, Toronto, 1896–1914"., in Linda Kealey *Women at Work*, pp. 214–15.
97. Ibid., p. 220
98. White, op. cit., p. 17.
99. Ramkhalawansingh, op. cit., 297–301.
100. White, op. cit., p. 18.

Chapter 5
Monopoly Capital and the Post World War II Problematique

THE SECOND WORLD WAR repeated in Canada what happened in the First World War so far as women's paid employment was concerned. Large numbers of women joined the labour force to replace the men who were in the armed forces and to fill the new jobs created during the war. The female participation rate rose from 24.4 percent in 1939 to 33.2 percent in 1945.[1] This increase in women's participation created once again the same sort of problems as arose in the aftermath of the First World War. The federal government created a subcommittee to make recommendations on women's post Second World War problems. The committee predicted that these would be solved either by the return of women to home and farm or by their entrance into new jobs in the trades and service sector, public administration and new industries. They recommended the introduction of family allowances payable to women and the training of household workers. Other initiatives such as the federal civil service regulations restricting the employment of married women also set a brake to women's continuing labour-market participation. By 1946, just one year after the war, the women's participation rate had dropped to 25.3 percent as woman after woman left the work-force to "hide in the household".

While there have always been some women in the labour force, there has been a dramatic increase in the number of women working for pay or profit since the early 1950's. In spite of this increase, women remain segregated in the least attractive and lowest paid jobs. As in the earlier part of the present century, women are now doing the same sort of wage work; only their number has increased but the segregation has continued. This change (increase) in participation and lack of change in segregation has to be understood, as we shall try to do in the sequel, in terms of the overall nature of the economic development process in Canada and in the capitalist world as a whole. There have been considerable shifts in industries and occupations along with the phenomenal growth in female labour force participation. But the segregation of women in specific industries and occupations characterized by low skill, low pay, low productivity and low prospects for advancement has been the stable feature of women's paid work throughout the century. We need to understand the structural changes in the Canadian economy (the shifts in industrial and occupational compositions), the kind of jobs that these changes have offered to women (the demand for women's labour power) and reasons why women have accepted these offers (supply of women's labour power).

1. Structural Changes in the Canadian-cum-world Capitalism

Broadly speaking, the nineteenth century represented the first stage of English capitalism after the transition from feudalism was completed by the end of the eighteenth century. This first stage was that of competitive capitalism. From the latter quarter of the nineteenth century, English capitalism assumed its modern monopoly stage. Other capitalist countries including Canada have also undergone this two-stage historical motion. Canada fell under the sway of United States monopoly capitalism in the last quarter of the nineteenth century as a result of MacDonald's national policy. Marx[2] was the theorist of the first (competitive) stage of capitalism. Taking the cue from Hilferding,[3] Lenin[4] set the stage for the study of the second phase and was followed, after a long interval, by Sweezy–Baran[5] and Braverman.[6]

At the competitive phase, the various forms of capital—money capital, commercial capital and industrial capital—had somewhat independent, autonomous existences. The commercial capitalists and industrial capitalists often enough were the same people but they rarely formed an interlocked group with the money capitalists. The latter gradually gained prominence to become what Hilferding called *finance capitalists*. With the rise of finance capital, came the cartels and combines that, as Lenin saw, gave rise to the phase of monopoly capitalism (imperialism), the system that created the global market and international capital.

It is the internal organization of monopoly capital that is of interest to us insofar as women's questions are concerned. Under monopoly capitalism, the various forms of capital—money capital (finance and banking), commercial capital (department store chains) and industrial capital (giant corporate manufacturing)—are integrated through ownership of equity in each other's empires. As capital concentrates, fewer and fewer firms dominate the market. The giant corporation is characterized by (a) heavy capital investment per worker, (b) high labour productivity, (c) growing control over a complex production-cum-marketing network, sometimes through vertical integration (from raw material production to retailing), and (d) take-over of firms with single industries (horizontal integration) and across industries (conglomerates and holding companies). Some of these giants are multinational corporations dominating the world market. One of the peculiarities of monopoly capitalism is that it does not eliminate small firms; in fact, thousands of small firms co-exist with the giants but they are allowed only a small share of the market.

By 1965, while there were over 170,000 corporations in Canada, as well as many thousands of unincorporated individual proprietary concerns active in business, the 174 largest corporations held 50 percent of total corporate assets (Canada, Department of Consumer and Corporate Affairs, 1971: 3). There are foreign-based (American) giant multinationals with branch plants in Canada. The dominant Canadian corporations operating on a national, if not international, scale are price-makers and not price-takers. Through corporate planning they are able to neutralize quite a bit of the instability of the market to which the earlier competitive capitalism was a regular victim.

The monopoly sector firms often provide the best-paying jobs because, on the one hand, worker-productivity is high due to higher capital investment per worker and, on the other, because, as price-makers, they can pass on cost increases to the consumer. The strong unions in this sector and the collective bargaining process also contribute to its high wage levels. The resulting cost-push leads to higher prices, the burden of which falls on the back of the consumer. However, the clerical and sales workers in this sector, most of whom are women, are by-passed in wage negotiations. The industries in this sector, notably mining, oil and gas production, forestry, utilities, and parts of manufacturing, have not been substantial creators of new jobs. Between 1961 and 1974, only 34.0 percent of the new jobs were created in mining, quarries and oil wells, forestry, utilities, finance, insurance and real estate, and manufacturing, and not all the firms in these industries were in the monopoly sector. Of the new jobs, 39.2 percent were created in the service industries alone and another 17.8 percent in trade (Canada, Economic Council of Canada, 1976: 98).

A second feature of monopoly capitalism is that the monopoly sector does not account for the entire economy. Certain lines of production are organized competitively. Historically, most of the industries established in the earlier competitive phase fall under the domination of a few giant firms. A second development accompanying the rise of monopoly capitalism is the phenomenal expansion of the service and trade industries which were inadequately developed in the phase of competitive capitalism. However, their competitive character is not lost in the process of this expansion. They continue to be characterized by relatively low capital investment, and hence low productivity, per worker, by low pay and by the absence of unions. As we have seen, in terms of job creation these two industries alone were responsible for 57 percent of the new jobs in Canada between 1961 and 1974. Most of the construction industry in Canada is in the competitive sector and so are the agriculture, fishing and trapping industries. In the 1961–74 period, the construction industry provided 7.4 percent of the new jobs while agriculture, fishing and trapping together accounted by 1974, for a loss of 6.5 percent of the 1961 jobs (Canada, Economic Council of Canada, ibid.). There have been substantial productivity gains in construction where pay is now relatively high and where unions are strong. Though most of the construction industry is competitive, there are some very large firms enjoying some monopoly power.

A third feature of monopoly capitalism is BIG GOVERN-MENT. If "anarchy of production" and *laissez-faire* are the major characteristics of competitive capitalism, then "planning" and intervention by government are the hallmarks of monopoly capitalism, so much so that government becomes the "Committee of the Oligopolists". As a result, employment has grown rapidly in the state sector. In public administration alone, 8.3 percent of the new jobs were created during the period 1961–74 (Canada, Economic Council of Canada, ibid.). Public administration, state education and hospitals together accounted for 34 percent of the new jobs in the same period.[7] Rates of pay in this sector are higher than in the competitive sector for two reasons: the rise and militancy of state sector unions, and the ability of the government to meet the extra labour costs through increased taxation.

The phenomenal rise in women's paid work, after World War II, has happened in the competitive (mainly service and trade) and state sectors, not in the monopoly sector. Why has this been so? To answer this question, the concepts of the "reserve army of labour" and market segmentation have to be invoked. The former was used vaguely, here and there, in women's studies but it is Patricia Connelly[8] who first systematically applied it to the Canadian scene, following a lead from Braverman.[9] Let us now examine these issues.

2. *Reserve Labour*

In the process of capital accumulation, a surplus population of labourers emerges. Through what Marx called "relative surplus value", the extraction of more surplus labour within the fixed length of the working day becomes possible. Necessary labour decreases because, with rising labour productivity, workers can produce in a lesser time their subsistence needs in order to reproduce their labour power. This is made possible by the rising organic composition of capital. True enough, variable capital (employment of labour) increases but not as fast as constant capital. This causes the relative redundancy of a portion of the population—Marx's "reserve army of labour". Increasing numbers of workers are replaced by modern machinery and thrown into this reserve army.

The reserve army is not simply a consequence of capital accumulation; it is also a necessary condition for accumulation. Capital needs it. As Marx[10] put it: "If a surplus labouring population is a necessary product of accumulation or of the development of wealth on a capitalist basis, this surplus population becomes, conversely, the lever of capitalistic accumulation, nay, a condition of existence of the capitalist mode of production."

How does this need for surplus population as a condition of existence of the capitalist mode of production arise? The capitalist mode of production is characterized by "uneven development"; the capitalist must constantly be prepared to move into new lines of production as the opportunity arises. To make this possible he must have a large mass of labourers available for being drawn into new areas rather than having to displace workers from existing areas. As Marx[11] has it, as capital expands, it

thrusts itself frantically into old branches of production, whose market suddenly expands, or into newly formed branches, such as railways etc., the need for which grows out of the development of the old ones. In all such cases, there must be the possibility of throwing great masses of men suddenly on the decisive points without injury to the scale of production in other spheres.

The reserve army is created by making capital-intensive inventions and innovations and thereby rendering sections of the labour force relatively redundant. According to Marx,[12] the reserve army regulates wages in this way:

> The industrial reserve army, during the periods of stagnation and average prosperity, weighs down the active labour-army; during the periods of overproduction and paroxysm, it holds its pretensions in check. Relative surplus population is therefore the pivot upon which the law of demand and supply of labour works. It confines the field of action of this law within the limits absolutely convenient to the activity of exploitation and to the domination of capital.

During the period of "stagnation and average prosperity", there is an abundance of labour relative to constant capital and the reserve army presses wages down and thereby induces the employed labour to struggle only to protect their jobs rather than their wages. In times of expansion and "overproduction and paroxysm", the reserve army is drawn down as a result of the capitalists' increased need for labour power. This causes wages to rise and threatens profit. The capitalists now guard themselves, according to Marx,[13] as follows: "a smaller part of revenue is capitalized, accumulation lags, and the movement of rise in wages receives a check."

This means that Department I (machinery producing sector) suffers a cut-back and labour force employed in that sector now begins to join the reserve army. The newly unemployed cannot maintain, any longer, their earlier levels of consumption. This reduced level of demand for consumer goods causes a cut-back in Department II (consumer goods sector). The laid-off workers from this sector now join the reserve army. A chain reaction is thus set in motion.

Marx talked about three forms of the reserve army of labour: floating, latent and stagnant. The floating form is to be found in the centres of industry. Labour-replacing innovations and technical progress embodied in new machinery renders a part

of the work-force redundant. The displaced workers now join
the reserve army. The latent form is found in agriculture. With
the introduction of capitalist forms of production and
machinery, farm workers are displaced. The displaced labour
moves out of the farm areas and into the cities looking for
work. The stagnant form consists of those whose employment
is "extremely irregular". "It is characterized by maximum of
working-time and minimum of wages."[14] Due to its irregular
employment, the stagnant portion of the reserve army "fur-
nishes to capital an inexhaustible reservoir of disposable
labour power. Its conditions of life sink below the average
normal level of the working class; this makes it at once the
broad basis of special branches of capitalist exploitation."[15]

The stagnant form of the reserve army merges with the
"lowest sediment" of the surplus population—the paupers.
As Marx vividly put it, "Pauperism is the hospital of the active
labour-army and the dead weight of the industrial reserve
army... But capital knows how to throw [this weight] for the
most part, from its own shoulders onto those of the working
class and the lower middle class."[16]

We have seen that the reserve army regulates wages through
competition with the active army—by (a) being available to
work for lower wages than those prevailing during periods of
stagnation and average prosperity, and (b) being available for
employment during periods of expansion which necessarily
involve rising wages.[17]

To examine the usefulness of the concept of reserve army in
the study of the woman question, we need to study the structure of the labour market created during the monopoly stage
of capitalism.[18]

3. Segmentation

A labour market is segmented when it is composed of non-
competing groups, with each group confined to its own segment. The importance and prevalence of non-competing
groups offer the basic criticism of the competitive assumptions

of neoclassical (orthodox) economic theory.[19] An early explanation of this phenomenon was given by Adam Smith[20] and John Stuart Mill.[21] On Adam Smith's explanation of wage differentials Mill[22] wrote:

> A well known and very popular chapter in Adam Smith [*Wealth of Nations*, Book 1, Chapter 10] contains the best exposition yet given of [wage differentials].... The differences, he [Smith] says, arise partly from the policy of Europe [mercantilism], which nowhere leaves things at perfect liberty and partly from certain circumstances in the employment themselves.... First, the agreeableness or disagreeableness of the employments themselves; secondly, the easiness and cheapness, or the difficulty and expense of learning them; thirdly, the constancy or inconstancy of employment in them; fourthly, the small or great trust which may be reposed in those who exercise them; and fifthly, the probability or improbability of success in them.

The allusion to mercantilism here really means a departure from perfect competition. Smith thus makes imperfect competition one explanation of wage discrimination. The other is the nature of the employments in terms of the five characteristics listed. Adam Smith thought that an equitable principle of compensation in the presence of any one of these characteristics will cause a wage differential. The first characteristic will require a more arduous job to be paid better than a less arduous one. The second will imply that a job requiring higher skill (human capital) will be paid more than one requiring lower skill. The third characteristic will require an irregular job to be paid at a higher rate than a regular one. To this Mill[23] reacted:

> These inequalities of remuneration, which are supposed to compensate for the disagreeable circumstances of particular employments, would, under certain conditions, be natural consequences of perfectly free competition: and as between

employments of about the same grade and filled by nearly the same description of people, they are, no doubt, for the most part, realized in practice. But it is altogether a false view of the state of facts, to present this as the relation which generally exists between agreeable and disagreeable employments. The really exhausting and the really repulsive labours, instead of being better paid than others, are almost invariably paid the worst of all, because performed by those who have no choice.... The undesirable [labourers] must take what they can get. The more revolting the occupation, the more certain it is to receive the minimum of remuneration, because it devolves upon the most helpless and degraded, on those who from squalid poverty, or from want of skill and education, are rejected from all other employments. Partly from this cause, and partly from the natural and artificial monopolies, ...the inequalities of wages are generally in an opposite direction to the equitable principle of compensation erroneously represented by Adam Smith as the general law of remuneration of labour. The hardships and earnings, instead of being directly proportional, as in any just arrangements of society they would be, are generally in inverse ratio to one another.

Mill agrees that under perfect competition the compensatory wage differentials would exist in the equitable direction. But he takes Smith to task for assuming capitalism to be a regime of perfect competition. Reality was far from perfect competition as Mill saw it. This is one side of the story—the demand for labour. For non-compensatory (discriminatory) wage differentials, Mill invokes the supply of labour—the "most helpless and degraded" and "those who from squalid poverty, or from want of skill and education, are rejected from all other employments".[24] Here he is referring to what nowadays are called segmented labour markets. Today's women, for instance, with their low skill and education and restriction to the service and trade sectors, would fit in this description.

Although recognized by Mill even in his days, labour-market segmentation is particularly characteristic of monopoly capitalism. John T. Dunlop[25] and Clark Kerr[26] were the first to give prominence to the concepts of internal and external labour markets. Dunlop and Kerr viewed the growth of large firms and unions as promoting internal (within-firm) labour markets that were only weakly linked with the external (between-firm) labour markets. These two authors and others maintained a sceptical view of neoclassical models of perfect competition, the rational "economic man" and maximizing behaviour by households and firms. They believed that the complexity of the modern economy, the growing role of government regulation, and the growth of other anti-competitive institutions such as bureaucratic corporations and unions, all served to undercut whatever basis had previously existed for the application of neoclassical models of perfect competition.

The work of Dunlop and Kerr was followed by that of Thurow[27] and Thurow and Lucas[28] who opposed their "job competition" theory to the neoclassical "wage competition" theory. The main elements of their theory are: (a) the number and type of job slots are technologically determined, (b) the workers' skills and their reservation wages are almost irrelevant in determining the number and type of job positions actually filled, (c) wages are in fact rigid and queues of workers at fixed wages constitute the supply of labour, and (d) employers use screening devices to hire workers based on their trainability and adaptability. The theory emphasizes the within-firm (internal) labour market as the locus of decisions about allocations, promotions and on-the-job training—all of which are relatively insulated from the external labour markets.

Segmentation theory based on the internal (within-firm) and external (between-firm) dichotomy of the labour market has been extended to the dual labour-market (DLM) theory by Doeringer,[29] Piore,[30,31] Harrison,[32] Harrison and Sum.[33] In this theory, the economy is viewed as comprising two labour markets. The primary labour market (PLM) is characterized by unionized jobs in large firms in the monopoly sector and those in the public sector with high wages, good fringe benefits, stability, promotion possibility and job security. These jobs are also part of the internal (within-firm) labour markets. This means that only entry level jobs in a PLM setting are open to the general competition of the labour market; other jobs are filled by promotion, and thus there is an opportunity for upward mobility in terms of wages. These are the "good" jobs. The secondary labour market (SLM) contains the "dead-end" jobs which pay relatively low wages, have poor working conditions and little job stability in terms of continuous full-time work. The SLM jobs are in the residual competitive sector (trade, services, competitive manufacturing, declining industries, small-scale unorganized workplaces).

Since only the entry level jobs in the primary labour market are open to general competition, there is limited mobility from the SLM to the PLM. Once in the SLM, people thus tend to be locked into it. The SLM jobs are typically in the competitive sector of the economy. As the demand for products of this sector is highly unstable, SLM workers gradually take on the unstable work habits and tastes for work which are inimical to steady employment. For example, Piore speaks of secondary workers' "inability to show up for work regularly and on time" and of their "life patterns and role models" that "foster behavioural traits antagonistic to primary employment". Harrison points to "life styles" of SLM workers that make them "psychologically as well as technically" unable to move out of the SLM ghetto. Women, non-whites, immigrants and teenagers are disproportionately found in SLM jobs.

The key features of the DLM approach are an emphasis on the structure of demand for labour power by capitalists rather than work characteristics and workers' employment preferences. Contrary to neoclassical theory, workers are not paid according to their skill/human capital characteristics and their "marginal productivity". Wages do not equilibrate supply of and demand for labour. Internal labour markets allocate many of the jobs with insulation from the external markets. Much empirical evidence[34] has been found in support of this scenario throughout the Western world. Particularly intriguing is the DLM position that years of schooling and vocational training and other characteristics that economists associate with worker "productivity" have almost no influence on the employment prospects of large numbers of urban employees. Evidence of the ineffectiveness of both educational resources and educational achievement on income and occupational attainment has been found in many studies.[35]

These writers on segmentation have been called in-stitutionalists.[36] They see the origin of segmented labour markets in the attempts by firms and workers to insulate themselves from the inherent demand instabilities in capitalism by capturing the stable portions of markets; thus, the instability becomes concentrated in the competitive product markets and in the secondary labour markets. There is a tendency for large monopolistic firms to develop in the stable portions of the product markets and small competitive firms in the residual unstable portions. The extent of division of labour and development of technology diverge between the two sectors, dualism in the product market being transmitted to the labour market. Fluctuating or small product markets in the competitive sector limit the division of labour and restrict the development of internal markets. Unstable product demand thus fosters unstable labour demand. Entirely the opposite is obtained in the monopoly sector. The PLM/SLM division, in this approach, is also furthered by institutional factors such as industrial unions sheltering PLM workers' employment via collective bargaining and protective legisla-tion.

The institutionalists emphasize the facts of life in segmented labour markets. They have not, however, provided an analyti-cal framework for the origin and working of the segments. To say that there are stable and unstable portions of the product market and that the monopolists grab the former is to explain nothing. Where do these portions come from? Where do the monopolists originate and how do they grab the stable portions of the market?

Marxists have broached the segmentation problem via a structural-historical approach. Taking the cue from the definitive work on monopoly capital by Sweezy and Baran,[37] Harry Braverman[38] first launched a frontal attach on the labour process under capitalism and helped explain the DLM problems in fundamental terms. He locates labour-market segments in the occupational and industrial shifts brought about by monopoly capitalism itself.

Take the industries directly concerned with the fabrication of goods (manufacturing, contract construction, mining, lumbering, fishing, mechanical industries). These are the arena of typical men's jobs—production jobs. A revolution in management and production techniques has caused an unprecedented occupational shift in these industries. In pre and early capitalist epochs, the worker was a craftsman, a thinker and an actor simultaneously. The competitive phase of capitalism preserved quite a bit of this unity of conceptualization and execution in the person of the worker. With monopoly capital, this unity was ruptured; conceptualization was taken to the "office" and execution remained on the shop floor. Technical engineers, chemists, scientists, architects, draftsmen, designers—forming about 3 percent of the total labour force—were now charged with the "skill" aspect of production. The worker now became just an "operative" doing a repetitive, monotonous operation which he learnt in a brief spell of time ranging from a few hours to a few months. The old proprietor-capitalist gave way to the giant corporation managed by executives—the "company men" of Sweezy and Baran.[39] Before these executives now lies a shadow replica of the entire process of production in paper form. This brings into being, besides the technical staff, a huge clerical labour force. Since management now carries on the production process from its desktops, conducting on paper a parallel process that physically takes place on the floor, an enormous mass of record keeping and calculating comes into being. Materials, work in progress, finished inventory, labour and machinery are subject to meticulous time and cost accounting. Each step is detailed, recorded and controlled from above and worked up into reports giving a cross-sectional picture, often on a daily basis, of the production process. This work is attended to by armies of clerks with their typewriters and data processing equipment.

Monopoly capital arises through concentration of former individual capitals in a specialized stratum of the capitalist class. This institutionalization, as opposed to the personalization, of capital causes an immense growth in the scale of management operation, the first requirement of which is the engineering organization just discussed. Soon this engineering organization gives way to the marketing apparatus—the national and international marketing organizations. Sales, advertising, promotion, correspondence, orders, commissions, sales analysis, etc., are organized in departments and sub-departments, calling forth another set of armies of clerks and their bosses. One major task of the marketing apparatus is what Thorsten Veblen[40] called "quantity-production of customers", meaning assured market (induced demand) creation or reduction of the autonomous (uncertain) part of demand. To achieve this, the engineering department becomes subservient to the marketing department; styling, design, packaging, etc., become a marketing demand although done by production engineering divisions.

Apart from marketing, monopoly capital causes an overall change in the structure of management. The competitive capitalist's simple "line" organization—a direct chain of command over operations from executive head through superintendent and foremen—now gives way to a complex of "staff" organizations. Administration, a labour process conducted for the purpose of control within the corporation, becomes the keynote of the giant corporation. Here the clerk becomes the counterpart of the production worker.

A third aspect of monopoly capitalism is social coordination. As vast economic empires, the giant firms need corporate planning as a key device for calculating and monitoring the profit flow. The government becomes the "committee of the oligopolists" in the sense that these corporate plans need to be coordinated by the government through fiscal, monetary and other means. The state tries to (a) maintain "effective demand" by government expenditure, (b) defend international capital via *policing* of the *world* (permanent war mobilization), (c) manage poverty and insecurity through welfare payments, and (d) provide public services such as education, health, postal, police, prisons, etc. This last aspect (d) partly contributes to the production of the commodity, *labour power*. Through the school system now, child-rearing and socialization, tasks formerly done mainly in the pre-capitalist family, take place. A vast public sector manned by clerks and bureaucrats thereby arises to help fill the gaps in the corporate economy.

Clerical workers, both in the corporation and the state, not only come increasingly from families of factory background but more and more they are merged within the same living family—the husband a factory operative and the wife an office clerk. Both have the same general level of (secondary) education (which as we shall see later have little to do with job requirements) and a specialized dexterity in body motion to do a specialized job. The clerk belongs to the proletariat as much as the operative does.

We have talked about the occupational shift caused by the rise of the "office" both within the giant corporation and the government in the epoch of monopoly capitalism. We now turn to industrial shifts. As a result of capital accumulation, although absolute employment has increased in the goods fabricating industries, relative employment, measured as the percentage of total non-agricultural employment, has declined. More and more agricultural population also have been rendered redundant. This has been due to the labour-displacing technical progress which we earlier discussed in connection with the reserve army of labour. This "freed" population from industry and agriculture have three places to go: (a) the reserve army of labour, (b) the newly formed branches of production, and (c) the branches of "non-production". (a) and (b) are Marx's coinage as we saw earlier. Non-production is an industrial sub-sector that has arisen with monopoly capital as discussed by Sweezy and Baran.[41] It covers industries whose only function is the struggle over the allocation of the social surplus among the various segments of the capitalist class. Let us elaborate.

Monopoly capital has created the "Universal Market" and the "Service Economy".[42] Industrial capitalism began with a limited range of goods that were circulated through the market, that became commodities. The Universal Market converts all goods and an increasing number of services into commodities. Most of the jobs in the service sector are labour-intensive and less susceptible to technological change than the processes of most goods-producing industries. Thus, while relative employment in manufacturing shrinks, labour piles up in the service industries and confronts forms of pre-monopoly competition among the many firms that proliferate in these industries. This is the field of employment—"the newly formed branches of production"— which, along with clerical work, has attracted large numbers of women out of the household. The bulk of this service work is concentrated in two areas: (a) cleaning and building care, and (b) kitchen and food service. The newly formed branches of production refer essentially to these service industries.

As to "the branches of non-production", one has those (unproductive) activities that are involved in distributing the surplus value created solely by productive labour under the auspices of industrial capital, i.e., in what Marx called the "sphere of production". These activities are in the "sphere of circulation" under the auspices of commercial and financial capital. They distribute the surplus value created in the sphere of production; they themselves do not create surplus value. The profit of the commercial capitalists, the interest on financial capital, wages of labourers employed by these two latter capitals, ground rent, etc., have to be paid out of the surplus value that, in the first place, accrues to industrial capital; the balance is the profit of the industrial capitalist class. These branches of non-production were insignificant in the competitive phase of capitalism. Under monopoly capitalism, however, these are vast operations, often transnational, and employ a vast number of sales clerks, mostly women.

4. Discrimination

Discrimination in the labour market against a section of the labour force may take place in several ways. It may be effected by the employer or by a dominant group of employees or by a collusion of both against the victims. There are two basic forms of discrimination in the neoclassical economic theory: wage discrimination and job discrimination. Wage discrimination takes place when equally able (productive) workers receive unequal wages. Job or occupational discrimination occurs when different jobs (occupations) with unequal wages and other benefits are awarded to equally able workers. Let us review the basic neoclassical literature in this regard and see how far it can explain discrimination against women.

There are competitive models of wage discrimination of two types: deterministic and statistical. In the deterministic variant, a production function with only one skill level is postulated. Workers are equally able—they may vary in skin colour, sex, ethnicity, etc. Discrimination here reflects "tastes" against a group of the labourers and is effected by the employer only by paying different wages. This model has been developed by Arrow[43] and Becker.[44] Arrow also incorporated in his model the case of employee discrimination, e.g., discrimination by foremen against black floor workers. He has shown that this variant also results in an unequal wage structure and is technically similar to pure employer discrimination. Arrow's basic conclusion is that, in the long run, a discriminator will be driven out of business by non-discriminating competitors who will employ low-cost workers. Since discrimination has been a steady phenomenon, Arrow admits that the competitive model has some "limitation".

Arrow[45] and Phelps[46] developed the statistical theory of employer discrimination under competitive assumptions. The employer who seeks to maximize expected profit will discriminate against women (blacks) if he is uncertain about their qualification but believes them, for whatever reason including male chauvinism, to be less qualified than males (whites) and if the cost of gaining information about their qualification is excessive. The cost of this uncertainty (i.e., the cost of reducing this uncertainty by collecting additional information) is shifted from the employer to the affected group—women (blacks).

As to non-competitive models of wage discrimination, Milton Friedman[47] argued that discrimination tends to increase as the monopolistic powers of the producer increase but he dismissed the idea of any significant divergence from atomistic competition in any market. Similarly, Alchian and Kessel[48] suggested that discrimination by a monopolistic producer was possible if (a) the monopolist were willing to forgo money profits in order to indulge in this taste for discrimination, (b) the barriers to entry were to prevent "buying out" of the monopolists, and (c) the monopoly were regulated and money profits controlled in such a way that there was room from discrimination at no loss of profit. They also believed, like Friedman, in the general validity of atomistic competition. In other words, they are unable to explain discrimination since they deny the validity of the very assumption—monopolistic behaviour—with which they explained it in the first place. Janice F. Madden[49] has produced a model of monopsony where the employer is a monopsonist (sole buyer of labour) though he may or may not be monopolist in the product market. In her monopsony model, discrimination follows if (a) labour is divided into separate pools (males–females, for example), and (b) these labour groups have different wage elasticities of supply of labour.

As to job or occupational discrimination, the pioneer work on this is by Millicent Fawcett[50] who advanced the "over-crowding hypothesis". She contended that trade union rules, employer prejudices and social custom denied skilled occupations to women, causing overcrowding of women in unskilled occupations and thereby inducing a downward pressure on their wages. Edgeworth[51] extended this analysis by suggesting that men were unwilling to work for less than a family wage whereas females, being generally subsidized by their families and with fewer dependants, were ready to work for less. These labour supply characteristics led, under competitive assumptions, to lower wages for females. According to the "human capital" model,[52] applicable to both job and wage discrimination, the amount of market-oriented investment by females, who expect to commit less time to the labour market, is less than that of males. As such female productivity, and hence wages, will be less.

All these neoclassical models are based on the premise that labour, as a "factor of production", is paid its marginal productivity. This red herring of neoclassical economic theory, the marginal productivity theory of distribution, has long been the subject of empirical-institutional criticism as we saw in the last section. Besides, the production function itself is not a very operational notion. As a matter of fact, there are a finite number of techniques of production available to a firm. This factor alone makes the notion of marginal physical product nebulous. Furthermore, in order to compute marginal productivity, i.e., the value of the marginal physical product, the price of the product must be known. But in the world of imperfect foresight and uncertainty, how would the price be known to the firm? In real life, therefore, the wages paid to the workers are determined by institutional factors mainly, and not by any general theory which can be routinely applied by a firm.

Even if the marginal productivity theory is accepted for the sake of argument, there is a fundamental inadequacy in the neoclassical discrimination theory. As we have seen, most of this theory concerns a given employer who discriminates between, say, two groups of workers. It is discrimination within the same firm, whether wage-based or occupation-based. While this kind of intra-firm discrimination indeed exists, what concerns women most is their confinement to the low-paying secondary market segment in contrast to the high-paying primary segment. As a matter of fact, even if there is no intra-firm discrimination, it is the primary–secondary wage differential resulting from industrial segregation and sex-typing that is at the heart of the women question. This is the very point that neoclassical theory evades because of its inability to recognize the very existence of the phenomenon of market segmentation, which stems from its original inability to recognize anything but atomistic competition.

With these theoretical underpinnings regarding the reserve army, segmentation and discrimination, we now examine the Canadian scene.

5. The Canadian Scene

5.1 Occupational and industrial shifts

Let us first examine the DLM structure in Canada by documenting the occupational and industrial shifts that have taken place in Canada since World War II. We first define two concepts introduced by Armstrong and Armstrong.[53] Consider the percentage of all workers in a given occupation (industry) that are females. Let us call this percentage the "degree of sex-typing" (DST) in that occupation (industry). If this percentage or degree exceeds 50, then the occupation (industry) will be called a female occupation (industry); if the degree is less than 50, the occupation (industry) will be designated a male one. We now define the "degree of female concentration" (DFC) in a given occupation (industry) to be the percentage of all female workers that are in the given occupation (industry). We wish to build up time series data of these key variables, DST and DFC, so as to be able to identify the historical pattern of the ghettoization of women accompanying the occupational and industrial shifts that Canada has experienced.

Table 5A in the Appendix at the end of this chapter gives the degree of sex-typing for selected years in the period 1948–81 in each of thirteen occupations: managerial, professional, clerical, transportation, communication, commercial, financial, service, agriculture, primary occupations, manufacturing and technical trades, construction, labourers and unskilled workers. Next, Table 5B gives the degree of sex-typing for selected years in the period 1946–81 in each of the following industry groups: agriculture, primary, manufacturing, construction, transportation-communication-public utilities, trade-commerce, finance-insurance-real estate, service and public administration. While these two tables directly give the degree of sex-typing, they do not give the degree of female concentration. We, therefore, calculate the latter by combining these two tables with Table 2A of the Appendix to Chapter 2. Table 2A gives the total number of female workers in the labour force while Tables 5A and 5B give the total number of female workers in each occupation and industry, respectively. Expressing these latter occupation-specific and industry-specific female work-force as percentage of the total female labour force of Table 2A, we get the degree of female concentration in each occupation (industry). In Table 5.1 below, we collect the figures for the degree of concentration and degree of sex-typing in each occupation. Similarly, in Table 5.2, the data on the degree of concentration and the degree of sex-typing in each industry are assembled.

Table 5.1 shows what kind of work women do in the labour market. Clerical work is found to be the occupation with the highest female concentration. The degree of female concentration in this occupation has increased from 25.9 in 1949 to 33.6 in 1981 on a more or less rising path. It is unmistakably the number one female job with the degree of sex-typing increasing from 56.3 in 1949 to 78.3 in 1981 along a rising trend. The second-ranking female occupation is service, with the degree of sex-typing rising from 50.4 in 1949 to 55.4 in 1981. The degree

Table 5.1: FEMALE CONCENTRATION AND SEX-TYPING IN OCCUPATIONS, CANADA, 1949–81 (selected years)

Year	Managerial 1		Professional 2		Clerical 3		Transportation 4		Communication 5		Commercial 6	
	DFC	DST	DFC	DST	DFC	DST	DFC	DST	DFC	DST	DFC	DST
1949	3.8	11.2	9.9	36.1	25.9	56.3	-	-	2.4	40.9	12.4	41.4
1951	3.9	10.9	10.3	35.3	27.7	56.7	-	-	2.5	43.5	11.6	41.8
1953	3.5	8.5	13.2	40.7	27.8	58.0	-	-	3.3	47.0	11.4	39.7
1958	3.6	10.7	13.2	38.2	29.7	62.8	-	-	2.4	42.4	10.4	39.0
1960	3.4	11.1	15.5	42.5	28.5	62.1	-	-	2.3	40.9	10.6	40.3
1963	3.5	11.0	14.6	40.4	29.2	63.7	-	-	1.8	57.9	8.7	35.3
1967	3.6	12.4	16.8	43.1	29.9	67.8	-	-	1.5	55.4	8.1	38.3
1972	4.0	14.3	16.5	41.2	31.2	72.0	-	-	1.2	50.0	7.6	38.8
1974	2.5	16.0	17.7	47.0	32.2	73.0	0.3	2.8	-	-	9.1	32.3
1975	3.1	18.6	18.5	48.3	33.4	74.9	0.3	3.1	-	-	9.6	33.9
1980	4.4	25.2	17.4	49.3	31.7	78.2	0.5	5.7	-	-	9.5	39.6
1981	5.2	27.7	18.3	49.8	33.6	78.3	0.6	6.1	-	-	9.9	40.2

Year	Service		Agriculture		Manufacturing Mechanical Trades		Construction		Labourers and Unskilled Workers		DOG
	DFC 7	DST	DFC 8	DST	DFC 9	DST	DFC 10	DST	DFC 11	DST	12
1949	16.8	50.4	11.8	11.8	15.0	18.8	-	-	-	-	65.0
1951	17.3	51.0	8.4	9.9	15.8	20.4	-	-	-	-	66.9
1953	18.8	51.9	4.2	5.5	14.8	19.0	-	-	0.9	3.6	71.2
1958	20.6	55.3	3.8	7.5	11.8	17.3	-	-	0.8	3.5	73.9
1960	21.2	56.2	2.7	6.6	10.9	17.0	-	-	0.9	4.3	75.8
1963	21.9	57.8	-	-	12.4	14.6	-	-	0.9	5.5	74.4
1967	22.0	59.3	-	-	11.5	14.1	-	-	0.9	6.7	76.8
1972	20.2	59.1	2.3	14.1	10.4	14.9	-	-	1.0	8.8	75.5
1974	16.3	51.4	2.1	14.7	10.3	18.2	-	-	-	-	75.3
1975	15.3	49.4	2.8	20.2	9.1	18.1	-	-	-	-	76.8
1980	16.6	54.0	2.6	23.1	8.6	19.1	0.2	1.2	-	-	75.2
1981	18.7	55.4	2.7	24.2	9.6	20.2	0.2	1.3	-	-	80.5

NOTE: For primary occupations, these values of DFC and DST, available for 1981 only, are 0.1 and 2.0, respectively.

DOG = Sum of DFC of (a) Service, (b) Clerical, (c) Professional and (d) Commercial
    = degree of occupational ghettoization.

SOURCE: Derived from Table 5A.

Table 5.2: FEMALE CONCENTRATION AND SEX-TYPING IN INDUSTRY, CANADA, 1949-81 (selected years)

Year	Agriculture 1		Primary Industries 2		Manufacturing 3		Construction 4		Transportation Communication Public Utilities 5	
	DFC	DST	DFC	DST	DFC	DST	DFC	DST	DFC	DST
1949	11.8	11.8	-	-	23.2	19.8	-	-	4.0	10.9
1951	8.4	10.0	-	-	23.2	20.2	-	-	4.3	11.1
1953	4.2	5.6	-	-	23.3	19.7	-	-	4.5	11.1
1958	3.8	7.6	-	-	19.5	19.7	0.8	2.6	4.2	12.3
1960	2.8	6.8	-	-	17.9	19.7	0.7	2.8	4.1	13.0
1963	-	-	-	-	17.8	21.5	-	-	4.7	14.7
1965	3.4	15.0	-	-	22.5	23.8	1.2	4.7	6.2	16.7
1967	3.0	13.1	-	3.2	16.8	22.7	0.8	3.8	4.1	14.6
1972	2.5	15.6	-	-	14.8	23.6	0.8	4.8	3.8	15.3
1974	2.2	16.1	0.3	5.2	14.1	24.2	0.9	5.4	3.9	17.1
1975	2.9	22.2	-	-	12.5	24.4	1.1	6.6	4.1	18.3
1980	2.7	26.4	0.6	10.1	12.2	26.8	1.2	8.7	4.0	20.8
1981	2.9	27.6	0.8	10.8	13.3	27.8	1.4	8.9	4.4	22.4

| Year | Trade Commerce | | Finance Insurance Real Estate | | Service | | Public Administration | | DIG |
	DFC 6	DST	DFC 7	DST	DFC 8	DST	DFC 9	DST	10
1949	18.4	31.9	5.4	42.0	34.6	45.5	-	-	-
1951	19.2	32.2	5.9	44.6	36.2	45.3	-	-	-
1953	20.1	29.5	5.8	43.9	40.0	48.3	-	-	-
1958	18.8	29.7	6.3	18.5	42.5	50.3	-	-	-
1960	19.0	32.2	6.3	45.6	45.4	49.9	-	-	-
1963	17.7	31.3	6.4	46.9	28.6	59.0	4.2	21.0	-
1965	17.3	38.2	10.7	54.4	64.9	59.0	7.7	27.3	-
1967	17.2	33.4	6.3	47.2	44.2	60.6	4.5	24.0	72.2
1972	17.3	36.2	6.8	51.9	30.7	58.6	-	-	-
1974	17.0	37.5	5.8	54.5	40.5	59.0	5.1	28.9	68.4
1975	17.5	39.2	7.4	57.1	40.5	58.7	5.7	31.5	71.1
1980	17.1	43.2	7.7	58.7	40.4	60.5	5.5	34.0	70.7
1981	18.0	43.2	7.9	61.4	44.1	61.1	6.1	36.8	76.1

NOTE DIG = Sum of DFC of (a) Trade-Commerce, (b) Finance, Insurance and Real Estate, (c) Service and (d) Public Administration

= degree of industrial ghettoization.

SOURCE: Derived from Table 5B.

of female concentration in this occupation was more or less on a rising track through the fifties and sixties, increasing from 16.8 in 1949 to the all-time highest figure of 22 in 1967. Then it began a descent and reached rock bottom, 15.3, in 1975, after which it began increasing and reached the figure of 18.7 in 1981.

The third important occupation for women is professional work where the degree of sex-typing increased from 36.1 in 1949 to 49.8 in 1981. It is not a female job yet, but promises to become one. The degree of female concentration has increased from 9.9 in 1949 to 18.3 in 1981. However, the broad 'professional' category is misleading. Most women in this category are teachers, nurses and para-professionals, not doctors, engineers, and other top professionals.

Commercial occupations constitute the fourth important job category for women with the degree of sex-typing hovering around the figure 40 during the period 1969–81. The degree of female concentration fell from 12.4 in 1949 to 7.6 in 1972 and then began rising and reached the value 9.9 in 1981.

These four occupations—clerical, service, professional and commercial—are women's job-ghettos. To give a quantitative expression to this, we define the "degree of occupational ghet-toization" (DOG) as the percentage of all women workers that are in these occupations, i.e., the sum of the degrees of female concentration in these four occupations. DOG figures for the period 1949–81 are given in the last column of Table 5.1. It is seen that the degree of occupational ghettoization has systematically increased from 65 in 1949 to 80.5 in 1981.

Communication is an occupation where the degree of sex-typing increased from 40.9 in 1949 to 57.9 in 1963 and then declined to 50 in 1972. The figures for subsequent years are not available. It does seem like a female occupation since a majority of communication workers have been women since the early sixties. Yet this is not where a substantial section of the female labour force is to be found. The degree of female concentration is very low here. From 2.4 in 1949 it fell to 1.2 in

1972. To a large extent, this has been due to labour-displacing technological progress.

In managerial occupations, the percentage of women has significantly improved. In these male jobs, the degree of sex-typing increased from 11.2 in 1949 to 27.7 in 1981. The degree of female concentration, though always remaining low, has increased from 3.8 in 1949 to 5.2 in 1981. At any rate, this progress is significant and is likely to be sustained as more and more women are getting higher education leading to managerial, and also higher professional occupations.

In manufacturing and mechanical trades, the degree of sex-typing was around 18 in the fifties, remained around 14 in the sixties and early seventies and then began improving. From 18.2 in 1974, it reached 20.2 in 1981. The degree of female concentration has declined from 15.0 in 1949 to 9.6 in 1981.

Sex-typing in agriculture was on the descent in the fifties, DST falling from 11.8 in 1949 to 6.6 in 1960. From the early seventies DST began climbing and stood at 24.2 in 1981. This must have been due mainly to men shifting from agriculture to urban jobs. The degree of female concentration fell from 11.8 in 1949 to 2.7 in 1981. Women's participation in the other occupations—transportation, construction, labour and un-skilled work—was negligible from the point of view of both sex-typing and concentration.

Turning now to industrial shifts, it is clear from Table 5.2, that the service sector is the prime industrial ghetto for women. The degree of female concentration here has increased from 34.6 in 1949 to 44.1 in 1981 although behaving somewhat erratically in 1963, 1965 and 1972, taking the extreme values 28.6, 64.9 and 30.7, respectively. The degree of sex-typing, however, assumed an ascending trend, rising from 45.5 in 1949 to 61.1 in 1981. The second-ranking sector is finance, insurance and real estate. The DFC here is rather low, rising from 5.4 in 1949 to 7.9 in 1981. But it is a female industrial group with a degree of sex-typing fairly similar to that of service, rising from 42.0 in 1949 to 61.4 in 1981, though exhibiting the pathological value 18.5 in 1958. Trade and commerce is the third important sector to which women had been drawn. Here the DFC hovered around 18 throughout the period 1949–81 while the DST increased from 31.9 to 43.2. Public administration is the fourth in importance with DST rising from 27.3 in 1965 to 36.8 in 1981. The DFC here has been low, starting at 7.7 in 1965 and ending up at 6.1 in 1981. The percentage of all women workers that are in these four industrial sectors is called here the degree of industrial ghettoization (DIG) and is obtained by adding the DFC's of these four sectors. It is presented at the last column of Table 5.2. DIG has been upward of 70 during 1965–81, with the exception of the year 1974 when it took the value 68.4. In 1981, slightly over 76 percent of all women workers were employed in these four sectors.

Women were "visible minorities" in three other sectors. In manufacturing, the DFC decreased from 23.2 in 1949 to 13.3 in 1981 while the DST increased from 19.8 in 1949 to 27.8 in 1981. In agriculture, the DFC decreased from 11.8 in 1949 to 2.9 in 1981. In this sector, the degree of sex-typing had a falling trend in the fifties starting at 11.8 in 1949 and hitting the bottom 6.8 in 1960. Then a more or less rising trend set in reaching the value 27.6 in 1981. Finally, in transportation, communication and public utilities, the DFC was more or less static around the figure 4 but DST increased from 10.9 in 1949 to 22.4 in 1981 along a rising track.

With this identification of industrial and occupational segregation of women in the Canadian economy, we turn to the discriminating consequences flowing from this labour market dualism.

5.2 Discrimination

We document now the fact that women have faced both occupational and wage discrimination in Canada. Women are segregated into low-paying occupations and within each occupation women earn less than men. Table 5C brings out these facts very vividly for the period 1931–80. Take first two female occupations—clerical and service. In terms of Table 5.1, all other occupations are male. Table 5C of the Appendix to this chapter unmistakably shows that all male jobs, except farming and labourers, paid more to each sex than the two female jobs in each year. Within the professional category, there are male professionals—doctors, lawyers, engineers, accountants, etc.—and female professionals—teachers, nurses, etc. Within sales (commercial occupations) again, there are men's jobs— managers, senior salesmen, etc.,—and women's jobs, e.g., salesgirls. Although the aggregated data of Table 5C cannot show it, these female jobs under the professional and sales categories pay much less than the male jobs within these two categories.

We have demonstrated that women's ghetto jobs pay much less than typical male jobs. We now examine wage discrimination within each occupation.

Table 5C shows that, within each occupation and for each year, women earned a lot less than men on the average. To quantify this wage discrimination, we present in Table 5.3 women's earnings as a percentage of corresponding men's earnings in each occupation. Let us call this percentage the (women's) earnings ratio. The following tendencies are then seen.

The earnings ratio in the managerial occupation has more or less improved along a rising trend starting at 19.3 in 1931 and ending at 52.5 in 1980. In the professional category, the ratio modestly increased from 54.7 in 1931 to 57.8 in 1980. In the principal women's occupation, clerical work, the earnings ratio has worsened, falling, through a few zig-zags, from 72.0 in 1931 to 61.0 in 1980. In sales, the ratio has changed from 41.4 in 1931 to 43.3 in 1980 in an oscillatory fashion. In another female occupation, namely, service, the earnings ratio has increased from 33.6 in 1932 to 46.1 in 1980. In farming, the ratio fell from 57.6 in 1931 to 40.7 in 1979. In processing and machining, the earnings ratio has fallen from 50.0 in 1931 to 46.6 in 1980. In product fabrication, it rose from 44.5 in 1972 to 54.8 in 1980. In transport, the ratio decreased from 66.0 in 1931 to 53.9 in 1980. Women fared somewhat better as "labourers" where their earnings ratio fell from 76.8 in 1931 to 66.3 in 1961. As

Table 5.3: WOMEN'S EARNINGS AS PERCENTAGE OF MEN'S EARNINGS, CANADA, 1931–80

Year	Managerial	Professional	Clerical	Sales	Service	Farming	Processing & Machining	Product Fabrication	Transport	Labourers	Miners and Craftsmen
	1	2	3	4	5	6	7	8	9	10	11
1931	19.3	54.7	72.0	41.4	33.6	57.6	50.0	-	66.0	76.8	-
1941	19.5	49.3	65.7	38.5	27.6	46.8	47.5	-	63.4	64.1	-
1951	33.8	58.3	71.4	44.4	35.8	-	55.9	-	63.4	69.2	-
1961	29.6	56.4	69.2	37.1	41.2	37.0	72.1	-	62.6	66.3	-
1965	39.8	49.7	61.5	31.5	36.9	-	-	-	-	-	43.3
1967	41.1	49.3	62.0	33.2	39.2	-	-	-	55.2	-	46.6
1969	43.2	52.1	61.0	30.3	37.0	-	-	-	-	-	46.0
1971	46.1	55.2	59.3	33.5	40.6	-	-	-	49.2	-	44.9
1972	48.1	55.3	59.9	32.4	34.4	-	54.5	44.5	44.9	-	-
1973	52.8	52.1	61.4	32.2	37.7	33.6	46.1	45.2	46.0	-	-
1974	50.8	55.0	61.3	38.2	40.0	-	48.4	45.7	46.2	-	-
1975	55.4	53.6	61.9	34.3	39.6	35.7	50.9	46.0	48.0	-	-
1976	51.4	52.6	58.3	39.2	40.5	-	50.3	48.8	50.5	-	-
1977	55.6	56.0	60.5	42.6	44.9	42.5	51.2	47.1	53.0	-	-
1978	52.0	58.1	64.4	36.8	43.1	-	44.1	49.7	59.0	-	-
1979	57.6	57.0	62.1	42.6	47.1	40.7	49.8	52.6	52.7	-	-
1980	52.5	57.8	61.0	43.3	46.1	-	46.6	54.8	53.9	-	-

SOURCE: Derived from Table 5C.

miners and craftswomen, they didn't do that well, their earnings ratio falling from 46.6 in 1967 to 44.9 in 1971.

We can therefore conclude that wage discrimination has not only been severe against women but has also increased during the last half a century in several occupations, including the principal female occupation—clerical work. Most of the occupations women held were, as we saw in the last section, in four classes: service, finance-insurance-real estate, trade-commerce, and public administration.

5.3 Education, Demography and Women's Work

From Table 2A, Chapter 2, we saw that the percentage of the women in the Canadian labour force secularly increased from 13.4 in 1911 to 41.1 in 1982. In this section, we seek to relate this phenomenal increase in women's labour force participation to their levels of education and certain demographic characteristics and thereby try to explain the demand for and supply of female labour.

Table 5D in the appendix to this chapter gives the labour force by sex and educational attainment for the years 1960, 1965, 1975–81. Four levels of education are considered: (a) 0–8 years of schooling, (b) some high school/completion, (c) some post-secondary/diploma, and (d) university degree. From this table, we derive Table 5.4 below showing the percentage of labour force by sex and educational attainment. It is clear that, at each level of education, the female percentage of the labour force has systematically increased and the male percentage decreased. At educational levels *a, b, c* and *d*, female percentages increased, respectively, to 30.2, 42.9 and 34.3 in 1981 from the base year values 17.4, 33.1, 34.7 and 20.3 in 1960. As shown earlier, women have been concentrated in four occupations: clerical, service, commercial and professional. Logically, therefore, their educational levels should match the needs of these occupations. An affirmation of this is found in Table 5.5 below which is also derived from Table 5D. As this table shows, the percentage of female workers with 0–8 years of education systematically decreased from 30.96 in 1960 to 11.31 in 1981,

Table 5.4: PERCENT OF TOTAL LABOUR FORCE BY EDUCATIONAL ATTAINMENT, BY SEX, BY YEAR 1960, 1965, 1975–81

Year	0–8 Years			Some High School/ Completion			Some Post-Secondary/ Diploma			University Degree		
	Total in Labour Force	Percent Male	Percent Female	Total in Labour Force	Percent Male	Percent Female	Total in Labour Force	Percent Male	Percent Female	Total in Labour Force	Percent Male	Percent Female
1960	2815	82.6	17.4	2874	66.9	33.1	248	65.3	34.7	281	79.7	20.3
1965	2615	79.6	20.4	3502	65.4	34.6	356	66.0	34.0	370	75.7	24.3
1975	2022	72.7	27.3	4706	59.8	40.2	2322	58.4	41.6	924	70.6	29.4
1976	1944	72.2	27.8	5044	59.2	40.8	2249	57.4	42.6	969	70.7	29.3
1977	1868	72.2	27.8	5325	59.3	40.7	2277	56.4	43.6	1028	69.5	30.5
1978	1899	71.3	28.7	5606	58.5	41.5	2295	55.9	44.1	1082	67.8	32.2
1979	1892	70.6	29.4	6021	58.3	41.7	2139	55.1	44.9	1154	67.1	32.9
1980	1806	70.7	29.3	6215	57.5	42.5	2272	54.6	45.4	1229	66.2	33.3
1981	1799	69.8	30.2	6274	57.1	42.9	2444	54.0	46.0	1312	65.7	34.3

SOURCE: Calculated from Table 5D.

Table 5.5: PERCENTAGE DISTRIBUTION OF FEMALE LABOUR FORCE OVER LEVELS OF EDUCATION IN YEARS, 1960, 1965, 1975–1981

Year	0–8 years	Some high school/completion	Some post-secondary	University Degree
1960	30.96	60.03	5.42	3.59
1965	27.29	61.93	3.18	4.60
1975	14.97	51.39	26.25	7.39
1976	14.07	53.58	24.96	7.40
1977	13.00	54.27	24.87	7.86
1978	12.88	54.97	23.93	8.22
1979	12.61	56.96	21.80	8.62
1980	11.47	57.31	22.35	8.87
1981	11.31	55.98	23.36	9.35

SOURCE: Derived from Table 5D.

while the percentage of women with university degrees increased secularly from 3.59 in 1960 to 9.35 in 1981. In the category some high school/completion, the percentage decreased from 60.03 in 1960 to 55.98 in 1981 through some oscillations, though always remaining above 50. The percentage of female workers with some post-secondary education or diploma increased from 5.42 in 1960 to 23.96 in 1981. The inescapable conclusion is that more and more women have been receiving higher education beyond high school level. The percentage of women workers with some post-secondary/diploma or university degree has increased from 9.01 in 1960 to 32.71 in 1981, a 263.04 percent increase in 21 years or an annual growth rate of 12.53 percent.

Women's participation in the labour market is just another way of expressing the economist's concept, 'supply of female labour power'. In order to participate in a given labour market, a woman must have a given educational qualification required by an employer, regardless of whether or not the job itself requires it. The higher the level of education required by the job, the more intensely the woman must have committed herself to the job prior to making the necessary investment of time and money in the specific education. Higher education as a filter would then seem to imply the hypothesis that the two variables, level of education and participation rate, move in the same direction. Without implying any causality, for the time being, let us see if the hypothesis is borne out by the data. Those in Table 5.6 indeed do so. The table provides data at four levels of education: (i) 0–8 years, (ii) high school, (iii) some university, and (iv) university. For each of the years 1971, 1976–81, we find that the levels of education and women's participation rate move in the same direction. When the level of education increases, the participation rate increases also. Given the reasons why a job is wanted, the necessary education is acquired. Education then appears to be the cause of participation, although it is actually an intermediate link between the causes and the effect (participation).

Let us look at education vis-a-vis unemployment. Except for 1971, in every other year Table 5.6 shows a negative correlation between level of education and unemployment rate. Even for 1971 this observation is validated if we drop any one of the two levels: 0–8 years and high school. This, again, implies no causal connection which we must seek at the demand side of the labour market.

We have seen above that women have been receiving increasingly higher levels of education in order to provide an educated female labour force. On the demand side, we have seen, the higher the level of education, the higher the employment rate. What then is the connection between education and work?

In the last few decades, the notion that modern advanced technology needs workers with higher skills and, hence, more years of education than ever before has become firmly rooted in the popular mind. The fact of the matter, according to Braverman,[54] taking his cue from Marx, is that the average worker has been deskilled. As we have seen earlier, in the discussion on monopoly capital, the scientific-technological revolution has indeed caused an unprecedented advance in knowledge in the aggregate; specialists are today the sole repositories of expert knowledge in special branches of

Table 5.6: WOMEN IN THE LABOUR FORCE BY LEVEL OF SCHOOLING, CANADA, 1971–81

Level of Schooling	Population 15 years and over (in thousands) (1)	Labour Force (2)	Participation Rate (3)	Unemployment Rate (percent) (4)
1971–TOTAL	7,649	3,053	39.9	8.8
0–8 years	2,468	630	25.5	8.3
High School	4,533	2,018	44.5	9.3
Some University	421	256	60.9	8.1
University degree	227	148	65.2	6.0
1976–TOTAL	8,570	3,859	45.0	8.4
0–8 years	2,142	541	25.2	9.1
High School	4,317	2,066	47.9	9.4
Some post-secondary	706	381	53.9	7.8
Post-secondary cert. or dip.	977	584	59.8	6.0
University degree	428	287	67.0	5.4
1977–TOTAL	8,767	4,022	45.9	9.5
0–8 years	2,085	521	25.0	11.0
High School	4,515	2,181	48.3	10.6
Some post-secondary	727	412	56.7	9.0
Post-secondary cert. or dip.	975	591	60.6	6.4
University degree	466	317	68.1	5.1
1979–TOTAL	9,016	4,406	48.9	8.8
0–8 years	2,104	556	26.4	10.0
High School	4,813	2,511	52.2	9.8
Some post-secondary	604	361	59.8	8.3
Post-secondary cert. or dip.	956	600	62.7	6.1
University degree	538	380	70.7	5.1
1980–TOTAL	9,178	4,613	50.3	8.4
0–8 years	2,057	529	25.7	10.1
High School	4,943	2,643	53.5	9.4
Some post-secondary	639	394	61.7	7.8
Post-secondary cert. or dip.	974	637	65.4	5.6
University degree	566	409	72.3	4.8

	(1)	(2)	(3)	(4)
1981–TOTAL	9,329	4,811	51.6	8.3
0–8 years	2,053	544	26.5	9.9
High School	4,942	2,693	54.5	9.4
Some Post-secondary	698	435	62.3	7.6
Post-secondary				
cert. or dip.	1,030	689	66.9	5.7
University degree	607	450	74.1	4.7

1971–81: Women in the labour force with High School education
increased by 33.4 percent.
Women with some post-secondary or university education
increased by 33.9 percent.
And women with university degrees in the labour force
increased by 75.8 percent. From 1976–81, women with university
degrees increased in the labour force by 56.8 percent.

Labour Force Composition
1971:   73 percent of the women in the labour force had a level of
schooling of High School or less.
23 percent had some post-secondary or university education.
1981:   67.3 percent of the women in the labour force had a level of
schooling of High School or less.
32.7 percent had some post-secondary or university education.

Analysis:
(1) growing numbers of women with post-secondary and
university education in the 1970's.
(2) increased participation of these women in the labour force.
(3) decreased unemployment rate of these more educated
women.

SOURCE: Statistics Canada, *The Labour Force*, Cat. 71–001, December Issues
for 1971, 1975–81.
NOTE: Figures were not available for 1978.

science. Once the worker was a thinker-doer, in possession of
all the knowledge and skill his job demanded. Today, the
thinking part of labour has left the shop floor and moved to
the office. The worker needs to learn a specific dexterity, a
limited and repetitious operation which he can learn in a few
months at most. The very fact that an operative is seen beside
a complex machine does not mean that he is in possession of
all the knowledge stored in it. In fact, he knows hardly anything about it. He only pushes buttons and turns knobs.

The worker is thus not really skilled, but he appears so because he is "educated". Today, a high school diploma is necessary for most jobs, whether in factory or office. The schooling process has been lengthened although most factory jobs require only 6th grade competency in arithmetic, spelling, reading, writing and speaking. With six years spent in the basics, a few weeks to months to learn the operation of the machine should be enough. Yet, a high school diploma, the reward for twelve to thirteen years of "study", is a "ticket of admission to almost any kind of job".[55] The job-content does not need the diploma but the employer uses it as a device to screen job applicants.

Beneath this form, this screening device, lies hidden the essence of the lengthening of the schooling period. Monopoly capital cannot employ the entire population that is currently in the labour force. It cannot afford, therefore, to further aggravate the situation by an early entry of youth into the labour market. The strategy of longer years at school postpones action on the unmanageable problem; it is a device to manipulate the current labour supply. More positively, the school under monopoly capital has taken over the child socialization role from the farm, family, community and church. Apart from learning the three R's, the child is imparted special education for conformity to the rules of society and obedience to the law. This is an added reason for the lengthening of schooling.

The high school "kids" have to be trained by university-educated teachers. To train the trainers, a university professoriate needs to be built up. Besides, an army of scientists and technologists is needed to man the giant corporation, especially its design and other R and D activities. The enlarged school system has thus given birth to a higher education industry furnishing employment for a considerable mass of teachers and construction and service workers. This industry is vertically and horizontally linked with many other industries. The closing of a single segment of this industry will lead to a social crisis. The schools, as caretakers of children and young people, are indispensable for family functioning, community stability and social order in general. Child socialization, employment postponement and catering to the inter-industrial linkages just described, together provide the rationale for the "ticket" that the employer uses as a screening device, although the job itself does not quite need it. Higher unemployment rates among early quitters from school are the result of this screening which is itself rationalized by the socio-economic considerations just outlined.

So far as women are concerned, this screening device has another cutting edge. There is discrimination against women due in part to patriarchy, in part to male competition. A woman may need more than a high school diploma as her ticket to a job even in her ghetto. In general, a woman would seem to need a level of education higher than that a man would need in order to be considered for an equal job at a lower pay. Her participation may be premissed on this higher level of education. A lower level of education thus serves as a disincentive to her entering the job market itself because she knows that the ticket she lacks would pre-empt her selection for the job(s) she seeks. This is a demand-side reason why level of education and participation rate move in the same direction. We now proceed to discussing some supply-side reasons for this positive correlation between level of education and participation rate.

When a woman participates in a labour market, she offers a certain kind of labour. What are the determinants of this supply? Before launching into a theoretical answer to this question, let us consider some figures. The Supplementary Bulletin of the 1976 Census of Canada, *Economic Characteristics, Female Labour Force*, gives Canadian women's labour-market participation rates in 1976 by level of schooling, marital status, age groups and presence of children. There are seven levels of schooling: less than grade 9, grades 9–10, grade 11, grades 12–13, post-secondary non-university (total and with certificate or diploma), some university, and university degree. We shall refer to the first five levels as the "non-university category" and the latter two as the "university category". The table first gives the participation rates of all Canadian women workers broken down into several age groups with each age group subdivided into four sub-groups on the basis of presence of children, i.e., (a) no children, (b) some children, (c) some children under 6, and (d) all children age 6 and over.

The total Canadian women workers are then divided into: single (never married) and ever-married. Participation rates of each of these two categories are given by age groups and presence of children similar to the case of total Canadian women workers. Thereafter, the "ever-married" is subdivided into (a) "married, husband present", (b) "married, husband absent", and (c) "widowed and divorced".

From the census data which, owing to limitations of space in the present format, cannot be here reproduced, the following tendencies emerge:

(a) For each demographic group and educational category, level of education and participation rate move in the same direction.

(b) For most demographic groups, level of education (university and non-university taken together) and participation rate move in the same direction.

(c) For each educational level and most age-marriage groups, the participation rate of a group with no children is higher than that of a group with some children.

(d) For each educational level and most age-marriage groups, the participation rate of a group with all children age 6 and above is higher than that of a group with some children under 6.

From the 1976 Census Bulletin mentioned above, we collected in Table 5.7 the consolidated data for all educational levels and all age groups. It will be seen that the total female work-force in 1976 was 3,827,515 of which 2,265,600 were "married with husband present". In percentage terms, married women with husbands present in this total female work-force were 59.2. The next highest group consists of 1,147,160 single (never married) female workers constituting 30.0 percent of

Table 5.7: **TOTAL POPULATION, LABOUR FORCE AND PARTICIPA-TION RATE OF CANADIAN WOMEN IN THE YEAR 1976**

	Total Population (1)	Labour Force (2)	Participation Rate (3)
(a) TOTAL CANADA	8,425,380	3,827,515	45.5
No children	4,707,640	2,172,220	46.0
Some children	3,717,740	1,655,300	44.5
Some children under 6	1,437,750	548,455	37.0
All children age 6 and over	2,230,495	2,206,845	49.5
(b) *Single*	2,020,810	1,147,160	56.5
No children	1,995,235	1,131,360	57.0
Some children	33,575	15,795	47.0
Some children under 6	21,900	8,585	39.0
All children age 6 and over	11,670	7,215	61.5
(c) *Ever-married*	6,396,570	2,680,355	42.0
No children	2,712,400	1,040,855	38.5
Some children	3,684,170	1,639,505	44.5
Some children under 6	1,465,350	539,870	37.0
All children age 6 and over	2,218,820	1,099,635	49.5
(d) *Married Husband Present*	5,168,735	2,265,600	43.5
No children	1,818,725	811,090	44.5
Some children	3,340,015	1,454,505	43.5
Some children under 6	1,389,795	505,610	36.5
All children age 6 and over	1,950,220	948,900	48.5
(e) *Married Husband Absent*	259,665	144,920	53.5
No children	135,635	72,430	53.5
Some children	134,030	72,485	54.5
Some children under 6	47,445	21,510	45.0
All children age 6 and over	86,585	50,970	58.5
(f) *Widowed and Divorced*	958,178	299,845	28.5
No children	748,045	157,330	21.0
Some children	210,125	112,510	53.5
(g) *Widowed*	777,265	153,695	19.5
No children	661,640	100,955	15.0
Some children	115,625	52,740	45.5
Some children under 6	7,785	2,665	34.5
All children age 6 and over	107,835	50,080	46.0

	(1)	(2)	(3)
(h) *Divorced*	180,905	116,145	64.0
No children	86,405	56,380	65.0
Some children	94,500	59,765	63.0
Some children under 6	20,320	10,085	49.5
All children age 6 and over	74,180	49,685	67.0

SOURCE: Collected from Supplementary Bulletin, 1976 Census of Canada, *Economic Characteristics, Female Labour Force.*

the total female labour force. The percentages of "married, husband absent", "widowed" and "divorced" were 3.8, 4.0 and 3.0, respectively. In the "single" category, 436,350 were aged 15–19 years and 378,395 aged 20–24. These 814,745 unmarried young women constituted 71 percent of the total unmarried female workers and 21.3 percent of the total female labour force. Thus, 80.5 percent of the female work-force were either unmarried youth (21.3 percent) or married with husband present (59.2 percent).

Participation rate is heavily influenced by family situation. Compare, for instance, "married, husband present" with "married, husband absent". The participation rate of the former is 43.5 against 53.5 of the latter. These ten percentage points of difference must be accounted for by the "husband-factor". In the former case, the husband normally brings home his wages. In the latter case, the woman may or may not get a sum from the absent husband in the form of a remittance (separation allowance). In normal cases, the remittance from the absent husband will be far less than his wages. The wife in this case has to work harder than a wife with husband present, regardless of the number of children. Divorcees have the highest participation rate in each of the four categories of presence of children primarily because alimony is a poor substitute for a full wage. Widows without children have a participation rate of 15.0 percent while widows with some children have a rate of 45.5 percent. This is a reversal of the normal situation where the participation rate is higher if there are no children. This apparent anomaly is due to the fact that a widow with children is among the "unfortunates". She needs extra money for the children and it has to come from her own paid work.

Let us now try to add a theoretical note concerning the determinants of women's labour market participation, the supply of female labour power. According to neoclassical theory, the supply of labour is determined by maximizing the utility of leisure and income earned through work at the given wage rate. The labour supply then becomes an increasing function of the single variable—the wage rate. The end result is the simplistic statement: the higher the wage rate, the higher the labour supply. As our empirical analysis above shows, the situation is far more complex. Let us take the married women with husband present. Here, a family decision is involved. When the wife in this family does paid work, it implies that the husband is not bringing home a family wage sufficient for the standard of living the family wishes to have. The wife balances her time between domestic work and paid work. Obviously an assessment is made between the contribution to family standard of living that an hour of domestic work in the margin makes with the contribution that will be made by a marginal hour in paid work. The opportunity cost of an hour of domestic work to her is the forgone wage. This comparison is subjectively made, without the aid of a computer or a hired mathematician. It is the end result of a saga, the final step in the decision making. The major issues are the family situation, the number and age-structure of the children, the size of the husband's wages and the extent to which the husband's wages may be stretched by domestic work and so on. For widows and divorcees, the income accruing from pension, alimony, etc. becomes the counterpart of husband's wages. Presence of children in the family and this income are crucial determinants of their labour supply. The unmarried young woman without children may come closest to the neoclassical simplicity. She has no family to worry about.

We conclude this section by adding a final note on the demand for women's labour. We have seen how the development of capitalism has brought women to the secondary labour market and how women, especially married women, have become a permanent force in this market. The capitalist's demand for female labour in these competitive sectors—service, finance, trade and other "non-productive" industries—are best described by the reserve army concept as described earlier in this chapter. The great majority of the married women who are not yet participating in the labour market form the latent reserve—termed the "institutionalized inactive reserve army of labour" by Connelly[56]—available for capital for its further expansion if and when that takes place.

5.4 Women and Industrial Unions

In the final section of Chapter 4, it was mentioned that, in the pre-1930 period, unions in Canada were craft unions. These unions were organized among skilled workers in construction, transportation, mining and some parts of manufacturing. These industries were men's preserves and, with the further development of these industries under monopoly capitalism, the craft unions gave way to what have been called "industrial unions". As we saw, with monopoly capitalism came industrial dualism and segmented labour markets. The industrial unions, as the reincarnation of the earlier craft unions, were entrenched in blue collar production jobs. Some women were employed in these jobs, especially in clothing and textile industries even at the early stages of industrialization. But the trend for women's employment in white collar jobs in service, finance, trade and public administration was established only during the first two decades of the twentieth century. Industrial dualism and labour-market segmentation were initiated in these early years. In subsequent decades, dualism-segmentation took firmer roots. Women remained confined to the same ghettos though a qualitative change took place with their unprecedented entry into these sectors as regular members of the labour force.

The industrial and occupational shifts that we discussed earlier in this chapter have major implications for the union movement. The percentage of workers has been declining in the monopoly sector industries which have been traditionally well unionized while that in the new industries in the public and the competitive tertiary sectors has been increasing. These industries, being new, could not have a history of unionization. Let us now get a quantitative picture of unionization resulting from these industrial and labour-market shifts.

Table 5.8 gives for the year 1977 the percentage of women workers in each industry division (degree of sex-typing) and the percentage of all workers in each industry division that is unionized (degree of unionization). Degree of sex-typing, i.e., the percentage of women workers, does not seem to bear any correlation with degree of unionization. Similar evidence was also given by Julie White[57] for the year 1976. We also notice from this table that the traditional male industries—manufacturing, transportation, construction—primarily have very high degrees of unionization, as expected, because of the long history of unionization in these industries. Three of the women's ghettos—service, finance and trade—have very low degrees of unionization. The relatively high value 29.0 for service is primarily due to teachers and nurses. Teachers and nurses who are employees of the government are highly unionized as are employees in public administration.

Table 5.8: **DEGREE OF SEX-TYPING AND DEGREE OF UNIONIZA-TION, CANADA, 1977**

Industry	Degree of Sex-Typing	Degree of Unionization
Service	59.5	29.0
Finance	57.3	1.5
Trade	40.0	7.9
Public Administration	32.5	65.8
Manufacturing	25.0	46.0
Transportation	19.3	53.7
Construction	7.4	47.9
Agriculture	25.0	0.6
Other Primary	7.9	41.9

SOURCE: Table 18, p. 91 in Naomi Hersom and Dorothy E. Smith, a collection of articles on women and work, Ottawa, 1981, unpublished.

Table 5E gives union membership by industry and sex for the period 1966–80. It is seen that in almost every year the percentage of women among unionized workers in male industries is significantly less than the corresponding male percentage. Similarly, the male percentage of unionized workers in the female industries—service and finance—is significantly less than the corresponding female percentage for most of the years. Table 5E also shows that the rate of union growth among women is much higher than among men. In fact, total male union membership increased from 1,572,686 in 1966 to 2,159,969 in 1980, an increase of 587,283 in 14 years, implying an annual growth rate of 2.7 percent. Female union membership increased from 322,716 in 1966 to 932,883 in 1980, an increase of 610,167, implying an annual growth rate of 13.5 percent. Comparing these rates of union growth with the participation growth rates discussed in Chapter 2, we see that participation growth rates and union growth rates move in the same direction. Yet, as Tables 5.9 and 5.10 show, compared to men, women are less unionized. Table 5.9 shows that, apart from the abnormal year 1975, the female percentage of union members has secularly increased from 17.0 in 1966 to 30.2 in 1980. This means that the higher growth rate of unionization

Table 5.9: **PERCENTAGE OF FEMALE UNION MEMBERS, CANADA, 1966–80**

Year	Percent Union Members, Female
1966	17.0
1969	21.1
1971	23.5
1972	24.2
1973	24.6
1974	25.3
1975	16.8
1977	28.6
1979	29.3
1980	30.2

SOURCE: Collected from Table 5E.

Table 5.10: **PERCENTAGE OF UNIONIZED WORKERS, CANADA, 1966–80**

Year	Percent Male Workers Unionized	Percent Female Workers Unionized
1966	30.3	14.5
1969	26.6	29.3
1971	31.3	19.6
1972	30.3	19.5
1973	32.5	19.2
1974	32.5	19.5
1975	20.0	6.9
1976	31.8	19.6
1977	34.0	22.2
1979	31.5	20.2
1980	31.3	20.2

SOURCE: Derived from Tables 2A and 5E

among women is raising the female share of union membership. Even so, this share in 1980 is only 30.2 percent as compared to the male share of 68.8 percent. Again, from Table 5.10, we see that the proportion of unionists among female workers is, in the main, less than that among male workers. This fact combined with the earlier finding of a significantly higher union growth rate among women suggests that there are still barriers to women's unionization. We now address ourselves to examining these barriers.

At the end of Chapter 4, we listed several barriers to women's unionization during the period of craft unions. As we saw earlier, in the 1930's, industrial unions emerged in the place of the craft unions. As the economy further developed, these barriers continued, however, to stand in the way of women. The pace and direction might have changed but the essence remained, as Julie White[58] has documented. We make below some supplementary remarks to White's excellent analysis.

Let us first take family socialization and societal attitudes as barriers to women's unionization. White tried to argue that, had female passivity and disinterest together with sexual discrimination by trade unions been responsible for the lower degree of female unionization, then one would expect that a high proportion of women in an industry would lead to a low degree of unionization of *all* workers. By "degree of unionization" she meant the proportion of unionized workers among all workers in the industry concerned. She found no such correlation for the year 1976 and we found none either for the year 1977. On this ground, White dismisses female passivity and trade union discrimination as serious determinants of women's lower unionization. The very high rate of growth of unionization among women that we have documented above also militates against the suggestion of female passivity as a major barrier to women's unionization. We shall postpone the discussion on the role of unions, employer opposition and legislation to the next chapter.

Job fragmentation and market segmentation still remain the principal barriers to women's unionization. A precondition for unionization is the gathering together of large masses of workers in the same workplace. Such large congregations of workers take place in monopolistic firms, not in atomistic competitive firms. Women are concentrated in the service, finance, trade and public administration. So far as service is concerned, women's unionization in health and education has been very high compared with that in public administration. These are areas where large masses of workers are gathered together by various levels of government, by public monopolies. A lot of service work is still personal with only a handful of workers in the workplace. The same is true with finance as any branch of any bank or financial institution will testify. In trade also, sales clerks work in isolation. Apart from public administration and public-cum-community service, the other areas—personal service, trade and finance—are in private sectors with most of the features of competitive capitalism of the nineteenth century. Union activity in a competitive industry is almost a contradiction in terms. These sectors have low rates of unionization not only among women but also among men.

The competitive structure, with small groups of workers under the employment of an atomistic competitor, shields these sectors from the "menace" of unionization.

As to the monopoly sector industries, the industrial unions here organize blue collar workers. The women who work here are mostly clerks whom the blue collar workers have little incentive to organize nor can they, working in isolation, organize themselves.

In conclusion, we may say that the mode of production of labour power lurks behind these forms of female employment. Labour power is still not produced capitalistically. True, some of the ingredients like food, personal service, health and education that go into the production of labour power have come under the sway of the recent phase of monopoly capitalism on a scale unknown to any other phase before. Yet, women's domestic work is the key input in preparing this commodity, labour power. A lot of women's paid work is an extended version of the domestic chores, like cooking, cleaning, caring, nursing and teaching, that used to be done entirely in the private home a few decades ago and are still done to a significant extent by today's wife-mother. Women are shut out from the principal private arena of union activity—production jobs. Monopoly capital and the industrial union have colluded to channel women to where capital goes in its expansionary journey. So far it has not been in places amenable to organized activities.

REFERENCES

1. Pat Armstrong and Hugh Armstrong, *The Double Ghetto: Canadian Women and Their Segregated Work.*
2. Karl Marx, *Capital: A Critique of Political Economy,* Volumes 1–3, Edited by F. Engels.
3. Rudolf Hilferding, *Finance Capital: A Study of the Latest Phase of Capitalist Development.*
4. V.I. Lenin, *Imperialism—The Highest Stage of Capitalism.*
5. Paul Sweezy and Paul Baran, *Monopoly Capital: An Essay on the American Economic and Social Order.*

6. Harry Braverman, *Labor and Monopoly Capital: The Degradation of Work in the Twentieth Century*, 1974.
7. Ibid., p. 22.
8. Patricia Connelly, *Last Hired, First Fired: Women and the Canadian Labour Force.*
9. Ibid., p. 385.
10. Marx, op. cit., p. 632.
11. Ibid.
12. Ibid., p. 639.
13. Ibid., p. 620.
14. Ibid., p. 643.
15. Ibid.
16. Ibid., p. 644
17. Connelly, *Last Hired First Fired*, op. cit., Chapters 3 and 4.
18. Ibid., p. 56.
19. Ibid.
20. Adam Smith, *The Wealth of Nations.*
21. John Stuart Mill, *Principles of Political Economy*, Volume 1, Revised edition.
22. Ibid., p. 369.
23. Ibid., p. 372.
24. Ibid., p. 377
25. John T. Dunlop, "The Task of Contemporary Wage Theory", in *New Concepts in Wage Discrimination*, edited by George W. Taylor and Frank C. Pierson, pp. 117–39; *Industrial Relations Systems.*
26. Clark Kerr. "Labor Markets: Their Character and Consequences", *American Economic Review*, May 1950, pp. 278–91. "The Balkanization of Labor Markets", in *Labor Mobility and Economic Opportunity*, edited by E.W. Bakke *et al.* pp. 92–110.
27. Lester C. Thurow, "The Determinants of the Occupational Distribution of Negroes", in *The Education and Training of Racial Minorities: Proceedings of a Conference; Poverty and Discrimination*; "Education and Economic Inequality", *The Public Interest*, Summer 1972, Vol. 28, pp. 66–81; *Generating Inequality.*
28. Lester C. Thurow and Robert E.B. Lucas, *The American Distribution of Income: A Structural Problem.*
29. Peter B. Doeringer, "Determinants of the Structure of Industrial Type Internal Labor Markets", *Industrial Labor Relations Review*, Jan. 1967, 20(2), pp. 206–20; "Manpower Programs for Ghetto Labor Markets", in *Proceedings of the Twenty-first Annual Meeting of the Industrial Relations Research Association.*
30. Michael J. Piore, *Internal Labor Markets and Manpower Analysis.*
31. Michael J. Piore, "On-the-Job Training in the Dual Labor Market", in *Public-Private Manpower Policies*, edited by Arnold R. Weber, Frank Cassell and Woodrow L. Ginsberg, pp. 101–32; "Notes for a Theory of Labor Market Stratification", in *Labor Market Segmentation* edited by R. Edwards *et al.*, pp. 125–50.

236   WOMEN, UNIONS AND THE LABOUR MARKET

32. Bennett Harrison, *Education, Training, and the Urban Ghetto;* "Education and Underemployment in the Urban Ghetto", *American Economic Review,* Dec. 1972, 62(5), pp. 796–812; "Ghetto Economic Development, A Survey", *Journal of Economic Literature,* March 1974, 12(1), pp. 1–37.
33. Bennett Harrison and Andrew Sum, "The Theory of 'Dual' or Segmented Labor Markets", *Journal of Economic Issues,* Vol. 13, No. 3, September, 1979.
34. Harrison and Sum, ibid., and R. Loveridge and A. Mok, *Theories of Labor Market Segmentation.*
35. James S. Coleman *et al., Equality of Educational Opportunity ("The Coleman Report");* Herbert Gintis, "Education, Technology and Characteristics of Worker Productivity", *American Economic Review,* May 1971, 61(2), pp. 266–79.
36. Martha MacDonald, "The Labour Force of Labour Market Segmentation Analysis: The Unanswered Questions" in N. Hersom and D. Smith eds., *Women and the Canadian Labour Force,* pp. 165–208.
37. Sweezy and Baran, op. cit.
38. Braverman, op. cit.
39. Sweezy and Baran, op. cit.
40. Thorsten Veblen, *Absentee Ownership and Business Enterprise in Recent Times,* pp. 305–06.
41. Sweezy and Baran, op. cit.
42. Braverman, op. cit., pp. 281–2.
43. Kenneth J. Arrow. "The Theory of Discrimination", in *Discrimination in Labor Markets,* edited by O. Ashenfelter and A. Rees, pp. 3–33.
44. Gary S. Becker, *The Economics of Discrimination.*
45. Arrow, op. cit.
46. E.S. Phelps: "The Statistical Theory of Racism and Sexism", *American Economic Review,* 1972, 62(4), pp. 659–61.
47. Milton Friedman, *Capitalism and Freedom.*
48. A.A. Alchian and R.A. Kessel, "Competition, Monopoly and the Pursuit of Pecuniary Gain", in *Aspects of Labor Economics: A Conference of the Universities,* pp. 156–75.
49. Janice F. Madden, *The Economics of Sex Discrimination,* pp. 70–73.
50. Millicent G. Fawcett, "Equal Pay for Equal Work", *Economic Journal,* 28 (March 1918), pp. 1–6.
51. F.Y. Edgeworth, "Equal Pay to Men and Women for Equal Work", *Economic Journal* 32 (December 1922), 431–57.
52. J. Mincer and S. Polachek, "Family Investments in Human Capital: Earnings of Women", *Journal of Political Economy,* March/April, 1974, 82(2). Part II, pp. S76–S108.
53. Armstrong and Armstrong, op. cit., p. 23.
54. Braverman, op. cit., pp. 424–47.
55. Ibid., p. 438.
56. Connelly, op. cit.
57. Julie White, *Women and Unions,* p. 31.
58. Ibid., pp. 29–51.

APPENDIX

to

Chapter Five

Table 5A: FEMALE LABOUR FORCE PARTICIPATION BY OCCUPATION BY YEAR, CANADA, 1948–81 (THOUSANDS) (SELECTED YEARS)

OCCUPATION	1948			1949			1951			1953		
	Total	Female	Percent	Total	Female	Percent	Total	Female	Percent	Total	Female	Percent
Managerial	254	29	11.4	375	42	11.2	422	46	10.9	496	42	8.5
Professional	287	100	34.8	305	110	36.1	343	121	35.3	386	157	40.7
Clerical	505	282	55.8	513	289	56.3	577	327	56.7	569	330	58.0
Transportation	335	-	-	343	-	-	333	-	-	343	-	-
Communication	63	24	38.1	66	27	40.9	69	30	43.5	83	39	47.0
Commercial	397	128	32.2	333	138	41.4	328	137	41.8	340	135	39.7
Financial	32	-	-	27	-	-	32	-	-	29	-	-
Service	376	185	49.2	371	187	50.4	400	204	51.0	430	223	51.9
Agriculture	1,183	158	13.4	1,122	132	11.8	998	99	9.9	903	50	5.5
Primary Occupations	136	-	-	133	-	-	169	-	-	139	-	-
Manufacturing and Mechanical Trades	911	157	17.2	886	167	18.8	911	186	20.4	921	175	19.0
Construction	259	-	-	347	-	-	323	-	-	315	-	-
Labourers and unskilled workers	205	-	-	163	-	-	238	-	-	305	11	3.6

OCCUPATION	1958			1960			1963			1967		
	Total	Female	Percent	Total	Female	Percent	Total	Female	Percent	Total	Female	Percent
Managerial	494	53	10.7	505	56	11.1	589	65	11.0	693	86	12.4
Professional	510	195	38.2	598	254	42.5	675	273	40.4	917	395	43.1
Clerical	699	439	62.8	752	467	62.1	857	546	63.7	1,038	704	67.8
Transportation	376	-	-	374	-	-	-	-	-	-	-	-
Communication	85	36	42.4	93	38	40.9	57	33	57.9	65	36	55.4
Commercial	395	154	39.0	432	174	40.3	462	163	35.3	501	192	38.3
Financial	50	-	-	56	-	-	-	-	-	-	-	-
Service	552	305	55.3	619	348	56.2	708	409	57.8	874	518	59.3
Agriculture	746	56	7.5	682	45	6.6	-	-	-	-	-	-
Primary Occupations	146	-	-	137	-	-	-	-	-	-	-	-
Manufacturing and Mechanical Trades	1,005	174	17.3	1,050	179	17.0	1,585	232	14.6	1,924	272	14.1
Construction	336	-	-	328	-	-	-	-	-	-	-	-
Labourers and unskilled workers	346	12	3.5	352	15	4.3	309	17	5.5	315	21	6.7

OCCUPATION	1972			1975			1980			1981		
	Total	Female	Percent	Total	Female	Percent	Total	Female	Percent	Total	Female	Percent
Managerial	817	117	14.3	614	114	18.6	815	205	25.2	905	251	27.7
Professional	1,181	486	41.2	1,409	681	48.3	1,626	801	49.3	1,768	881	49.8
Clerical	1,279	921	72.0	1,639	1,228	74.9	1,871	1,463	78.2	2,063	1,615	78.3
Transportation	-	-	-	389	12	3.1	437	25	5.7	445	27	6.1
Communication	70	35	50.0	-	-	-	-	-	-	-	-	-
Commercial	583	226	38.8	1,039	352	33.9	1,106	438	39.6	1,187	477	40.2
Financial	-	-	-	-	-	-	-	-	-	-	-	-
Service	1,010	597	59.1	1,137	562	49.4	1,414	764	54.0	1,627	901	55.4
Agriculture	488	69	14.1	504	102	20.2	519	120	23.1	534	129	24.2
Primary Occupations	-	-	-	120	-	-	153	-	-	198	4	2.0
Manufacturing and Mechanical Trades	2,055	306	14.9	1,855	336	18.1	2,064	395	19.1	2,278	461	20.0
Construction	-	-	-	648	-	-	650	8	1.2	750	10	1.3
Labourers and unskilled workers	352	31	8.8	-	-	-	-	-	-	-	-	-

SOURCES:

Historical Statistics of Canada: M.C. Urquhart and K.A.H. Buckley, Toronto, Macmillan Company of Canada Limited, 1965.
Women in the Labour Force, Facts and Figures, Labour Canada Women's Bureau, 1968, 1969, 1973 and 1975 editions.
Women in the Labour Force, Part I, Participation, Labour Canada, Women's Bureau, 1976, 1977, 1978–1979 editions.
The Labour Force, Statistics Canada, Catalogue 71–001, December issues 1980, 1981.
"The Occupational Composition of the Canadian Labour Force" Sylvia Ostry, *1961 Census Monograph Programme,* Dominion Bureau of Statistics, Ottawa, Canada 1967.

NOTES:

1. Where figures were less than 10,000 they were either not provided from various sources or not included.
2. Various sources have different breakdowns of occupational groupings—some groups have no calculated figures as they were not provided.
3. Figures for the years 1964, 1965, 1966, 1969, 1970, 1971, 1973 are not available in the categories/format which would correspond with the rest of the data in this table. For some of the years mentioned, these data were not available at all.

Table 5B: PERCENT FEMALES EMPLOYED BY INDUSTRY AND YEARS*, 1946–81 (SELECTED YEARS)

Years	Transportation, Communication, Public Utilities			Trade, Commerce			Finance, Insurance, Real estate			Service			Public administration		
	Total both sexes employed (000's)	Total females employed (N)	Per-cent females employed	Total (000's)	(N) (000's)	Per-cent	Total (000's)	(N) (000's)	Per-cent	Total (000's)	(N) (000's)	Per-cent	(Both Sexes) Total (000's)	(N) (000's)	Per-cent
1946	369	39	10.6	567	195	34.4	125	51	40.8	778	349	44.8	-	-	-
1949	411	45	10.9	642	205	31.9	143	60	42.0	849	386	45.5	-	-	-
1951	459	51	11.1	705	227	32.2	157	70	44.6	942	427	45.3	-	-	-
1953	476	53	11.1	806	238	29.5	157	69	43.9	982	474	48.3	-	-	-
1960	515	67	13.0	966	311	32.2	226	103	45.6	1,494	745	49.9	-	-	-
1963	597	88	14.7	1,062	332	31.3	254	119	46.9	1,306	535	59.0	371	78	21.0
1965	773	129	16.7	940	359	38.2	410	223	54.4	2,284	1,348	59.0	582	159	27.3
1967	657	96	14.6	1,214	405	33.4	313	149	47.2	1,719	1,041	60.6	442	106	24.0
1972	730	112	15.3	1,410	511	36.2	385	200	51.9	2,194	908	58.6	-	-	-
1974	790	135	17.1	1,575	590	37.5	448	202	54.5	2,388	1,407	59.0	613	177	28.9
1975	820	150	18.3	1,649	646	39.2	478	273	57.1	2,537	1,490	58.7	670	211	31.5
1980	901	187	20.8	1,830	790	43.2	608	357	58.7	3,079	1,862	60.5	740	252	34.0
1981	953	214	22.4	2,005	867	43.2	616	378	61.4	3,476	2,123	61.1	805	296	36.8

* Public administration category not added: 1946–60, 1961, 1962.

Year	Agriculture			Primary Industries[1] Forestry, Fishing, Min. etc.			Manufacturing			Construction[2]		
	Labour Force Total Females & Males (000's)	Females in labour force (N)	Percent of females in labour force	Females & males Total (000's)	(N) Females (000's)	Percent Females	Females & males Total (000's)	Number females (000's)	Percent Females	Total (000's)	Number females (000's)	Percent Females
1946	1,246	200	15.7	141	-	-	1,239	245	19.8	238	-	-
1949	1,114	132	11.8	167	-	-	1,310	259	19.8	343	-	-
1951	991	99	10.0	208	-	-	1,356	274	20.2	347	-	-
1953	898	50	5.6	188	-	-	1,401	276	19.7	349	-	-
1960	675	46	6.8	185	-	-	1,488	293	19.7	430	12	2.8
1963	-	-	-	-	-	-	1,552	333	21.5	-	-	-
1965	467	70	15.0	-	-	-	1,968	468	23.8	548	26	4.7
1967	542	71	13.1	217	7	3.2	1,747	396	22.7	473	18	3.8
1972	481	75	15.6	208	-	-	1,858	438	23.6	501	24	4.8
1974	473	76	16.1	235	12	5.2	2,024	490	24.2	598	32	5.4
1975	486	108	22.2	-	-	-	1,890	462	24.4	610	40	6.6
1980	477	126	26.4	297	30	10.1	2,105	565	26.8	619	54	8.7
1981	507	140	27.6	351	38	10.8	2,302	640	27.8	740	66	8.9

[1] Other primary industries total both sexes includes males only, since the number of females is less than 10,000. Percent would be less than 1 percent. This applies to 1946–60, 1962; 1972—no available figures.

[2] 1946–56 females are not included in total figures since the number of females is less than 10,000.

For Sources see next page

SOURCES: *The Labour Force*, Dec. 1979, Table 69, p. 85, Cat. 71–001.
The Labour Force, Dec. 1980, Table 77, p. 97, Cat. 71–001.
The Labour Force, Dec. 1981, Table 71, p. 96, Cat. 71–001.
The Labour Force, Dec. 1977, Table 57, p. 70, Cat. 71–001.
Women in the Labour Force, 1978–79, Part I, Table 27a, p. 78 (1968 and 1978).
Women in the Labour Force, 1977, Part I, Table 25a & 25b, pp. 62 & 63 (1967, 1966 & 1976).
Women in the Labour Force, 1976, Part I, Table 23, p. 55 (1965 and 1975).
Women in the Labour Force, 1973, Table 23, p. 47 (1962 and 1972).
Women in the Labour Force, 1969, Table 10, p. 14 (1963).

Table 5C: AVERAGE EARNINGS BY OCCUPATION AND SEX[1], 1931, 1941, 1951, 1961, 1963, 1965, 1967–80

Year	Managerial		Professional		Clerical		Sales		Service		Farming	
	Males $	Females $	Males $	Females $	Males $	Females $	Males $	Females $	Males $	Females $	Males $	Females $
1980 Average Earnings	27,486	14,436	23,050	13,331	15,276	9,318	16,825	7,294	12,211	5,630	9,961	(2)
Average Income	30,508	15,882	24,660	14,375	16,343	10,333	18,614	8,350	13,629	6,658	12,349	(2)
1979 Average Earnings	23,665	13,637	20,577	11,738	13,822	8,590	16,032	6,828	11,400	5,365	11,253	4,580
Average Income	25,277	14,576	22,011	12,631	14,673	9,369	18,102	7,732	12,857	6,248	13,371	5,685
1978 Average Earnings	23,192	12,067	18,869	10,697	12,751	7,887	14,709	5,421	10,305	4,445	9,908	(2)
Average Income	25,365	12,841	20,004	11,691	13,233	8,741	16,577	6,509	11,517	5,273	11,009	(2)
1977 Average Earnings	19,995	11,117	17,209	9,634	12,036	7,287	13,380	5,703	9,975	4,482	8,789	3,739
Average Income	21,051	11,964	18,205	10,491	12,865	7,925	14,724	6,389	11,037	5,156	10,568	4,808

contd on p. 246

[1] For notes and sources, *see* p. 251.

	Managerial		Professional		Clerical		Sales		Service		Farming	
1976 Average Earnings	21,936	11,277	17,242	9,078	10,934	6,374	13,308	5,216	9,303	3,766	8,744	(2)
Average Income	23,643	12,016	18,343	9,657	11,727	6,843	14,484	5,781	10,279	4,285	10,372	(2)
1975 Average Earnings	17,850	9,891	15,154	8,123	9,455	5,852	12,056	4,130	8,336	3,301	7,946	2,839
Average Income	18,968	10,614	16,084	8,656	10,266	6,326	13,088	4,670	9,300	3,817	9,308	3,988
1974 Average Earnings	16,225	8,237	13,044	7,178	8,400	5,150	10,897	4,160	7,405	2,962	7,214	(2)
Average Income	17,682	8,736	14,065	7,690	9,010	5,557	11,872	4,469	8,157	3,423	8,546	(2)
1973 Average Earnings	14,346	7,576	12,299	6,413	7,374	4,531	9,205	2,967	6,506	2,454	5,798	1,951
Average Income	15,390	8,080	12,911	6,758	7,867	4,824	10,035	3,323	7,135	2,805	6,591	2,565
1972 Average Earnings	12,807	6,161	10,922	6,037	6,775	4,056	8,477	2,747	6,275	2,157	4,320	(2)
Average Income	13,614	6.619	11,486	6,291	7,229	4,275	9,161	3,175	6,776	2,506	5,012	(2)

contd. on p. 247

1971 Average Earnings	10,711	4,941	11,095	6,120	6,504	3,859	6,755	2,262	5,326	2,163	3,609	(2)
Average Income	11,823	5,439	11,711	6,339	6,898	4,069	7,251	2,479	5,746	2,390	4,254	(2)
1969 Average Earnings	9,873	4,262	9,622	5,012	5,495	3,352	6,071	1,841	5,104	1,890	3,407	(2)
Average Income	10,767	4,506	10,080	5,188	5,851	3,477	6,497	2,153	5,489	2,083	3,885	(2)
1967 Average Earnings	8,594	3,530	8,604	4,246	5,025	3,118	5,374	1,782	4,168	1,633	2,982	(2)
Average Income	9,260	3,729	9,029	4,381	5,274	3,227	5,665	1,918	4,490	1,763	3,386	(2)
1965 Average Earnings	7,501	2,987	7,133	3,549	4,255	2,617	4,682	1,477	3,462	1,278	2,634	(2)
Average Income	8,145	3,153	7,479	3,718	4,475	2,708	4,888	1,573	3,726	1,393	2,988	(2)
1961 Average Earnings	6,721	1,993	5,507	3,104	3,381	2,339	3,89(3)	1,443(3)	2,797	1,153	1,637(5)	606
1951	3,604	1,220	3,011	1,756	2,166	1,546	2,28(3)	1,014(3)	1,800	644	940(5)	(6)
1941	2,508	490	1,746	861	1,113	731	1,219(3)	468(3)	844	233	399(5)	185
1931	2,903	559	1,978	1,083	1,153	830	1,294(3)	530(3)	897	301	408(5)	235

Year	Processing and Machinery		Product Fabrication		Construction		Transport		Labourers		Miners and Craftsmen	
	Males $	Females $	Males $	Females $	Males $	Females $	Males $	Females $	Males $	Females $	Males $	Females $
1980 Average Earnings	17,363	8,089	16,092	8,822	16,050	(2)	15,725	8,482				
Average Income	18,695	9,145	17,276	9,878	18,036	(2)	16,877	9,398				
1979 Average Earnings	15,326	7,635	14,904	7,846	14,985	(2)	14,660	7,728				
Average Income	16,286	8,511	15,991	8,659	16,562	(2)	15,750	8,548				
1978 Average Earnings	13,644	6,019	13,506	6,712	12,807	(2)	13,001	7,677				
Average Income	14,838	7,039	14,439	7,583	14,251	(2)	14,049	8,693				
1977 Average Earnings	13,107	6,705	13,017	6,131	12,508	(2)	12,223	6,472				
Average Income	14,098	7,491	14,031	6,958	13,813	(2)	13,185	7,187				

1976 Average Earnings	12,107	6,089	11,890	5,804	12,149	(2)	11,938	6,029
Average Income	12,946	6,616	12,672	6,401	13,562	(2)	12,747	6,458
1975 Average Earnings	10,287	5,238	10,586	4,870	11,110	(2)	10,385	4,987
Average Income	11,153	6,037	11,385	5,505	12,242	(2)	11,178	5,484
1974 Average Earnings	9,270	4,485	9,426	4,307	9,809	(2)	9,491	4,389
Average Income	9,983	4,825	10,081	4,638	10,755	(2)	10,169	4,670
1973 Average Earnings	8,382	3,867	8,301	3,751	8,785	(2)	8,144	3,746
Average Income	8,861	4,195	8,735	4,032	9,548	(2)	8,649	3,968
1972 Average Earnings	7,788	4,244	7,598	3,381	7,894	(2)	7,399	3,326
Average Income	8,185	4,468	8,020	3,631	8,527	(2)	7,963	3,597

	Processing and Machinery		Product Fabrication		Construction		Transport		Labourers*		Miners and Craftsmen	
1971 Average Earnings	(7)	(7)	(7)	(7)	(8)	(8)	6,775	3,333	4,306	(2)	7,171	3,223
Average Income	(7)	(7)	(7)	(7)	(8)	(8)	7,148	3,550	4,675	(2)	7,582	3,407
1969 Average Earnings	(7)	(7)	(7)	(7)	(8)	(8)	5,941	(2)	3,778	(2)	6,181	2,841
Average Income	(7)	(7)	(7)	(7)	(8)	(8)	6,263	(2)	4,058	(2)	6,524	2,920
1967 Average Earnings	(7)	(7)	(7)	(7)	(8)	(8)	5,131	2,835	3,406	(2)	5,427	2,527
Average Income	(7)	(7)	(7)	(7)	(8)	(8)	5,402	2,876	3,668	(2)	5,702	2,598
1965 Average Earnings	(7)	(7)	(7)	(7)	(8)	(8)	4,536	(2)	2,900	(2)	4,682	2,027
Average Income	(7)	(7)	(7)	(7)	(8)	(8)	4,772	(2)	3,070	(2)	4,908	2,072
1961 Average Earnings	2,513[4]	1,813[4]	(4)	(4)	(4)	(4)	3,451	2,160	2,186	1,449	3,971	(2)
1951	2,260[4]	1,264[4]	(4)	(4)	(4)	(4)	2,135	1,353	1,555	1,076	2,399	(2)
1941	1,013[4]	481[4]	(4)	(4)	(4)	(4)	1,030	653	607	389	1,116	(2)
1931	936[4]	468[4]	(4)	(4)	(4)	(4)	1,067	704	488	375	782	(2)

*(recorded categories)

NOTES:

[1] Includes full and part-time workers unless otherwise specified
[2] Sample inadequate for reliable estimate
[3] Commercial and financial category (reading—change by Stats Canada to Sales)
[4] Manufacturing and construction category—see processing and machining for totals (recording—change by Stats Canada)
[5] Agriculture, Logging and Fishing—combined and averaged.
[6] Less than $500
[7] See Miners and Craftsmen for these years (recording by Stats Canada)
[8] See Labourers for these years (recording by Stats Canada)
[9] No data available for these non-census years 1970, 1968 and 1963 from sources listed in this table.

SOURCES:

1971–1980   *Income Distributions by Size in Canada* 13–207
1980—pp. 72–73, Table 43
1979—p. 113, Table 60
1978—p. 72, Table 43
1977—p. 110–111, Table 58
1976—p. 73, Table 42
1975—p. 103, Table 57
1974—p. 65, Table 43
1973—p. 101, Table 57
1972—p. 61, Table 43
1971—p. 102, Table 64 (microfiche 13–207)

1969   *Income Distributions by Size in Canada* 13–544
p. 54, Table 37

1967   *Income Distributions by Size in Canada* 13–534
p. 5556, Table 42

1965   *Income Distributions by Size in Canada* 13–528
p. 44, Table 31

1931, 1941, 1951, 1961:
Changes in the Occupational Composition of the Canadian Labour Force 1931–1961
Noah M. Meltz L2-26/2
Economics and Research Branch,
Dept. of Labour

Table 5D: LABOUR FORCE BY EDUCATIONAL ATTAINMENT, BY SEX, BY YEARS (THOUSANDS) 1960, 1965, 1975–81

Year	0–8 Years			Some High-School Completion			Some Post-Secondary/ Diploma (1)			University Degree			Total Female
	Total	Males in Labour Force	Females in Labour Force	Total	Males in Labour Force	Females in Labour Force	Total	Males in Labour Force	Females in Labour Force	Total	Males in Labour Force	Females in Labour Force	
1960	2815	2324	491	2874	1922	952	248	162	86	281	224	57	1586
1965	2615	2081	534	3502	2290	1212	356*	235	121	370	280	90	1957
1975	2022	1471	551	4706	2815	1891	2322	1356	966	924	652	272	3680
1976	1944	1404	540	5044	2988	2956	2249	1292	957	969	685	284	3837
1977	1868	1349	519	5325	3258	2167	2277	1284	993	1028	714	314	3993
1978	1899	1354	545	5606	3279	2327	2295	1282	1013	1082	734	348	4233
1979	1892	1336	556	6021	3510	2511	2139	1178	961	1154	774	380	4408
1980	1806	1277	529	6215	3572	2643	2272	1241	1031	1229	820	409	4612
1981	1799	1255	544	6224	3581	2693	2444	1320	1124	1312	862	450	4811

(1) Includes some University, some Post-Secondary Education and / or Certificate or Diploma.
*Includes Some University Education only.

SOURCE: Statistics Canada, *The Labour Force.* Cat 71–001, December Issues for 1960, 1965, 1975–81.

Table 5E: UNION MEMBERSHIP BY INDUSTRY AND SEX FOR 1966–80

Industry	Total Members	Males	Females	Percentage Male	Percentage Female
1980					
Agriculture	509	323	186	63.5	36.5
¹Other Primary	93,903	91,662	2,241	97.6	2.4
Manufacturing	887,115	719,028	168,087	81.0	19.0
Construction	274,731	272,973	1,758	99.4	0.6
²Transportation	441,191	353,314	87,877	80.1	19.9
Trade-Commerce	150,159	96,748	43,411	64.4	35.6
Finance	14,760	5,348	9,412	36.3	63.7
Service	688,467	250,945	437,522	36.5	63.5
Public Administration	503,940	333,884	170,056	66.3	33.7
³Other	38,077	35,744	2,333	93.9	6.1
TOTAL	3,092,852	2,159,969	932,883	69.8	30.2
1979					
Agriculture	504	310	194	61.5	38.5
¹Other Primary	96,354	94,436	1,918	98.0	2.0
Manufacturing	910,890	733,105	177,795	80.5	19.5
Construction	261,195	259,929	1,266	99.5	0.5
²Transportation	427,774	346,255	81,519	81.0	19.0
Trade-Commerce	135,499	88,917	46,582	65.6	34.4

1979 (contd)	Total	M	F	% M	% F
Finance	13,294	5,175	8,119	39.0	61.0
Service	638,840	236,485	402,355	37.0	63.0
Public Administration	508,531	340,144	168,387	66.9	33.1
³Other	42,871	40,631	2,240	94.8	5.2
TOTAL	3,035,752	2,145,387	890,365	70.7	29.3
1977					
Agriculture	2,980	2,504	476	84.0	26.0
¹Other Primary	99,419	97,049	2,370	97.6	2.4
Manufacturing	868,870	704,331	164,539	81.1	18.9
Construction	302,954	299,862	3,092	99.0	1.0
²Transportation	439,416	363,283	76,133	82.7	17.3
Trade-Commerce	132,050	86,277	45,773	65.4	34.6
Finance	7,884	2,856	5,028	36.2	63.8
Service	781,470	345,225	436,245	44.2	55.8
Public Administration	460,126	308,278	151,848	70.0	30.0
³Other					
TOTAL	3,095,301	2,209,797	885,504	71.4	28.6
1976					
Agriculture	334	229	105	68.6	31.4
¹Other Primary	90,486	88,578	1,908	97.9	2.1
Manufacturing	834,844	669,364	165,480	80.2	19.8

Construction	281,551	280,260	1,291	99.6	0.4
²Transportation	401,098	331,548	69,550	82.7	17.3
Trade-Commerce	127,787	82,624	45,163	64.7	35.3
Finance	13,151	5,581	7,570	42.4	57.6
Service	527,202	210,669	316,533	40.0	60.0
Public Administration	461,807	319,320	142,487	69.2	30.8
³Other	40,462	39,912	550	98.6	1.4
TOTAL	2,778,722	2,028,085	750,637	73.0	27.0

1975

Agriculture	143	108	35	75.5	24.5
¹Other Primary	68,229	67,208	1,021	98.5	1.5
Manufacturing	669,103	533,258	135,845	97.7	2.3
Construction	266,149	265,292	857	99.7	0.3
²Transportation	207,793	193,903	13,890	93.3	6.7
Trade-Commerce	97,220	61,984	35,236	63.8	36.2
Finance	5,900	2,754	3,146	46.7	53.3
Service	141,853	78,186	63,667	55.1	44.9
Public Administration	21,193	21,089	104	99.5	0.5
³Other	34,249	33,236	1,013	97.1	2.9
TOTAL	1,511,832	1,257,018	254,814	83.2	16.8

1974

Agriculture	456	335	121	73.5	26.5
¹Other Primary	90,111	86,967	3,144	96.5	3.5
Manufacturing	860,572	693,932	166,640	80.7	19.3

256 WOMEN, UNIONS AND THE LABOUR MARKET

1974 (contd)	Total	M	F	%M	%F
Construction	285,802	284,882	920	99.7	0.3
[2]Transportation	394,346	328,300	66,046	83.3	16.7
Trade-Commerce	108,259	72,728	35,531	67.2	22.8
Finance	7,786	2,424	5,362	31.2	68.8
Service	483,607	201,237	282,370	41.6	58.4
Public Administration	415,420	301,275	114,145	72.5	27.5
[3]Other	36,473	33,813	2,660	92.7	7.3
TOTAL	2,682,832	2,005,893	676,939	74.7	25.3
1973					
Agriculture	311	160	151	51.5	48.5
[1]Other Primary	83,238	82,240	998	98.8	1.2
Manufacturing	853,586	689,030	164,556	80.7	19.3
Construction	277,989	276,868	1,121	99.6	0.4
[2]Transportation	381,686	323,313	58,373	84.7	15.3
Trade-Commerce	96,490	62,870	33,620	65.2	34.8
Finance	4,882	1,845	3,037	37.8	62.2
Service	459,561	189,806	269,755	41.3	58.7
Public Administration	386,352	286,644	99,708	74.2	25.8
[3]Other	36,017	31,475	4,542	87.4	12.8
TOTAL	2,580,112	1,944,251	635,861	75.4	24.6

1972

Agriculture	177	131	46	74.0	26.0
¹Other Primary	73,525	71,947	1,578	97.8	2.2
Manufacturing	778,556	629,997	148,559	80.9	19.1
Construction	261,008	259,906	1,102	99.6	0.4
²Transportation	357,845	302,611	55,234	84.6	15.4
Trade-Commerce	94,639	63,240	31,399	66.8	33.2
Finance	4,485	2,766	1,719	61.7	38.3
Service	429,822	178,687	251,135	41.6	58.4
Public Administration	337,160	252,958	84,202	75.0	25.0
³Other	39,984	39,374	610	98.5	1.5
TOTAL	2,377,201	1,801,617	575,584	75.8	24.2

1971

Agriculture	534	418	116	78.3	21.7
¹Other Primary	73,914	73,441	473	99.4	0.6
Manufacturing	775,448	632,780	142,668	81.6	18.4
Construction	245,962	244,884	1,078	99.6	0.4
²Transportation	354,801	301,820	52,981	85.1	14.9
Trade-Commerce	96,556	68,870	27,686	71.3	28.7
Finance	2,963	1,319	1,644	44.5	55.5
Service	418,453	174,976	243,477	41.8	58.2
Public Administration	352,935	268,572	84,363	76.1	23.9
³Other	53,616	49,964	3,652	93.2	6.8
TOTAL	2,375,182	1,817,044	558,138	76.5	23.5

1969	Total	M	F	%M	%F
Agriculture	1,448	1,314	134	90.8	9.2
¹Other Primary	*	*	*	-	-
Manufacturing	778,723	630,960	147,763	81.0	19.0
Construction	220,078	219,015	1,063	99.5	0.5
²Transportation	351,880	307,159	44,721	87.3	12.7
Trade-Commerce	95,535	71,627	23,908	75.0	25.0
Finance	7,813	4,471	3,342	57.2	42.8
Service	326,807	143,847	182,960	44.0	66.0
Public Administration	328,615	263,880	64,735	80.3	19.7
³Other	**	**	**	-	-
TOTAL	2,217,646	1,748,411	469,235	78.9	21.1
1966					
Agriculture	5	5	5	-	-
¹Other Primary	5	5	5	-	-
Manufacturing	736,905	607,177	129,728	82..4	17.6
Construction	197,281	195,712	1,569	99.2	0.8
²Transportation	334,805	297,750	37,055	88.9	11.1
Trade-Commerce	51,186	36,613	14,573	71.5	28.5
Finance	5	5	5	-	-
Service	169,525	88,854	80,671	52.4	47.6
Public Administration	286,301	230,014	56,287	80.4	19.6
³Other	**	**	**	-	-
TOTAL	1,895,402	1,572,686	322,716	83.0	17.0

NOTES:

[1]*Other Primary* includes: forestry, fishing and trapping, mines, quarries and oil wells.
[2]*Transportation* includes: transportation, communication and other utilities.
[3]*Other* includes: pensioners, unemployed, etc.
* No data available from the sources listed for 1967, 1968, 1970 and 1978.
** No figures for these categories from the sources listed.
Industries with few females have not been included therefore the all industries total does not equal columns for 1969 and 1966.

SOURCES:

1980, *Corporations and Labour Unions Returns Act*, Part 2, 71–202, Annual, p. 62, Table XLI. Note percent of females also available as: percent by industry of total female membership, females as a percent of industry membership, and percent of females of total union membership.
1979, As above, p. 62, Table XLI.
1977, *Women in the Labour Force, Facts and Figures*, Part 2, 1977 ed., p. 5, Table 1.
1976, *Corporations and Labour Unions Returns Act*, Part 2, 71–202, Annual, p. 69, Table 27A.
1975, As above, p. 70, Table 27B.
1974, As above, p. 68, Table 27A.
1973, As above, p. 68, Table 27A.
1972, As above, p. 68, Table 27A.
1971, As above, p. 68, Table 27A.
1969, *Women in the Labour Force, Facts and Figures*, 1971, p. 37, Table 16.
1966, *Women in the Labour Force, Facts and Figures*, Part 3, 1977.

Chapter 6
Testing the Hypotheses
*A Statistical Analysis of Labour Market and
Institutional Barriers*

IN THE PRECEDING chapters, our review of the existing literature on unionization and an extensive ideological, historical
and theoretical analysis of the female labour process under
capitalism have led us to formulate several structural and
institutional barriers to women's unionization. These barriers
have been specified in the form of six hypotheses in Chapter 1.
Insofar as these hypotheses are the result of an analysis of a
historical process, their confirmation or otherwise has already
been made with the help of historical data—the concentrated
expression of all social and economic forces. Our historical
analysis has pointed out the primacy of structural factors as
the major barriers to women's unionization.

The present is also history. As such, we have used contemporary published information as much as it has been possible
to do so. It would have been ideal, for example, to have
first-hand information from workers, union members and
union executives on their own perception of the barriers to
women's unionization and see if they confirm our six
hypotheses. A random sample representative of all these persons including the ones who have failed to unionize or become
union executives, though ideal, has been beyond the realm of
possibility for the purpose of this study. We have therefore
limited ourselves to the union executives listed in the *Directory
of Labour Organizations, Canada, 1982*. This gives the most recent
list of executives of unions which are affiliated with a central
labour congress and of those not affiliated but subject to collective bargaining legislation.

A questionnaire concerning the hypotheses, a copy of which
is appended at the end of this chapter, was sent out to the
officers of these unions. The questionnaire was pre-tested

earlier on 30 union executives in the Edmonton area. Out of this list, we received 453 valid responses which, strictly speaking, do not constitute a random sample from the population of union executives in general. But, as often done in social science research, we shall employ statistical procedures of testing hypotheses in analysing the data from this somewhat "systematic" sample. The very large size of the sample is an added justification for our use of standard statistical procedures.

The questionnaire responses generated several tables regarding experience and opinion data on the perception of union executives regarding barriers to women's unionization. From a statistical point of view these responses concern multinomial distributions and, as such, only confidence intervals and tests of proportions based on the standardized normal variable Z will be needed for testing the six hypotheses.

6.1: Hypothesis 1

Hypothesis 1 states that:

> Union executives perceive that education is a key factor in unionization of women.

The null hypothesis stating "It is not the case that education is a key factor in unionization of women" was tested by several indicators, chosen to measure the relevance of education for the unionization of women workers.

All the respondents were asked (Question No. 32) to indicate how important they thought a relatively higher level of education/training was for women workers seeking union membership successfully. Their responses were categorized from "most important" to "not important at all". From Table 6.1 it is clear that 25 percent of the respondents felt that education was a very important, though not the most important, factor in unionization of women workers. Another 6 percent thought that it was "*the* most important" factor in women successfully joining unions. So, altogether, 31 percent, or about one-third of the respondents indicated that education was "very important or most important" for women wanting to join unions. However, 30 percent of the sample members said that education was "not very important" and 34 percent of the respondents said that it was "not important at all". Hence altogether 64 percent of them did not perceive a higher level of education as relevant to women workers' successfully seeking union membership.

In order to test the significance of the difference between these two proportions, the Z-test was conducted. The calculated Z-value was equal to 7.0. Since this value is larger than the critical value of 1.96 at .05 level of significance, the difference is significant. The finding from this hypothesis can be stated thus: Education is not perceived to be a key variable in unionization of women workers by the majority of the union executives; and the converse of this would seem to be true, namely, that a lack of a relatively high level of education would not be perceived as a crucial barrier for women workers seeking union membership.

This particular finding gets support from other findings in this investigation. For example, in answer to the questions about the most important labour-market and institutional barriers (Questions 41 and 42), only 14 out of 453 or 3 percent of the respondents stated "lack of skill/training" as a most important labour-market barrier, and only 15 or 3 percent stated "low education" as the most important institutional barrier. Other barriers were perceived to be far more crucially related to women's unionization than education. For example, "employer opposition" was perceived by the union executives as the most important labour-market barrier (chosen by 35 percent) followed by "job fragmentation" (29 percent). Similarly "societal expectation" was selected as the most important institutional barrier by 28 percent of the respondents, followed by "family socialization" (25 percent).

The data for sex breakdown presented in Table 6.1 indicate that there is some difference in the perceptions of male and

Table 6.1: FREQUENCY AND PERCENTAGE DISTRIBUTION OF UNION EXECUTIVES' PERCEPTION OF IMPORTANCE OF EDUCATION IN WOMEN SEEKING UNION MEMBERSHIP, BY SEX, 1983

Categories of Answers	Total		Male		Female	
	Freq.	Percent	Freq.	Percent	Freq.	Percent
1. Most important	25	6.0	18	6.0	7	6.0
2. Very but not the most important	111	25.0	76	23.0	35	31.0
3. Not very important	135	30.0	104	32.0	31	28.0
4. Not important at all	152	34.0	116	35.0	36	32.0
5. Undecided	16	4.0	13	4.0	3	3.0
9. DK/NA	0	0.0	0	0.0	0	0.0
0. No response	3	1.0	3	1.0	0	0.0
Total	442	100.0	330	101.0	112	100.0

female union executives regarding the importance of education. Thirty-one percent of women as compared with 23 percent of men feel that education is very important and 6 percent of both believe that it is important for unionization of women workers. So a total of 37 percent of women as compared to 29 percent of men find education very or most important for women workers successfully seeking union membership. However, 59 percent of women as compared with 67 percent of men think it is not very important or not important at all. This also does not confirm the hypothesis, but does show that union women executives perceive education as slightly more relevant to unionization of women than union men executives do.

In order to make sharper inferences about the population from the sample data of Table 6.1, we have derived the following non-simultaneous two-sided 95 percent confidence intervals (Table CI–1).

From Table CI–1, we conclude with 95 percent confidence:

(a) Among all union executives, 27 to 35 percent perceive higher education as important in women workers seeking union membership successfully. Among male executives

Table CI–1

Sex	Parameter	Confidence Interval
(a) Male & Female	P_1—proportion of all executives who perceive education as important	.31 ± .04
	P_2—proportion of all executives who perceive education as not important	.64 ± .04
	P_2–P_1	.33 ± .06
(b) Male	P_1—proportion of male executives who perceive education as important	.29 ± .05
	P_2—proportion of male executives who perceive education as not important	.67 ± .05
	P_2–P_1	.38 ± .08
(c) Female	P_1—proportion of female executives who perceive education as important	.37 ± .09
	P_2—proportion of female executives who perceive education as not important	.60 ± .09
	P_2–P_1	.23 ± .14

the corresponding percentage is between 24 and 34 while among female executives it is between 28 and 46.

(b) Among all union executives, 60 to 68 percent do not perceive education as important in women workers seeking union membership successfully. Among males, the percentage is betwen 62 and 72 while among females it is between 51 and 69.

(c) Among all union executives, those who do not perceive education as important in women workers seeking union membership successfully have a majority of 27 to 39 percent over those who do. The corresponding percentage among males lies between 31 and 45 while among females it lies between 9 and 37.

Another direct indicator of the importance of education for unionization of women workers was explored in the following question (Question No. 34): "Relative to other factors, how important was *your* education/training in *your* seeking union membership?" Both men and women answered this question. The responses, which are presented in Table 6.1A, and again categorized from "most important" to "not important at all", show that for 32 percent of the sample, relative to other factors, education was "very important but not the most important" factor in their unionization, and another 10 percent thought it was "most important". Thus, altogether 42 percent of the respondents admitted that education was important in their own case. However, 55 percent of the sample did not find their education important in their seeking union membership. Hence this hypothesis is not confirmed.

Again a Z-test was conducted and the computed Z score value was 2.4 which is larger than the critical value of 1.96 at .05 level of significance, and indicates that the difference between the two proportions is significant. Our finding again is that education is perceived as not relevant by a majority of women in their own seeking of union membership.

Table 6.1A: FREQUENCY AND PERCENTAGE DISTRIBUTION OF UNION EXECUTIVES' PERCEPTION OF HOW IMPORTANT ONE'S EDUCATIONAL TRAINING IS RELATIVE TO OTHER FACTORS IN MOTIVATING ONE TO SEEK UNION MEMBERSHIP, BY TOTAL AND SEX, 1983

Categories of answers	Total		Male		Female	
	Freq.	Percent	Freq.	Percent	Freq.	Percent
1. Most important	43	10.0	25	8.0	18	16.0
2. Very but not the most important	145	32.0	107	32.0	38	34.0
3. Not very important	124	28.0	102	31.0	22	20.0
4. Not important at all	119	27.0	88	27.0	31	27.0
5. Undecided	4	1.0	3	1.0	1	1.0
9. DK/NA	2	0.5	1	0.5	1	1.0
0. No response	7	2.0	5	0.0	2	2.0
Total	444	100.5	331	99.5	113	101.0
Percentage of 453 questionnaires used:	98 Percent		73.1 Percent		25 Percent	

Table 6.1A also contains data on sex differences. According to this table 18 percent of women as against 8 percent of men say that education was most important in their own case. However, the percentages of men and women are nearly equal (32 and 34 percent) in the category of "very important but not most important". But only 20 percent of women as compared to 31 percent of men state that it was not very important. Hence altogether 50 percent of women perceived their education as very important or most important in their seeking union membership relative to only 40 percent of men. This hypothesis then gets a partial support from sex breakdown data, in that a larger percentage of women than men found education important for their unionization, though not most important. We can state our finding thus: Education is a relatively more important factor in the case of women union executives than men union executives.

Table CI–1A gives the non-simultaneous two-sided confidence intervals derived from Table 6.1A.

	Table CI-1A	
Sex	Parameter	Confidence Interval
(a) Male & female	P_1—proportion of all executives who perceive education as important	.42 ± .05
	P_2—proportion of executives who perceive education as unimportant	.55 ± .05
	P_2–P_1	.13 ± .08
(b) Male	P_1—proportion of male executives who perceive education as important	.40 ± .05
	P_2—proportion of male executives who perceive education as unimportant	.58 ± .05
	P_2–P_1	.18 ± .08
(c) Female	P_1—proportion of female executives who perceive education as important	.50 ± 0.9
	P_2—proportion of female executives who perceive education as unimportant	.47 ± .09
	P_1–P_2	.03 ± .13

We draw the following conclusions with 95 percent confidence:

(a) Among all union executives, 37 to 47 percent believe their own education was helpful in seeking their own union membership. Among the males the percentage lies between 35 and 45; among the females it lies between 41 and 59.

(b) Among union executives in general, 50 to 60 percent believe their own education was not helpful in their seeking union membership. Among males the corresponding percentage is between 53 and 63 while among females it is betwen 38 and 56.

(c) Among union executives in general, those who believe their education was not helpful in their seeking union membership have a majority of 6 to 20 percent over those who believe it was. Among the males this percentage lies between 10 and 26. Among the females, the difference between the proportions of those who believe their education was helpful and those who believe it was not lies between −.10 and .16.

6.2: *Hypothesis 2*

The second hypothesis states that:

Union executives perceive that women workers being clustered in low-paid, semi-skilled or unskilled occupations, with very little bargaining power, contributes to their low unionization.

Positive responses to the question (Question No. 21), "Do you agree that women workers being clustered in low-paid, semi-skilled occupations is primarily responsible for their low unionization?", were taken as the measure of occupational clustering in low-paid, semi-skilled occupations as an important barrier to unionization of women. The responses as presented in Table 6.2 were "agreed", "disagreed", and "un-

Table **6.2:** **FREQUENCY AND PERCENTAGE DISTRIBUTION OF UNION EXECUTIVES' PERCEPTION OF "OCCUPATIONAL CLUSTERING/LOW PAY/JOB FUNCTIONS THAT REQUIRED LITTLE SKILL" AS A BARRIER TO THE UNIONIZATION OF WOMEN; BY TOTAL AND SEX, 1983**

Categories of Answers	Total		Male		Female	
	Freq.	Percent	Freq.	Percent	Freq.	Percent
Agreed	210	47.5	153	46.0	57	52.0
Disagreed	194	43.0	155	47.0	39	35.0
Undecided	36	8.0	22	7.0	14	13.0
DK/NA	0	0.5	0	0.0	0	0.0
No Response	3	1.0	3	1.0	0	0.0
Total	443	100.0	333	101.0	110	100.0
Percent of 453 questionnaires used	97.8 Percent		74.0 Percent		24.0 Percent	

decided". The table indicates that of the 453 union executives who responded to this question, 215 or 48 percent indicated that this is the case, whereas 43 percent disagreed and 8 percent were undecided. In order to assess the significance of the difference between these proportions, the Z-test was conducted. The computed value of Z was equal to 1.17, which is below the critical value of 1.96 at .05 level of significance; hence the difference between these two proportions is not significant. This means that our data do not show whether or not the union executives perceive a relationship between the occupational clustering of women workers and their low unionization. Therefore our hypothesis cannot be taken as confirmed by these data.

When sex is considered as a factor, Table 6.2 shows that there is some difference between male and female responses, in that a larger percentage of women (52 percent) as compared with men (46 percent) agree with the stated proposition. Hence we can say that women union executives perceive women workers being clustered in low-paid occupations as contributing to their low unionization. Thus our hypothesis finds a partial confirmation from data showing a breakdown by sex.

From Table 6.2 non-simultaneous two-sided 95 percent confidence intervals have been derived (Table CI-2).

Table CI–2 allows us to draw the following conclusions with 95 percent confidence:

(a) Among union executives in general, the percentage of those who agree that being clustered in low-paid, semi-skilled or unskilled occupations contributes to low female unionization lies between 43 and 53. The percentage for males lies between 41 and 51 while that for females lies between 43 and 61.

Table CI–2

Sex	Parameter	Confidence Interval
(a) Male and Female	P_1—proportion of all executives who perceive occupational clustering as responsible for low female unionization	$.48 \pm .05$
	P_2—proportion of all executives who do not perceive occupational clustering as responsible for low female unionization	$.43 \pm .05$
	P_1-P_2	$.05 \pm .07$
(b) Male	P_1—proportion of male executives who perceive occupational clustering as responsible for low female unionization	$.46 \pm .05$
	P_2—proportion of male executives who do not perceive occupational clustering as responsible for low female unionization	$.54 \pm .05$
	P_2-P_1	$.08 \pm .08$
(c) Female	P_1—proportion of female executives who perceive occupational clustering as responsible for low female unionization	$.52 \pm .09$
	P_2—proportion of female executives who do not perceive occupational clustering as responsible for low female unionization	$.35 \pm .09$
	P_1-P_2	$.17 \pm .13$

(b) Among union executives in general, the percentage of those who disagree that being clustered in low-paid, semi-skilled or unskilled occupations contributes to low female unionization lies between 38 and 48. The corresponding male percentage lies betwen 49 and 59 while the female percentage lies between 26 and 44.

(c) Among all union executives, the difference between the proportions of those who agree that occupational clustering leads to low female unionization and those who do not lies between –.02 and .12. Among female union executives, those who agree that occupational clustering leads to low female unionization have a majority of 4 to 30 percent over those who disagree. Among males, those who disagree that such clustering leads to lower female unionization have a majority of 0 to 16 percent over those who agree.

6.3: *Hypothesis 3*

Hypothesis 3 states that:

Union executives perceive that job fragmentation, in the case of women unionizing, is a very strong deterrent, second only to employer's opposition.

Participants were asked (Question No. 22) if they thought that the fragmentary nature of their work made it difficult for women to be organized into a union. "Job fragmentation" was operationalized as working in small isolated places like restaurants, small stores, etc. The positive responses of union executives were to be the indicator of their perception of job fragmentation as a serious barrier to organizing women workers into a union.

The data for testing this hypothesis are presented in Table 6.3 and these indicate that a very large percentage (82 percent) of respondents think that job fragmentation is a strong deterrent to the unionization of women, whereas 14 percent think

Table 6.3: FREQUENCY AND PERCENTAGE DISTRIBUTION OF UNION EXECUTIVES' PERCEPTION OF "JOB FRAGMENTATION AND ISOLATED WORKPLACES" AS A BARRIER TO THE UNIONIZATION OF WOMEN, BY TOTAL AND SEX, 1983

Categories of Answers	Total		Male		Female	
	Freq.	Percent	Freq.	Percent	Freq.	Percent
Agreed	366	82.0	263	80.0	103	91.0
Disagreed	61	14.0	53	16.0	8	7.0
Undecided	17	4.0	15	4.0	2	2.0
DK/NA	0	0.0	0	0.0	0	0.0
No Response	3	0.5	3	1.0	0	0.0
Total	447	100.5	334	101.0	113	100.0
Percentage of 453 questionnaries used	98.7 Percent		73.7 Percent		25.0 Percent	

it is not. That this difference is significant can be seen from the large computed Z value of 29 percent at .002 level of significance. On the basis of this percentage difference in the perception of union executives, assessed in the form of positive and negative responses, we can say that job fragmentation is largely perceived by the union executives as a strong barrier to unionization of women. Hence our hypothesis is overwhelmingly confirmed.

An analysis of the data by sex, contained in Table 6.3, reveals that a higher percentage of women union executives (91 percent) as compared with men executives (80 percent) perceive job fragmentation to be a serious barrier in the unionization of women workers. The case of women executives' perception then offers even stronger support for this hypothesis. One likely reason for this percentage difference may be that more women executives than men executives organize women workers, hence they would face the difficulties in organizing women created by job fragmentation in larger numbers than men.

It is very significant that this hypothesis found such strong support from the opinion data of the union *executives*. In their leadership role many of them are involved in the actual organizing of women workers and would have had first-hand personal experience of the difficulties which constitute barriers to organizing women. Job fragmentation has long been considered a very important labour-market barrier to women workers being organized, since the organizers would rather spend their limited time and resources in organizing large numbers of workers within one big concentrated area of work, such as a factory or hospital, where it is not only easier to reach large numbers of workers, but peer pressure can induce workers to join unions. This is not possible in small isolated workplaces. Our data do support these general statements. On the basis of these data we can say that our hypothesis relating to union executives' *perception* regarding job fragmentation is confirmed.

Again confidence intervals give sharper results. Table 6.3 gives us non-simultaneous two-sided 95 percent confidence intervals as shown in Table CI-3.

This table yields the following conclusions with 95 percent confidence:

(a)   Among executives in general, 78 to 86 percent perceive job fragmentation as a deterrent to women's unionization. The corresponding figure for male executives is between 76 and 84 and for female executives between 86 and 96.

(b)   Among union executives in general, 11 to 17 percent do not perceive job fragmentation as a deterrent to women's unionization. The corresponding figure for male executives is between 12 and 20 and for female executives between 2 and 12.

(c)   Among union executives in general, those who perceive job fragmentation as a barrier to women's unionization have a majority of 63 to 73 percent over those who do not so perceive it. The corresponding percentage for male executives is between 58 and 70 while for female executives it is between 77 and 91.

Table CI–3

Sex	Parameter	Confidence Interval
(a) Male and Female	P_1—proportion of all executives who perceive job fragmentation as a deterrent to female unionization	$.82 \pm .04$
	P_2—proportion of all executives who do not perceive job fragmentation as a deterrent to female unionization	$.14 \pm .03$
	P_1–P_2	$.68 \pm .05$
(b) Male	P_1—proportion of male executives who perceive job fragmentation as a deterrent to female unionization	$.80 \pm .04$
	P_2—proportion of male executives who do not perceive job fragmentation as a deterrent to female unionization	$.16 \pm .04$
	P_1–P_2	$.64 \pm .06$
(c) Female	P_1—proportion of female executives who perceive job fragmentation as a deterrent to female unionization	$.91 \pm .05$
	P_2—proportion of female executives who do not perceive job fragmentation as a deterrent to female unionization	$.07 \pm .05$
	P_1–P_2	$.84 \pm .07$

6.4: Hypothesis 4

Hypothesis 4 states:

> Where there was a family member among union executives who was a trade unionist, a woman executive in that household would have had greater incentive to join a union.

This particular hypothesis, intended to assess the impact of family socialization and role-modelling on the attitude of women workers toward joining unions, was tested by the personal experience data of union executives. Since socialization affects both men and women, all the respondents were requested to report whether they had a family member, specifically father or mother or a friend, in a union (Question Nos. 9–11). The percentage of responses stating "yes" was taken as the measure of the impact of family socialization and role-modelling on the respondent.

The data in Tables 6.4, 6.4A and 6.4B show that while only 46 percent of the respondents said that their fathers were union members (44 percent men and 33 percent women) and 12 percent of the respondents said that their mothers were union members (12 percent of men and 15 percent of women), 72 percent of the respondents reported that they had, while 27 percent reported that they did not have, a family member or a friend as union member. The two latter percentages, given in Table 6.4B, give overwhelming support to this hypothesis. The Z-test on these proportions revealed a very large Z value of 21.42, confirming the significance of the difference between the two proportions.

The data in Table 6.4B on sex breakdown show that 78 percent of men compared to 59 percent of women reported having a union member among their relatives and/or friends. These data suggest that the majority of respondents had some-

Table 6.4: FREQUENCY AND PERCENTAGE DISTRIBUTION OF UNION EXECUTIVES IN CANADA WHOSE FATHER WAS A UNION MEMBER, BY TOTAL AND SEX, 1983

Categories of Answers	Total		Male		Female	
	Freq.	Percent	Freq.	Percent	Freq.	Percent
Yes	182	41.0	145	44.0	37	33.0
No	261	58.0	185	56.0	76	67.0
DK/NA	0	0.0	0	0.0.	0	0.0
No Response	3	1.0	3	1.0	0	0.0
Total	446	100.0	333	101.0	113	100.0
Percentage of 453 questionnaires used	98.5 Percent		73.5 Percent		25.0 Percent	

Table **6.4A: FREQUENCY AND PERCENTAGE DISTRIBUTION OF UNION EXECUTIVES IN CANADA WHOSE MOTHER WAS A UNION MEMBER, BY TOTAL AND SEX, 1983**

Categories of Answers	Total		Male		Female	
	Freq.	*Percent*	*Freq.*	*Percent*	*Freq.*	*Percent*
Yes	56	12.0	39	12.0	17	15.0
No	385	87.0	290	88.0	95	85.0
DK/NA	0	0.0	0	0.0	0	0.0
No Response	3	1.0	3	1.0	0	0.0
Total	444	100.0	332	101.0	112	100.0
Percentage of 453 questionnaires used	98.0 Percent		73.3 Percent		25.0 Percent	

Table **6.4B: FREQUENCY AND PERCENTAGE DISTRIBUTION OF UNION EXECUTIVES IN CANADA WITH EITHER FAMILY MEMBERS/FRIENDS WHO WERE UNION MEMBERS, BY TOTAL AND SEX, 1983**

Categories of Answers	Total		Male		Female	
	Freq.	*Percent*	*Freq.*	*Percent*	*Freq.*	*Percent*
Yes	323	72.0	258	78.0	65	59.0
No	117	27.0	71	21.0	46	41.0
DK/NA	0	0.0	0	0.0	0	0.0
No Response	3	1.0	3	1.0	0	0.0
Total	443	100.0	332	100.0	111	100.0
Percentage of 453 questionnaires used	98.0 Percent		73.3 Percent		25.0 Percent	

one as a role-model to create aspirations for becoming union members and even acquiring leadership positions. The fact that the percentage of women is lower than that of men is not surprising, since very few mothers of the respondents were found to be union members: furthermore, it is likely that, relative to men, not many women union executives, or women in general, would have come across other women unionists during their formative years who could socialize them into aspiration for joining unions simply because few women unionists existed.

Our finding then is: the majority of union executive members do have a family member and/or a friend in a union. This factor may be taken to mean that such socialization makes them less reluctant to join unions; hence family socialization has an impact on the motivation of "persons" to join unions.

Our hypothesis gets confirmed by a large percentage of women reporting having a friend or family member as a member of a union. Probably it would also be true that lack of family socialization and adequate role-models would be a barrier in the case of many women's joining unions.

It should, however, be noted that in this sample this particular factor is operative more often in the case of men (78 percent) than women (59 percent). This might mean, as will be argued later, that, relative to men, some women seek union membership more often out of their personal struggles and convictions rather than under the influence of family socialization.

In order again to make firmer conclusions, we calculate below non-simultaneous 95 percent two-sided confidence intervals from the data of Tables 6.4, 6.4A and 6.4B and present them in Tables CI–4, 4A and 4B.

From these tables, we conclude with 95 percent confidence:

1. The fathers of (a) 36 to 46 percent of union executives in general, (b) 39 to 49 percent of male union executives, and (c) 28 to 46 percent of the female union executives were union members.

Table CI–4

	Sex	Parameter	Confidence Interval
(a)	Male and Female	P_1—proportion of all union executives whose fathers were union members	.41 ± .05
		P_2—proportion of all union executives whose fathers were not union members	.58 ± .05
		P_2–P_1	.17 ± .07
(b)	Male	P_1—proportion of male executives whose fathers were union members	.44 ± .05
		P_2—proportion of male executives whose fathers were not union members	.56 ± .05
		P_2–P_1	.12 ± .08
(c)	Female	P_1—proportion of female executives whose fathers were union members	.37 ± .09
		P_2—proportion of female executives whose fathers were not union members	.76 ± .08
		P_2–P_1	.39 ± .13

Table CI–4A

	Sex	Parameter	Confidence Interval
(a)	Male and Female	P_1—proportion of all executives whose mothers were union members	.12 ± 0.3
		P_2—proportion of all union executives whose mothers were not union members	.87 ± .03
		P_2–P_1	.75 ± .04
(b)	Male	P_1—proportion of male executives whose mothers were union members	.12 ± .03
		P_2—proportion of male executives whose mothers were not union members	.88 ± .03
		P_2–P_1	.76 ± .05
(c)	Female	P_1—proportion of female executives whose mothers were union members	.15 ± .07
		P_2—proportion of female executives whose mothers were not union members	.85 ± .07
		P_2–P_1	.70 ± .10

Table CI–4B

Sex	Parameter	Confidence Interval
(a) Male and Female	P_1—proportion of all executives who had family members / friends as union members	.72 ± 0.4
	P_2—proportion of all executives who did not have family members / friends as union members	.27 ± .04
	P_1–P_2	.45 ± .06
(b) Male	P_1—proportion of male executives who had family members / friends as union members	.78 ± .04
	P_2—proportion of male executives who did not have family members / friends as union members	.21 ± .04
	P_1–P_2	.57 ± .06
(c) Female	P_1—proportion of female executives who had family members / friends as union members	.59 ± .09
	P_2—proportion of female executives who did not have family members / friends as union members	.41 ± .09
	P_1–P_2	.18 ± .14

2. The fathers of (a) 53 to 63 percent of union executives in general, (b) 51 to 61 percent of male union executives, and (c) 68 to 84 percent of female union executives were not union members.

3. Among all union executives, those whose fathers were not union members have a majority of 10 to 24 percent over those whose fathers were union members. The corresponding figure for male union executives is between 4 and 20 and for female union executives between 26 and 52.

4. The mothers of (a) 10 to 16 percent of union executives in general, (b) 9 to 15 percent of male union executives, and (c) 8 to 22 percent of female union executives were union members.

5. The mothers of (a) 84 to 90 percent of all union executives, (b) 85 to 91 percent of male union executives, and (c) 78 to

92 percent of female union executives were not union members.

6. Among all union executives, those whose mothers were not union members have a majority of 60 to 80 percent over those whose mothers were union members. The corresponding percentage for male union executives is between 71 and 81 and for female union executives between 60 and 80.

7. Among union executives in general, 68 to 76 percent had family members or friends as union members. The corresponding figures for male union executives lies between 74 and 82 and for female union executives between 50 and 68.

8. Among union executives in general, 23 to 31 percent did not have family members or friends as union members. The corresponding percentage for male union executives is between 17 and 25 and for female union executives between 32 and 50.

9. Among union executives in general, those who had family members or friends as union members have a majority of 39 to 51 percent over those who did not have them. The corresponding figure for male union executives is between 51 and 63 and for female union executives between 4 and 32.

6.5: Hypothesis 5

Hypothesis 5 states:

Union executives perceive that unionization of women will be facilitated if special legislation were to be passed. It would encourage women to form their separate bargaining units.

This hypothesis is based upon the assumption that very often women do not join unions because they do not perceive unions as adequate vehicles for meeting their demands. This was tested by opinion data. The respondents were asked two different questions to quantify two parts of the hypothesis:

(a) Do you think that special legislation should be passed encouraging women's unionization? (Question No. 35)
(b) Do you think there should be separate bargaining units for women? (Question No. 36)

The responses to both the questions were taken as a measure of their perceptions of the desirability of special legislation for encouraging women's unionization.

The data on the responses relating to special legislation, presented in Table 6.5, reveal that only 40 percent of the respondents felt that special legislation should be passed, whereas 44 percent did not agree. Another 15 percent were undecided on this issue.

To assess the significance of the difference between these two proportions the Z-test was conducted. The computed Z value was 1.2 which is below the critical value of 1.96 and this shows that the difference is not significant at .05 level of significance.

Table 6.5: FREQUENCY AND PERCENTAGE DISTRIBUTION OF UNION EXECUTIVES' PERCEPTION THAT SPECIAL LEGISLATION SHOULD BE PASSED TO ENCOURAGE WOMEN'S UNIONIZATION, BY TOTAL AND SEX, 1983

Categories of Answers	Total		Male		Female	
	Freq.	Percent	Freq.	Percent	Freq.	Percent
Agreed	178	40.0	131	40.0	47	42.0
Disagreed	198	44.0	153	46.0	45	40.0
Undecided	65	15.0	45	14.0	20	18.0
DK/NA	0	0.0	0	0.0	0	0.0
No Response	3	1.0	3	1.0	0	0.0
Total	444	100.0	332	101.0	112	100.0
Percentage of 453 questionnaires used	98.0 Percent		73.3 Percent		25.0 Percent	

Since the difference between these two proportions is not significant, the hypothesized relationship does not emerge. This means that we cannot say that, in general, union executives perceive that passing of special legislation would encourage unionization of women workers.

The analysis by sex of Table 6.5 does not reveal a very different picture. Forty percent of men union executives as compared with 42 percent of women executives were in favour of special legislation whereas 46 percent of men and 40 percent of women, respectively, were not. Again we cannot say that this hypothesis is even partially confirmed. At best we can say that union executives of both sexes are divided on this issue.

The data based on the responses to the second question relating to separate bargaining units, presented in Table 6.5A, have been categorized into "yes", "no" and "indifferent" categories. This table shows that a very small percentage, viz. 6 percent of the respondents, say "yes" whereas 85 percent say "no". Hence, on the basis of these data, our hypothesis is not confirmed. A large Z score with a computed value of 13.8 at the required level of significance shows that the difference

Table **6.5A:** **FREQUENCY AND PERCENTAGE DISTRIBUTION OF UNION EXECUTIVES' PERCEPTION THAT THERE SHOULD BE SEPARATE BARGAINING UNITS FOR WOMEN, BY TOTAL AND SEX, 1983**

Categories of Answers	Total		Male		Female	
	Freq.	Percent	Freq.	Percent	Freq.	Percent
Agreed	23	6.0	13	4.0	10	9.0
Disagreed	382	85.0	297	90.0	85	76.0
Undecided	38	9.0	21	6.0	17	15.0
DK/NA	0	0.0	0	0.0	0	0.0
No Response	3	0.5	3	1.0	0	0.0
Total	446	100.5	334	101.0	112	100.0
Percentage of 453 questionnaires used	98.5 Percent		74.0 Percent		25.0 Percent	

between the two proportions is highly significant and we can state that our findings are that union executives do not believe that there should be separate bargaining units for women workers.

To assess whether similar responses are found across the sex categories, data were analysed by sex. Table 6.5A reveals that, though in very small numbers, women are relatively more in favour of separate bargaining units than men, i.e., 9 percent of women as against 4 percent of men say that there should be separate bargaining units for women; however, 76 percent of the women and 90 percent of men are against it with 15 and 9 percent being undecided, respectively. Hence this hypothesis does not get even partial statistical support from the analysis of sex breakdown.

What can be said about this hypothesis after examining the analyses of the responses to both questions? It can be stated thus: although no clear perception of union executives emerges from these data about the desirability or undesirability of passing special legislation, there is a definite general opinion that separate bargaining units for women should *not* be formed.

Again, we give more precise conclusions. First, we present in Table CI-5 the non-simultaneous, two-sided 95 percent confidence intervals from Table 6.5.

From Table CI-5 the following conclusions can be drawn with 95 percent confidence:

(a) Among union executives in general, 35 to 45 percent think that special legislation should be passed encouraging women's unionization. The corresponding percentage for male union executives is between 35 and 45 and for female union executives between 33 and 51.

(b) Among union executives in general, 39 to 49 percent do not think that special legislation should be passed encouraging women's unionization. The corresponding percentage in the case of male union executives is between 41 and 51 and in the case of women union executives between 31 and 49.

Table CI–5

Sex	Parameter	Confidence Interval
(a) Male and Female	P_1—proportion of all union executives who favour legislation encouraging women's unionization	$.40 \pm .05$
	P_2—proportion of all union executives who do not favour legislation encouraging women's unionization	$.44 \pm .05$
	P_2-P_1	$.04 \pm .07$
(b) Male	P_1—proportion of male union executives who favour legislation encouraging women's unionization	$.40 \pm .05$
	P_2—proportion of male union executives who do not favour legislation encouraging women's unionization	$.46 \pm .05$
	P_2-P_1	$.06 \pm .08$
(c) Female	P_1—proportion of female union executives who favour legislation encouraging women's unionization	$.42 \pm .09$
	P_2—proportion of female union executives who do not favour legislation encouraging women's unionization	$.40 \pm .09$
	P_1-P_2	$.02 \pm .14$

(c) Among union executives in general, the difference between the proportions of those who think that special legislation encouraging women's unionization should be passed and those who do not think so lies between −.03 and .11. The corresponding difference for male union executives is between −.02 and .14 and for female union executives between −.12 and .16.

The two-sided 95 percent non-simultaneous confidence intervals are now given from the data in Table 6.5A.

We can now draw the following conclusions with 95 percent confidence (Table CI-5A):

Table CI–5A

Sex	Parameter	Confidence Interval
(a) Male and Female	P_1—proportion of all union executives who favour separate bargaining units for women	$.06 \pm .02$
	P_2—proportion of all union executives who oppose separate bargaining units for women	$.85 \pm .03$
	P_2-P_1	$.79 \pm .04$
(b) Male	P_1—proportion of male union executives who favour separate bargaining units for women	$.04 \pm .02$
	P_2—proportion of male union executives who oppose separate bargaining units for women	$.90 \pm .03$
	P_2-P_1	$.86 \pm .04$
(c) Female	P_1—proportion of female union executives who favour separate bargaining units for women	$.09 \pm .05$
	P_2—proportion of female union executives who oppose separate bargaining units for women	$.75 \pm .08$
	P_2-P_1	$.67 \pm .10$

(a)　Among union executives in general, 4 to 8 percent favour separate bargaining units for women. The corresponding figure for male union executives is between 2 and 6 and for female union executives between 4 and 14.

(b)　Among union executives in general, 82 to 88 percent oppose separate bargaining units for women. The corresponding figure for male union executives is between 87 and 93 and for female union executives between 67 and 83.

(c)　Among union executives in general, those who oppose separate bargaining units for women have a majority of 75 to 83 percent over those who support it. The corresponding figure for male union executives is between 82 and 90 and for female union executives between 57 and 77.

6.6: Hypothesis 6

Hypothesis 6, which sought to explore union discrimination, was stated in two parts:

(a) Union executives perceive that the attitude of male union members towards women's joining unions is either negative or indifferent.

(b) Union executives perceive that in bargaining for specific female issues there is reluctance or opposition from other male union members.

Each part was tested by a different set of data. Part (a) was tested on experience data gathered by asking union executives whether they found the attitude of union male members towards women's joining unions positive, negative or indifferent (Question No. 26). Their responses saying "negative" were to be taken as indicators of union discrimination.

Table 6.6, which contains data on union executives' perception of union discrimination, indicates that a fairly large percentage, viz., 56 percent of the respondents, found male members' attitude positive and only 7 percent found it negative. However, 31 percent of the sample did show their attitude to be indifferent. So altogether 38 percent of the respondents

Table **6.6: FREQUENCY AND PERCENTAGE DISTRIBUTION OF UNION EXECUTIVES' PERCEPTION OF "MALE MEMBERS' ATTITUDE" AS A BARRIER TO THE UNIONIZATION OF WOMEN, BY TOTAL AND SEX, 1983**

Categories of Answers	Total		Male		Female	
	Freq.	Percent	Freq.	Percent	Freq.	Percent
Positive	249	56.0	195	60.0	54	48.0
Negative	33	7.0	19	6.0	14	12.0
Indifferent	135	31.0	99	30.0	36	32.0
Undecided	20	4.0	12	4.0	8	7.0
DK/NA	1	0.5	1	0.5	0	0.0
No Response	3	2.0	3	1.0	0	0.0
Total	441	100.5	329	101.5	112	99.0
Percentage of 453 questionnaires used		97.3 Percent		73.0 Percent		25.0 Percent

experienced indifferent or negative attitudes of male union members towards women's joining unions.

To test the significance of the difference between these two proportions, the Z-test was conducted and the computed value of Z was 3.52 which is greater than the critical value at .05 level of significance which shows a larger percentage of union executives perceive members' attitude towards women's joining unions as positive. This means that statistically our hypothesis is not confirmed and our findings on these data would be that most of the union executives do not perceive that there is any sex discrimination on the part of male union members.

The data examined by sex breakdown reveal that the experiences of men and women executives differ. A greater percentage of union men executives, i.e., 60 percent, found male members' attitude positive as compared with only 48 percent of union women executives. Only 6 percent of men as against 12 percent of women found it negative, but an almost equal number stated (30 and 32 percent) that they were indifferent. It follows that more women than men experienced negative or indifferent attitudes among male members.

The data on part (b) of the hypothesis relating to male members' attitude, viz., "reluctance to bargain for female issues", contained in Table 6.6A support this finding. Again a large percentage, i.e. 68 percent of the respondents, indicated that they did not experience any reluctance on the part of male members to bargain for female issues. Only 23 percent of the respondents believed that there was such reluctance.

The Z score on the significance of the differences between these proportions which is equal to 5.84—well into the critical region at .05 level of significance—indicates that the differences between the two proportions is significant. This means that the majority of the union executives do not perceive that there is reluctance on the part of the male members to bargain for female issues. Thus our hypothesis is not confirmed.

Table **6.6A**: FREQUENCY AND PERCENTAGE DISTRIBUTION OF UNION EXECUTIVES' PERCEPTION OF MALE MEMBERS' RELUC-TANCE TO BARGAIN ON FEMALE ISSUES, BY TOTAL AND SEX, 1983

Categories of Answers	Total		Male		Female	
	Freq.	Percent	Freq.	Percent	Freq.	Percent
Agree	102	23.0	67	21.0	35	31.0
Disagree	304	68.0	229	73.0	75	66.0
DK/NA	20	5.0	17	6.0	3	3.0
No Response	5	4.0	5	1.0	0	0.0
Total	431	100.0	318	101.0	113	100.0
Percentage of 453 questionnaires used	95.0 Percent		70.2 Percent		25.0 Percent	

The sex breakdown of the data in Table 6.6A reveals important differences. Twenty-one percent of male and 31 percent of female union executives faced male reluctance in bargaining for female issues. A large percentage, 73 percent of men, as against 66 percent of women, reported that they did not face any reluctance on the part of male union members in bargaining for female issues. It follows that, though relatively more women than men faced reluctance on the topic under discussion, an altogether larger percentage of both sexes did not experience any such reluctance. Thus our hypothesis does not get much support from the data examined by sex either. Hence our finding is: Union executives (of both sexes) do not generally perceive that there is reluctance on the part of male union members in bargaining for female issues. It is then reasonable to conclude that unions are not perceived by the union executives as discriminating against women workers joining unions and bargaining for their issues.

Table 6.6 generates the following non-simultaneous two-sided 95 percent confidence intervals.

Table CI–6

Sex	Parameter	Confidence Interval
(a) Male and Female	P_1—proportion of all union executives who perceive male union members' attitude as positive	.56 ± .05
	P_2—proportion of all union executives who perceive male union members' attitude as negative or indifferent	.38 ± .05
	P_1–P_2	.18 ± .07
(b) Male	P_1—proportion of all male union executives who perceive male union members' attitude as positive	.60 ± .05
	P_2—proportion of all male union executives who perceive male union members' attitude as negative or indifferent	.36 ± .05
	P_1–P_2	.24 ± .08
(c) Female	P_1—proportion of all female union executives who perceive male union members' attitude as positive	.48 ± .09
	P_2—proportion of all female union executives who perceive male union members' attitude as negative or indifferent	.44 ± .09
	P_1–P_2	.04 ± .14

From Table CI–6, we can draw the following conclusions with 95 percent confidence:

(a) Among union executives in general, 51 to 61 percent perceive that male union members' attitude towards women's joining unions is positive. The corresponding percentage for male union executives is between 55 and 65, and for female union executives betwen 39 and 57.

(b) Among all union executives in general, 33 and 43 percent perceive that male union members' attitude toward women's joining unions is negative or indifferent. The corresponding percentage for male union executives is between 31 and 41 and for female union executives between 35 and 53.

(c) Among union executives in general, those who perceive that male union members' attitude towards women's joining unions is positive have a majority of 11 to 25 percent over those who perceive it to be negative or indifferent. The corresponding figure for male union executives is between 16 and 32 and for female union executives between −10 and 18.

Table 6.6A generates the non-simultaneous two-sided confidence intervals shown in Table CI–6A, from which we can draw the following conclusions with 95 percent confidence:

Table CI–6A		
Sex	*Parameter*	*Confidence Interval*
(a) Male and Female	P_1—proportion of all union executives who perceive male union members' reluctance	$.23 \pm .04$
	P_2—proportion of all union executives who do not perceive male union members' reluctance	$.68 \pm .04$
	P_2–P_1	$.45 \pm .06$
(b) Male	P_1—proportion of male union executives who perceive male union members' reluctance	$.21 \pm .04$
	P_2—proportion of male union executives who do not perceive male union members' reluctance	$.73 \pm .05$
	P_2–P_1	$.52 \pm .07$
(c) Female	P_1—proportion of female union executives who perceive male union members' reluctance	$.31 \pm .09$
	P_2—proportion of female union executives who do not perceive male union members' reluctance	$.66 \pm .09$
	P_2–P_1	$.35 \pm .13$

(a)   Among union executives in general, 19 to 27 percent perceive that in bargaining for specific female issues there is reluctance or opposition from male union members. The corresponding percentage among male union executives is betwen 17 and 25 and among female union executives between 22 and 40.

(b)   Among union executives in general, 64 to 72 percent do not perceive that in bargaining for specific female issues there is reluctance or opposition from male union members. The corresponding figure for male union executives is between 68 and 78 and for female union executives between 57 and 75.

(c)   Among union executives in general, those who do not perceive that in bargaining for specific female issues there is reluctance or opposition from male union members have a majority of 39 to 51 over those who do. The corresponding figure for male union executives is between 45 and 59 and for female union executives 32 and 38.

6.7 Summary of Findings

Six hypotheses were tested in the previous sections, all attempting to discover the factors which do and which do not constitute barriers to unionization of women. Before discussing and interpreting the findings from these tests, a brief summary of the findings from each hypothesis is presented below.

Hypothesis 1 concerning the union executives' perception of the relevance of education for the unionization of women was tested by two different indicators, and based on both, *statistically* it was not confirmed, which means that education was not perceived by the union executives as a very important factor in the unionization of women. However, when the data were examined by sex, more women union executives as compared with men union executives were found to believe that education was very important or most important for women workers successfully seeking union membership.

Hypothesis 2 testing union executives' perception of women workers being clustered into low-paid, semi-skilled or un-skilled occupations as forming a barrier to unionization was statistically again not confirmed by aggregate data. Yet the finding from the data with sex breakdown showed that more women than men perceived such occupational clustering as a barrier to unionization of women and the hypothesis got partial confirmation.

The findings from hypothesis 3 aimed at assessing union executives' perceptions on job fragmentation as a serious bar-rier to women workers being unionized, are that an over-whelming majority of union executives, both men and women, perceive job fragmentation as a serious barrier to women's unionization.

Hypothesis 4, designed to test the influence of socialization in adopting the role of a union member through role-models, which most women lack, shows that such influence does count, as the majority of union executives, both men and women (many more men than women), have some friends or family members as members of unions. So an absence of such role-models becomes a barrier to unionization in the case of women workers.

The findings from hypothesis 5 concerning union executi-ves' perception of the need for special legislation and separate bargaining units for women workers can be stated thus: union executives are divided on the issue of special legislation, so we cannot say whether in general the union executives perceive that passing of special legislation would encourage unioniza-tion of women workers; but on the question of separate bar-gaining units for women workers, union executives are unanimous in their belief that these should not be formed.

Hypothesis 6 was aimed at exploring the question of union discrimination in terms of male union members' (a) negative attitude towards women's joining unions, and (b) reluctance about bargaining for specific female issues. The test yielded the following results: in general, union executives do not perceive that there is any sex discrimination on the part of male union members either in terms of a negative attitude towards women's joining unions or in terms of reluctance about bargaining for female issues. An analysis of these data by sex revealed the same kind of difference between union men and women as was found earlier, namely, that though few in number, relatively more female union executives perceived union discrimination on both the above indicators than did male union executives.

6.8 Conclusions

From these findings three important conclusions emerge which we elaborate below.

1. Comparative Male-Female Perceptions of Barriers to Women's Unionization

Although our findings show that, according to the union executives' perception, some of the factors hypothesized above do while others do not constitute barriers to unionization of women workers, it should be noted that all the hypotheses find consistently more support from women executives than from men executives. This means that on all the hypothesized variables (whether statistically confirmed or not), women union executives show deeper and greater perception of the barriers to unionization of women workers than men executives do. This finding is not surprising in view of the fact that, (a) women executives would themselves have faced such barriers as *women* when seeking union membership and union executive positions, and (b) they would probably be involved more than men executives in an attempt to organize women and thus would have a deeper awareness of the factors which constitute barriers to women workers seeking union membership.

Regarding the representative character of the women union executives of our sample, it should be pointed out here that these women themselves have successfully achieved not only union membership but executive positions; hence, basically they have a success story to tell. Although they have displayed greater awareness of the barriers to women's unionization as compared to men, even they may not be cognizant of all the barriers in the way of women who tried to join or to form unions and failed. Ideally, the perceptions of the women who faced failure would have given us a greater understanding of the barriers in the way of women being unionized, but within the scope of this research, we could not include such women and draw a random sample from the whole population. We limited ourselves to the sub-population of the successful women, the women executives, because, on the one hand, they could be easily identified, having been listed in the *Directory of Labour Organizations*, 1982, and, on the other, they had, as leaders and executives, expert and direct knowledge of the barriers in organizing women workers into a union, or persuading them to join existing unions.

However, we can supplement our results by some case studies of failure. One such study (Joan Sangster, 1978) pointed out employer opposition, union ambivalence and the prevailing sexist attitude towards women as barriers to women's organizing attempts after the 1907 Bell Telephone Strike.[1] Organizing attempts by women in Toronto after the meat boycott in 1932 and the strike in the textile industry in Hamilton in 1929 were unsuccessful for similar reasons, as reported in another study (Dorothy King, 1974).[2] A recent study (SORWUC—Stores Office Retail Workers Union of Canada—1979) showed employer opposition, the protracted certification process and the opposition of the Canada Labour Congress (CLC) as the major barriers in unionizing bank women workers.[3] The structural factors underlying employer opposition and the obstructions of legal process are not much analysed in these case studies as we have done. The emphasis on sexist attitudes and union opposition in these studies is, however, not borne out by our analysis of union executive opinion data.

2. *The Primacy of Structural Barriers to Women's Unionization*

A closer examination of the findings from all the hypotheses reveals a pattern which is in conformity with the finding from our historical analysis in the preceding chapters, namely, the primacy of structural factors as barriers to female unionization. Most of the hypotheses which related to attitudinal and institutional barriers do not find as much support from the opinion data of the union executives as those which deal with labour-market (i.e. structural) barriers rooted in the nature and conditions of women's work. For example, the hypothesis about job fragmentation is overwhelmingly supported and that about occupational ghettoization is partially supported. On the other hand, the hypothesis regarding the (a) attitudes of male unionists to women's seeking union membership, (b) need for separate bargaining units for women, and (c) male union members' reluctance about bargaining for female issues are not supported at all. The hypotheses about special legislation and education do not find much support either. The conclusion drawn from these findings is that, in general, union executives perceive labour-market barriers as far more crucially related to the low unionization of women workers than the other kinds of barriers. To be sure, this is a verification by contemporary data of what we inferred from our earlier historical and theoretical analysis. As such, this conclusion must have very important theoretical implications and practical significance. This we shall discuss by way of concluding this study in Chapter 7.

3. *The Role of Education in Women's Unionization*

While most of the hypotheses discussed were drawn from existing literature on barriers to unionization of women, one hypothesis tested was unique, i.e. the one concerning union executives' perception of the relevance of education to unionization of women. As noted in Chapter 1, to date, this has not been studied in the Unionization/Industrial Relations literature. Yet, its importance is obvious from the fact that women in occupations which require relatively higher levels of education, e.g., teaching, nursing and public administration, are unionized far more successfully than those who are in semi-skilled or unskilled occupations like sewing, cleaning, cooking, waitressing and laundry work. Indeed, our aggregate data on education, labour force participation and unionization showed a positive correlation between education and participation, on the one hand, and, between participation and unionization, on the other. A visual image of this correlation is as follows:

Economy → Education → Labour Force → Unionization
Participation

The higher the level of the economy, the higher the level of education, and, hence, the higher the labour force participation rate and, consequently, the unionization rate.

As we can see from the contemporary history of unionization, organizations encompassing unskilled, less educated and thereby marginalized women workers like waitresses, bank tellers and saleswomen are facing the hardest battle against employer opposition, retaliation, intimidation, layoff and eventual firing compared to those organizing women with higher education and possessing scarce professional qualifications, e.g., nurses, paramedics (physiotherapists), nutritionists, dieticians, teachers and researchers. It is unfortunate that unsuccessful organizations are not listed in a systematic way in any labour bulletin. If we could sample them—organizations like SORWUC—would they also reject or at best partially support our hypothesis regarding the positive impact of education on women's unionization as the executives of the successful organizations in our sample have done?

This question invites a final note on education. Education is a filter; it connotes no causal relation in the diagram above. Nurses are better unionized than tellers not because nurses, as such, are more educated than tellers. More educated tellers would not be any more unionized than less educated tellers.

Less educated nurses will not be any less unionized than more educated ones. The point is: nursing is a unionizable job, bank-clerking is not. The former is a public or semi-public monopoly employing large congregations of nurses; the latter is a small bank branch hiring a few tellers and competing atomistically with other financial institutions. SORWUC and other similar unsuccessful organizations would also have probably rejected our hypothesis regarding education. Blue collar jobs in the monopoly sector don't need higher education, but they are the citadel of unionization. The fact that they have been unionizing more slowly than nursing, teaching and public administration in recent years, implies the decline of relative employment in the former and the rise in the latter. So, with a slump in the teaching, nursing and public administration industries, the picture may be totally reversed. Yet, like blue collar jobs, they will remain unionizable jobs whereas personal service, sales-clerking, bank-clerking, etc., will remain ununionizable.

For women to unionize, they have to work in places where unionization is possible. Competitive private sector jobs are not among such places. Surely, they don't want unionization for the sake of unionization. They want good jobs. They need higher education as a precondition to consideration for these jobs. Once in, it so happens that the job has a union with which the newcomer can identify. But here is the caveat. These good jobs are not thrown around in abundance. Beyond a certain level of highly educated manpower lies the spectre of unemployment. One may find no such job not even as a research or a teaching assistant. A young woman Ph.D. may end up as a bank teller, probably hiding her Ph.D. diploma for a while. Leave aside being unionized, she may not even be in the active army of labour in the first place; she may simply be in the stagnant reserve doing an irregular job as a tutor today, a bank teller tomorrow, and so on. To put it another way: granted that with higher education you can get a job that is already unionized, say nursing; how about the original question? Floor cleaning, bank-telling and sales-clerking do not need higher education. How can higher education help unionization in these jobs?

This last was perhaps an extreme example used merely to dramatize the case for the crucial role of the nature of the job itself, its structure as opposed to the form education imparts to it. This is not to deny the role of education as a raiser of consciousness. But what sort of education? We shall return to this question in our concluding chapter.

REFERENCES

1. Joan Sangster, "The 1907 Bell Telephone Strike: Organizing Women Workers", *Journal of Canadian Labour Studies*, 1978, vol. 3.
2. Dorothy King, "Women's Organization: Learning From Yesterday", in *Women at Work*, 1975.
3. SORWUC: *An Account to Settle*.

APPENDIX

to

Chapter Six

APPENDIX 6A

UNIVERSITY OF ALBERTA
FACULTY OF BUSINESS

Number _____ .   March 7, 1983

PERCEPTIONS OF MALE & FEMALE UNION EXECUTIVES OF THE INSTITUTIONAL AND LABOUR MARKET BARRIERS TO THE UNIONIZATION OF WOMEN

Please fill in the blanks or circle the appropriate response number. Add any additional information which may help clarify your response.

1. *Place of residence:* _____

                              City/Town   Province/State

2. *Age:* 1. Under 20   5. 36–40
            2. 20–25   6. 41–45
            3. 26–30   7. 46–50
            4. 31–35   8. 51–55
                                    9. 56 or above

3. *Sex:* 1. Male
            2. Female

4. *Present marital status:*   1. Single
                                    2. Married/Common law
                                    3. Divorced/Separated/Widowed

5. *Number of children:*   1. None
                                    2. One
                                    3. Two
                                    4. Three
                                    5. Four or More
                                    6. NA

6. *What is the highest level of education you have received?*
            1. less than grade 9
            2. some high school but no diploma
            3. high school diploma (university entrance)

    4. some post-secondary training (no diploma or degree)
    5. completed apprenticeship
    6. technical institute or community college diploma
    7. bachelors degree
    8. post-graduate degree

7. *What is your occupation? Please be specific.*

_____

8. *How many years have you been in paid employment?*
    1. One year
    2. 2–4 years
    3. 5–7 years
    4. 8–10 years
    5. 11–12 years
    6. 13–14 years
    7. 15 years or more

9. *Was your father a union member?*
    1. Yes
    2. No

10. *Was your mother a union member?*
    1. Yes
    2. No

11. *Was any member of your family or friend a union member?*
    1. Yes
    2. No

12. *What led you to become active in union work?* Please specify.

_____
_____
_____

13. *For how many years have you belonged to the union where you are currently an executive?*
    1. 2 years or less
    2. 3–5 years
    3. 6–8 years
    4. 9–11 years
    5. 12 years or more

14. *For how many years were you a rank and file member before being elected to a position?*
     1. 2 years or less
     2. 3–5 years
     3. 6–8 years
     4. 9–11 years
     5. 12 years or more

15. *Are the majority of your union members*
     1. male
     2. female
     3. or is your union mixed?

16. *What is the name of your union?*

     _____

17. *Is your union affiliated with*
     1. an international,
     2. national, or
     3. government employee union?

18. *What is your designation on the Union Executive Board?*
     1. President
     2. Vice-president
     3. Sec./Treas.
     4. Secretary
     5. Treasurer

_____

Do you agree with the following statements?

19. "One of the most important barriers to women being successfully unionized is the opposition of the employer."
     1. agree
     2. disagree
     3. undecided

20. "As a large number of women hold part-time jobs or temporary jobs, they have little incentive to join unions in order to improve their working conditions."
     1. agree
     2. disagree
     3. undecided

21. "Women workers being clustered in low paid, semi-skilled or unskilled occupations with very little bargaining power, is primarily

responsible for their low unionization."
1. agree
2. disagree
3. undecided

---

22. *Many women work in isolated work places like restaurants, kitchens, domestic places, small shops. Do you think that the fragmented nature of their work makes it difficult for them to be organized into a union?*
    1. yes
    2. no
    3. undecided

23. *Do you think that the societal expectation from women to play a submissive role in the family and in society stands in the way of their actively seeking union membership?*
    1. yes
    2. no
    3. undecided

24. *Is it true that women's low unionization is in part the result of their self-perception (created by society) as the weaker and dependent sex?*
    1. yes
    2. no
    3. undecided

25. *Do you think that the lack of easily available and affordable day care/evening care facilities is a significant factor in preventing women from being active in union work?*
    1. yes
    2. no
    3. undecided

26. *How do you find the attitude of male union members toward women joining unions?*
    1. positive
    2. negative
    3. indifferent
    4. undecided

27. *If negative, could you suggest what according to you, are the reasons for this attitude?*
    1. _____
    2. _____
    3. _____

4. _____

5. NA

28. *In bargaining for specific female issues, did you face reluctance and opposition from male union members?*
    1. yes
    2. no

29. *Do you think the existing unions and the collective bargaining process are adequate vehicles to meet their demands as women and as workers?*
    1. yes
    2. no
    3. undecided

30. *If no, could you suggest some other organizational means through which women workers could press for their demands?*

    1. _____
       _____
       _____

    2. NA

31. *Based upon your own experience, could you say that unions discriminate against women unionists?*
    1. yes
    2. no
    3. undecided

32. *For women workers to seek union membership how important is it for them to have a relatively high level of education or specific training?*
    1. most important
    2. very important but not the most important
    3. not very important
    4. not important at all
    5. undecided

33. *If important, could you specify in what ways does their education, skill or raining affect women workers' attitude towards unionization?*
    1. by increasing their labour force participation
    2. by creating job consciousness
    3. by fostering ambition to improve working conditions
    4. by creating aspiration to seek union leadership
    5. all of the above

    6. any other _____

7. undecided
8. NA

34. *Relative to other factors, could you state, how important has your education and/or training been in motivating you to become a union member?*
    1. most important
    2. very important but not the most important
    3. not very important ·
    4. not important at all
    5. undecided
    6. NA

35. *Do you think that some special legislation should be passed encouragin women's unionization?*
    1. yes
    2. no
    3. undecided

36. *Do you think industrial relations boards should allow separate bargaining units for women?*
    1. yes
    2. no
    3. undecided

37. *In you own case, did you face some barriers when you were seeking union membership?*
    1. yes
    2. no

38. *If yes, could you specify five most important barriers that you faced in joining the union?*

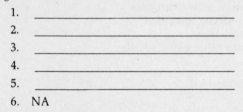

    1. _____
    2. _____
    3. _____
    4. _____
    5. _____
    6. NA

39. *Could you also specify the most important strategy you adopted to overcome those barriers.*
    1. obtained higher education
    2. took industrial relations courses
    3. became more active in union work
    4. upgraded your particular training

> 5.   any other, please specify
> 6.   NA

40. *Could you state what are the specific barriers which in YOUR KNOWLEDGE, other women workers are at present facing in joining a union?*

> 1.   _____

> _____

> _____

> 2.   NA

41. *In your opinion which one of the following labour market barriers is most crucially related to low unionization of women.*
>   1.   employer's opposition
>   2.   working in small, isolated places rather than in a large concern
>   3.   lack of skill/training
>   4.   temporary/part-time work involvement
>   5.   any other, please specify
>
> _____
>
>   6.   concentration in white collar jobs
>   7.   lack of skilled jobs in blue collar sector
>   8.   any other, please specify
>
> _____

42. *In your opinion, which one of the following institutional barriers is most crucially related to low unionization of women?*
>   1.   family socialization
>   2.   low education
>   3.   male unionist attitude
>   4.   societal expectation
>   5.   legislation
>   6.   any other, please specify
>
> _____
>
>   7.   undecided

Chapter 7
A Summing up and Some Unresolved Issues

7.1 *A Summing Up*

IN CHAPTER 1, we have critically examined the existing theories of unionization which are all couched in unisex terms, treating labourers as a homogeneous group. We have argued that women workers form a distinct group with some special problems that do not affect male workers. As such, existing theories have little validity so far as women are concerned. For this reason, we have emphasized the need for a new theory of unionization that incorporates specific feminine issues. To this end, we have made a preliminary attempt by laying down some groundwork as constructs for what we have called a "Barriers Theory of Unionization". We have emphasized the barriers to women's unionization and thus tried to answer why women often fail to unionize. This is what is relevant to women. A "positive" theory of unionization, like the existing theories, would ask why a group of workers unionize. We find this question secondary as a practical issue. Women are struggling to unionize because that is how they hope to have some control over their job situation and thereby improve the conditions of their work, including wages and benefits. Besides this "economism", women, in some cases, may even consider union as a weapon for class struggle against the capitalists. In this sense, the "female answer" to "why unionize" may not be different from the "male answer" which the existing theories have covered.

The building blocks of the suggested new theory are seen to be several structural (labour-market) and institutional barriers to women's unionization. These barriers have been identified both from our review of the existing literature on women workers and our own reflection on the constructs for the new theory. We have formulated six hypotheses about these barriers for testing later on, in Chapters 4–6, which do and which do not turn out to be "theses" on women's unionization—for checking which barrier is primary, which secondary.

In Chapter 2, we have established some historical trends in women's labour-market participation, unemployment and unionization vis-a-vis men. This serves several purposes. First, it gives a macro-picture of the historical evolution of the female work-force in the Canadian economy. Secondly, the quantitative measures of the size and rate of change in the characteristics of this labour force by age and sex, give the scale of the importance of the female component of the labour force. Finally, the trends in participation established in this chapter are later related in Chapter 5 to the trends in education and unionization of women.

Chapter 3 examines the sex-role ideology and its offshoots— patriarchy, male supremacy, family socialization for boys to be aggressive and girls submissive, social morality, etc.—via an examination of the institution, family, since the days of savagery. It thus places the institutional barriers to women's participation and unionization in perspective. It refutes the radical feminist thesis that patriarchy is an independent "structure" and the main cause of women's oppression at home and exploitation in the market. This is done by tracing the origin of patriarchy in the mode of production itself, by the overthrow of mother-right by men at a stage of development when accumulation of private property, such as cattle, became possible for the first time in human history. It shows how the dialectic of capital accumulation, under the capitalist mode of production, continued until recently to assign to the household the principal tasks involved in the production of labour power and sugar-coated this structural need with the trappings of the patriarchal ideology and thereby restricted women's full participation and unionization.

Chapter 3 includes a note on the "mothering" role of women in the nuclear family of contemporary monopoly capitalism. While some of the ingredients in the production of labour power have been brought to the marketplace, women are still left with the tasks of rearing and socializing children and managing the tensions of husbands. The chapter ends by noting that capital has channelled women in large numbers to secondary market segments where, as argued later in Chapter 5, the basic prerequisites of unionization are missing.

Chapter 4 describes, through case studies of the UK, the USA and Canada, the process of capitalist development till the 1930's and the gradual transfer of production of goods and services from households to factories and how young women were first drawn to the labour market and later packed back to the household after their marriage to be involved in the domestic production of labour power for the rest of their lives. It describes also the rise of craft unions and the erection of the labour-market and institutional barriers that were listed in Chapter 1 and how the latter were applied to bar the women workers from these unions. It shows how jobs and industries began to be sex-typed and how women began to be concentrated as pink and white collar workers in women's ghettos—services, finance, trade and public administration—and how structural barriers such as the fragmented nature of the jobs in segregated labour markets, employer opposition, trade union discrimination, etc. combined with institutional barriers like protective legislation and Victorian ideology to keep women out of the unions in the brief span of their pre-marriage labour-market participation.

Chapter 5 picks up the historical thread laid down in Chapter 4 and places it in the perspective of the process of development of monopoly capitalism. It describes the deepening and widening of the industrial and occupational shifts that were initiated earlier, in the pre-1930 period. It explains the rise of a huge public sector to coordinate corporate plans in the monopoly sector and the emergence of unproductive sectors—finance, trade, etc.—engaged in the distribution of the surplus value generated in the productive sectors. It gives a quantitative description of the re-entry of married women into the labour market *en masse* and as a permanent force. It explains how labour-displacing technological change in the monopoly sector keeps women and also the technologically evicted men away from the primary labour market in the monopoly sector and how they are channelled to the newly enlarged labour-intensive public sector and the competitive private sector. It lays bare the essence of wage and job discrimination against women in these structural shifts punctuated by market segmentation and sex-segregation.

Chapter 5 also notices that after the 1930's the earlier craft unions were replaced by industrial unions which were concentrated in the blue collar jobs, not in the white collar jobs in the services, finance, trade and public administration. Monopoly capital and industrial unions have created internal (intra-firm) labour markets insulated from external competition. As such these industrial unions should not be much concerned with what women, and also men, do or do not do in the latter's ghettos. The former type of trade union discrimination, therefore, should now have lost its meaning. Thus, these structural changes under monopoly capitalism themselves should have removed, or at least significantly weakened, this particular labour-market barrier. But it has not worked exactly that way. SORWUC is an example; the CLC did not help it financially when requested. On the contrary, it wanted SORWUC to affiliate with it and mildly opposed its status as an independent organization of bank workers. Yet, it must be said that SORWUC could have gone it alone, without any real opposition from organized labour, if the structural difficulties set by the finance industry had not prevented this. Attitudinal factors like women's disinterest in unions and lack of commitment to jobs and male sexist beliefs are, as shown in this chapter, no longer significant barriers to unionization of women.

In Chapter 5, it is argued that a major precondition of unionization is the large-scale concentration of workers in one workplace which is possible only under monopolistic conditions. Public sector jobs at various levels of government fulfil this condition. Teachers, nurses and employees in public administration are therefore highly organized. Permissive legislation is only an admission of a foregone conclusion. Contrarily, the competitive private sector—personal service, finance and trade—assemble small groups of workers. The employer can easily fire recalcitrant workers and replace them by drawing on the reserve army. Job fragmentation conveniently assists the employer by making it impossible for workers to get together from scattered places of work even to make a symbolic protest of the firing. Legislation encouraging women's unionization will be of no consequence here.

Similarly, with education. It is true that workers in public sector jobs are highly educated and unionized whereas those in private competitive sector jobs are less educated and hardly unionized. One may get therefrom the illusion that education is a cause of unionization. Education, of course, has a role in consciousness raising. But a group of Ph.D. bank tellers or D. Phil. salesgirls will hardly be able to unionize better than their less fortunate sisters who have a poor grade ten. Education is just a facilitator to carrying one to a better job in the public sector, which is unionized for reasons outlined earlier and not because of the higher education of its employees.

The keynote of this chapter is the primacy of structural barriers in women's unionization.

In Chapter 6, we have tested all the six hypotheses formulated in Chapter 1 with the help of a sample survey of union executives. The tests have found overwhelming support for our emphasis on structural barriers to women's unionization. Only one institutional barrier, lack of family socialization through union membership, has been found significant. In other words, if a family member/friend of a worker is a union member, then he/she is a "role-model" for the worker. But this is not a pure, separable institutional category; it overlaps the labour-market (structural) category. Regarding trade union discrimination, the survey tends to show its absence. However one case study, SORWUC, shows that elements of trade union discrimination persist to this day.

7.2 *Issues for Further Research*

1. In Chapter 3, we said that we could not explain the "natural division of labour" which confined women to home and let men gather food as hunters, fishermen, etc. For Marx and Engels, it was "natural", not social, and hence beyond explanation. Yet, the family even at that early stage of human evolution was at least a mini-society: it must have had some rationale for the "natural" division of labour. We pose the hypothesis here, for further testing, that the *mother's womb* was the most precious asset. The family would soon have been extinct if the women went hunting and were devoured or mutilated by beasts. When the gens arose, this might have even become a social concern.

2. We have pointed out in Chapter 5 that more and more women were being channelled to the "unproductive" sectors—trade and finance—whose function is to "struggle" over the distribution of surplus value generated in the productive sectors. Capitalists and workers alike in these unproductive sectors were paid out of this surplus value generated outside their own sphere. We saw that the differential remuneration between the productive and unproductive sectors was the essence which appeared in the form of lower wages for women. As Harry Braverman (op. cit., p. 420) says, "This difference between the capital laid out as wages for production workers and for commercial workers, Marx refers to as a 'difficulty'." Both Marx and Braverman seem to point out here a dominance–dependence relation between the productive and unproductive sectors as the cause of the wage differential between these two spheres. Yet, it remained a "difficulty" to Marx and neither Braverman nor anybody else has grappled with it. In neoclassical theory also, there seems to be very little discussion of profits and wages in the commercial sector. Indeed, in the neoclassical general equilibrium theory, there are producers only, no merchants. Interpreting merchants as producers of, say, "mercantile services" would not seem to

work. In Marxian theory, merchants and finance capitalists produce no service. Here is an area of important, but almost intractable, research. Women as the victims of "this difference between the capital laid out as wages for production workers and for commercial workers" should be seriously interested in this research problem.

3. A large research area concerns strategies women should pursue in their struggle for better working conditions. What should women do? We suggest some issues below:

(a) Should they struggle for more jobs in the better-paid public sector? This question raises the issue of the future economic growth of monopoly capitalism. As we have seen monopoly capital, if anything, evicts workers from blue collar production jobs. Under the regime of monopoly capital, the public sector has been expanding. But there is a limit to this expansion. This limit must be set by the growth potential of the productive sector, i.e., the monopoly sector itself. The research in this area should then concern the projection of manpower needs in the public sector. Women leaders and spokespersons often recommend that women should try to get more and more public sector jobs. But how many jobs will there be for women?

(b) A related question follows from this one. Should women struggle for higher education? Obviously, if x jobs are foreseeable in the public sector, then there is no point in significantly more than x women struggling for an education that will equip them for the x jobs. What should be the policy on educational planning for women? This is an area of research that follows from the research on (wo)manpower needs of the public sector.

One could extend the previous two questions to professional jobs in the private sector also.

(c) What strategy should women pursue vis-a-vis the unions? It is often suggested that women should try to join the existing unions and fight for executive positions in them. Some suggest independent unions for women; some suggest women's caucuses, and not separate unions, working in cooperation with existing unions. What are the prospects for such strategies? Our survey results show that union executives, male and female, do not see any union discrimination any more. But the "unsuccessful" women in SORWUC have a somewhat different story to tell. Aren't the industrial unions in collusion with monopoly capital? Have they really given up sexist attitudes? How far will they go to help women? These questions are important research issues.

4. The last research issue suggested concerns the private competitive sectors. Unionization there would, willy nilly, imply the prior introduction of monopolistic elements. What are the degrees of monopoly that are foreseeable in these sectors? Monopoly is a bad thing as neoclassical welfare economics tells us. Yet women want unions in these competitive sectors. Here are involved hosts of neoclassical equity–efficiency issues. Research on these items should be useful.

BIBLIOGRAPHY

Abbott, Edith, *Women in Industry.*

Abella, Irving, *Nationalism, Communism and Canadian labour, the CIO, the Communist Party and the Canadian Congress of Labour. 1935–1956.* Toronto: University of Toronto Press, 1973.

—— and David Miller, eds., *The Canadian Worker in the 20th Century.* Toronto, 1978.

Acker, Joan, "Women and social stratification: a case of intellectual sexism." *American Journal of Sociology,* 78:936–45, 1973.

——, "Issues in the sociological study of women's work." In Ann H. Stromberg *et al.,* eds., *Women Working, Theories and Facts in Perspective.*Op. cit.

—— and Donald R. Van Houten, "Differential recruitment and control: the sex structuring of organizations."*Administrative Science Quarterly,* 19:152–63, 1974.

Acton, Janice, Penny Goldsmith and Bonnie Shepard, eds., *Women at Work, Ontario 1850–1930.* Toronto: Canadian Women's Educational Press, 1974.

Advisory Council on the Status of Women, The Person Papers, *Fringe Benefits, and the Price of Maternity.* Ottawa, 1976.

Agarwal, Naresh C. and Harish C. Jain, "Pay discrimination against women in Canada: issues and policies." *International Labour Review,* 117:169–77, March-April 1978.

Alchian, A.A. and R.A. Kessel, "Competition, monopoly and the pursuit of pecuniary gain." In *Aspects of Labor Economics: A Conference of the Universities,* pp. 156–75. Princeton: National Bureau of Economic Research Committee, 1962.

Alexander, Milnor, "Women and the political economy." *Atlantis,* II(2): 131–9, Spring 1977.

Antons, Joseph R., Mark Chandler and Wesley Mellow, "Sex differences in union membership." *Industrial and Labour Relations Review,* 33(2): 162–9, January 1980.

Archibald, Kathleen, *Sex and the Public Service.* Ottawa: Queen's Printer, 1970.

Armstrong, Hugh and Pat Armstrong, "The segregated participation of women in the Canadian labour force, 1941–71." *Canadian Review of Sociology and Anthropology,* 12:370–84, 1975.

Armstrong, Pat and Hugh Armstrong, *The Double Ghetto: Canadian Women and Their Segregated Work.* Toronto: McClelland and Stewart, 1978.

Arrow, Kenneth J., "The theory of discrimination." In O. Ashenfelter *et al.,* eds., *Discrimination in Labor Markets,* pp. 3–33. Op. cit.

Ashenfelter, O. and A. Rees, eds., *Discrimination in Labor Markets.* Princeton: 1973.

Auchmuty, Rosemary, "Spinsters and trade unions in Victorian Britain." In Amy Curthoys *et al.,* eds., *Women at Work,* pp. 109–22. Op. cit.

316   WOMEN, UNIONS AND THE LABOUR MARKET

Axworthy, Lloyd, *The 1980's: A New Era of Opportunity for Women in the Labour Force.* Ottawa: Canada Ministry of Employment and Immigration, 1980.

Babcock, Barbara A., Ann F. Friedman, Eleanor H. Norton and Susan C. Ross, *Sex Discrimination and the Law: Causes and Remedies.* Boston: Little, Brown, 1975.

Bachynsky, Valerie, "Women and unions." *Perception,* 1: 5–6, April 1978.

Baer, Judith A., *The Chains of Protection.* Westport, Connecticut: Greenwood Press, 1978.

Bain, George S., "The growth of white-collar unionism and public policy in Canada." *Relations Industrielles/Industrial Relations,* 24: 243–73, 1969.

―――, *The Growth of White-collar Unionism.* London: Oxford University Press, 1970.

―――, *Union Growth and Public Policy in Canada.* Ottawa: Labour Canada, 1979.

――― and Forouk Elsheikh, "Trade union growth in Canada: a comment." *Relations Industrielles,* 31(3): 1976.

――― and ―――, "An inter-industry analysis of unionization in Britain." *British Journal of Industrial Relations,* 17: 137–57, 1979.

Bain George S. and R.J. Price, *Profiles of Union Growth: A Statistical Profile of Eight Countries.* Oxford: Blackwell.

Bairstow, Frances, *White-Collar Workers and Collective Bargaining* (mimeo). Preliminary report of a study prepared for the Task Force on Labour Relations. Montreal: 1968.

Baker, Elizabeth F., *Technology and Women's Work.* New York: Columbia University Press, 1964.

Baker, M. and Mary-Anne Robeson, "Trade Union reaction to women workers." *Canadian Journal of Sociology,* 6(1): (1981).

Bakke, E.W. *et al.*, eds., *Labor Mobility and Economic Opportunity.* New York: Wiley, 1954.

Bank Book Collective, *An Account to Settle: The Story of the United Bank Workers.* Vancouver: Press Gang Publications, 1979.

Bannon, Sharleen, "Chart story: women in the Canadian labour force." *Canadian Business Review,* II(3): 6–7, Summer 1975.

―――, "Women in the workplace." *The Labour Gazette,* xxxvi: 69–74, Feb. 1976.

―――, "Women unionists demand their share." *The Labour Gazette,* April 1976.

Barbash, Jack, "Unionizing low-paid workers." *Challenge,* 39–43, July-August, 1975.

Barker, D.L. and S. Allen, eds., *Dependence and Exploitation in Work and Marriage.* London: Longman, 1976.

Bayefsky, Evelyn, "Women and the status of part-time work: a review and annotated bibliography." *Ontario Library Review,* 61: 87–106, June 1977.

Becker, Gary S., *The Economics of Discrimination*. Second edition, Chicago: 1971.

Beechey, Veronica, "On patriarchy." *Feminist Review*, 3: 66–82, 1979.

Beneria, Lourdes, "Reproduction, production and the sexual division of labour." *Cambridge Journal of Economics*, 3: 203–25, 1979.

Benmouyal-Acoca, Viviane, *Le retour des femmes sur le marché du travail*. Quebec: Ministère du Travail et la Main-d'oeuvre, 1978.

Bennett, James E., "Equal opportunities for women: why and how companies should take action." *Business Quarterly*, 40: 22–9, Winter 1975.

———— and Pierre M. Loewe, *Women in Business: A Shocking Waste of Human Resources*. Toronto: Maclean-Hunter, 1975.

Berger, Peter L. and Mansfried Kellner, "Marriage and the construction of reality." In Rose Lamb Cosner, ed., *The Family: Its Structure and Functions*. Op. cit.

Berman, Barbara, "Alternative measures of structural unemployment." In A.M. Ross, ed., *Employment Policy and the Labour Market*, pp. 258–68. Op. cit.

Bibring, Grete, "On the passing of the Oedipus complex in a matriarchal family setting." In Rudolph M. Lowenstein, ed., *Drives, Affects and Behavior*. Op. cit.

Bickner, Mei Lang, *Women at Work: An Annotated Bibliography*. Los Angeles: UCLA, 1977.

Blackburn, R.M., *Union Character and Social Class*. London: B.T. Batsford, 1967.

———— and M. Mann, *The Working Class in the Labour Market*. London: Macmillan, 1979.

Blacklock, W.M., *Female Job Satisfaction: A Social Perspective*, 2 fiche. Ottawa: National Library of Canada, 1978.

Blau, Francine D., *Equal Pay in the Office*. Toronto: D.C. Heath, 1977.

Block, Ruth, "Sex and sexes in eighteenth century magazines." 1972.

Bossen, Marianne, *Employment in Chartered Banks, 1969–1975*. Advisory Council on the Status of Women and the Canadian Bankers' Association, 1976.

Bowen, Peter and Monica Shaw, "Patterns of white-collar unionization in the steel industry." *Industrial Relations Journal*, 3: 8–34, 1971.

Boyle, M. Barbara, "Equal opportunity for women is smart business." *Harvard Business Review*, 51: 85–95, May-June 1973.

Braverman, Harry, *Labor and Monopoly Capital: The Degradation of Work in the Twentieth Century*. New York: Monthly Review Press, 1974.

Brown, Richard, "Women as employees: some comments on research in industrial sociology." In D.L. Barker *et al.*, eds., *Dependence and Exploitation in Work and Marriage*. Op. cit.

Brown, Susan, "Trade union participation: a study of membership attitudes in the National Union of Bank Employees." Unpublished M.A. dissertation, University of Warwick, 1972.

Brownlee, W. Elliot and Mary M. Brownlee, *Women in the American Economy*. New Haven: Yale University Press, 1976.

Burman, Sandra, ed., *Fit Work for Women*. London: Croom Helm, 1979.

Burns, Robert K., "The comparative economic position of manual and white-collar employees." *Journal of Business*, 27: 257–67, 1954.

Burstein, M. *et al.*, *Canadian Work Values: Findings of a Work Ethic Survey and a Job Satisfaction Survey*. Ottawa: Information Canada, 1975.

Campbell, Marie, L., *Women and Trade Unions in B.C., 1900–1920: The Social Organization of Sex Discrimination*. Prepared for the Women's Research Centre, Vancouver: June 1978.

Carr, Shirley, "Women's year—a union role." *Canadian Labour*, xx: 2–6, 34, June 1975.

Chafe, William H., *The American Woman*. New York: Oxford University Press, 1972.

Child, J., R. Loveridge and M. Warner, "Towards an organizational study of trade unions." *Sociology*, 7: 71–91, 1973.

Chodorow, Nancy, "Mothering, male dominance, and capitalism." In Zillah R. Eisenstein, ed., *Capitalist Patriarchy: The Case for Socialist Feminism*. Op. cit.

Clark, Alice, *The Working Life of Women in the Seventeenth Century*. New York: Harcourt, Brace and Howe, 1920.

Clark, Melissa, "The status of women in relation to transitions in the mode of production." Occasional papers of the McMaster Sociology of Woman Programme, 128–64, Spring 1977.

Clement, Wallace, *The Canadian Corporate Elite*. Toronto: McClelland and Stewart, 1975.

Coleman, James S. *et al.*, *Equality of Educational Opportunity ("The Coleman Report")*. Washington: USGPO, 1967.

Collins, Kevin, *Women and Pensions*. Ottawa: Canadian Council on Social Development, 1978.

Collins, Thomas W., "Unionization in a secondary labour market." *Human Organization*, 36: 135–41, 1977.

Commons, John R., *Legal Foundations of Capitalism*. Madison: University of Wisconsin Press, 1924.

Connelly, M. Patricia, "Canadian women as a reserve army of labour." Toronto: University of Toronto, Ph.D. thesis, 1976. (Canadian thesis on microfiche no. 30337)

———, "The economic context of women's labour force participation in Canada." In Patricia Marchak, ed., *The Working Sexes*, pp. 10–27. Op. cit.

———, *Last Hired, First Fired: Women and the Canadian Labour Force*. Toronto: The Women's Press, 1978.

Conrad, J.D., *Women as Reserve Labour: The Nova Scotia Case*. Ottawa: National Library of Canada, 1978.

Cook, Alice H., "Women and American trade unions." *Annals of American Academy of Political and Social Science*, 375: 124–32, 1968.

———, "Corporate woman: up the ladder finally." *Business Week*, 58–68, 24 November 1975.

————, *The Working Mother: A Survey of Problems and Programs in Nine Countries.* Ithaca, New York: Cornell University, 2nd ed., 1978.

————, "Collective bargaining as a strategy for achieving equal opportunity and equal pay: Sweden and West Germany." In *Equal Employment Policy for Women*, pp. 53–78. Philadelphia, Pennsylvania: Temple University Press, 1980.

Cornish, Mary, "Women in trade unions." *This Magazine*, ix: 8–10, September-October 1975.

Cosner, Rose Lamb, ed., *The Family: Its Structure and Functions.* New York: St Martin's Press, 1974.

Cunningham, Ruth, *Non-traditional Occupations.* Toronto: Ontario Status of Women Council, 1978.

Curthoys, Amy *et al.*, eds., *Women at Work.* Canberra: Australian Society for the Study of Labour History, 1975.

dalla Costa, Mariarosa, *The Power of Women and the Subversion of the Community*, Bristol, England: Falling Wall Press, 1973.

Davies, Margery, "Women's place is at the typewriter: The feminization of the clerical labour force." In Richard Edwards *et al.*, eds., *Labor Market Segmentation.* Op. cit.

Dawson, Robert M., *The Civil Service of Canada.* London: Oxford University Press, 1929.

Deckhandt, Barbara, *The Women's Movement.* New York: Harper and Row, 1975.

Della Valle, P.A. and B. Meyer, "Changes in relative female: male unemployment—Canadian–United States comparison." *Relations Industrielles*, xxxi(3): 417–33, 1976.

Dennis, Barbara D., ed., *Industrial Relations Research Association, Proceedings of the Fifty-third Annual Meeting*, 1978.

Devereaux, M.S. and Edith Rechnitzer, *Higher-education Hired: Sex Differences in Employment Characteristics of 1976 Postsecondary Graduates.* Ottawa: Supply and Services, 1980.

Dewey, Lucretia M., "Women in labour unions." *Monthly Labour Review*, 94: 42–8, 1971.

Dixson, Miriam, *The Real Matilda.* Melbourne: Penguin, 1976.

Doeringer, Peter B., "Determinants of the structure of industrial type internal labor markets." *Industrial Labor Relations Review*, 20(2): 206–20, Jan. 1967.

————, "Manpower programs for ghetto labor markets." In *Proceedings of the Twenty-first Annual Meeting of the Industrial Relations Research Association.* Madison: Industrial Relations Research Association, University of Wisconsin, 1969.

Donner, Arthur and Fred Lazar, "An econometric study of segmented labor markets and the structure of unemployment: the Canadian experience." *International Economic Review*, 14(2): June 1973.

———— and ————, "The dimensions of Canadian youth employment: a theoretical explanation." *Industrial Relations Quarterly Review,* 31(2): 1976.

Drummond, Ian, "Labour markets and educational planning." In Arthur Kruger *et al.,* eds., *The Canadian Labour Market: Readings in Manpower Economics.* Op. cit.

Dubin, Robert, "Attachment to work and union militancy." *Industrial Relations,* 12: 51–64, 1973.

Dulude, Louise, *The Status of Women in Federal Crown Corporations.* Ottawa: Advisory Council on the Status of Women, 1977.

Dumas, Evelyn, *The Bitter Thirties in Quebec.* Montreal: Black Rose Books, 1975.

Dunlop, John T., "The development of labor organization: a theoretical framework." In R.A. Lester *et al.,* eds., *Insights into Issues.* Op. cit.

———, "The task of contemporary wage theory." In George W. Taylor *et al.* eds., *New Concepts in Wage Discrimination,* pp. 117–39. Op. cit.

Eastham, Kay, "Women on the move: affirmative action for women Crown employees in Ontario." *Canadian Business Review,* 3: 34–5, Spring 1976.

Eaton, J.K., *Union Growth in Canada in the Sixties.* Ottawa: Canada Department of Labour, Economics and Research Branch, 1976.

Edgeworth, F.Y., "Equal pay to men and women for equal work." *Economic Journal,* 32(4): 431–57, December 1922.

Edmonton Social Planning Council: Task Force on Women in the Alberta Labour Force. *Report,* Edmonton: Edmonton Social Planning Council, 1974.

Edwards, Richard, *Contested Terrain: The Transformation of the Workplace in the Twentieth Century.* New York: Basic Books, 1979.

———, Michael Reich and David M. Gordon, eds., *Labor Market Segmentation.* Lexington, Mass.: D.C. Heath, 1975.

Eichler, Margret, "A review of selected recent literature on women." *Canadian Review of Sociology and Anthropology,* 86–96, 1 Sept. 1972.

Eisenstein, Zillah, R., ed., *Capitalist Patriarchy: The Case for Socialist Feminism.* New York: Monthly Review Press, 1979.

Employers' Council of British Columbia: *Female Employment in Non-traditional Areas: Some Attitudes of Managers and Working Women.* Vancouver: Employers' Council of B.C., 1975.

Engels, Freidrich, "The origin of the family, private property and the state." In K. Marx and F. Engels, *Selected Works.* Op. cit.

———, *The Conditions of the Working Class in England.* London: Panther Books, 1969.

Epstein, Laurily Keir, *Women in the Professions.* Lexington, Massachusetts: D.C. Heath, 1975.

Equal Opportunities for Women in Public Employment: Federal–Provincial Conference November 1–3, 1976. Ottawa: Supply and Services Canada, 1976.

Equal Rights and Industrial Relations. Madison, Wisconsin: Industrial Relations Research Association, 1977.

Falk, Gail, "Women's Rights." *Law Reporter*, 1:54–66, Spring 1973.
Farber, Henry S. and Daniel H. Saks, "Why workers want unions: The role
of relative wages and job characteristics." *Journal of Political
Economy*, 88: 349–69, 1980.
Farley, Jennie, *Men, Women and Work Satisfaction on Campus*, pp. 17–33.
Ithaca, New York: New York State School of Industrial and Labor
Relations, Cornell University, 1974.
———, *Affirmative Action and the Woman Worker.* New York: AMACOM,
1979.
Fawcett, Millicent G., "Mr. Sidney Webb's article on women's wages."
Economic Journal, 1892.
———, Equal pay for equal work." *Economic Journal*, 28: 1–6, March 1918.
Feldberg, Roslyn L. and Evelyn Nakano Glenn, "Male and female: job
versus gender models in the sociology of work." *Social Problems*,
26: 524–38, 1979.
Firestone, O.J., "Canada's economic development, 1867–1952." Paper
prepared for the Third Conference of the International Association
for Research in Income and Wealth. Castelgandolfo, Italy: 1953.
Firestone, Shulamith, *The Dialectic of Sex.* New York: Bantam Books, 1970.
Fogarty, Michael P., *Sex, Career and Family: Including an International Review
of Women's Roles.* London: George Allen and Unwin, 1971.
Foner, Philip S., *Women and the American Labor Movement*, London: Collier
Macmillan Publications, 1979.
Fox, Bonnie, ed., *Hidden in the Household.* Toronto: The Women's Press, 1980.
Francis, Anne, "Action from the blueprint: The Royal Commission on
the Status of Women." *Canadian Business Review*, 2: 2–7, Summer
1975.
Frankfurt Institute for Social Research, *Aspects of Sociology.* Boston: Beacon
Press, 1972.
Freedman, Marcia, *Labor Markets: Segments and Shelters.* Montclair, N.J.:
Allanheld, Osmun, 1976.
Freger, Ruth, "The Jewish Labour Movement in Toronto in the twentieth
century." Ph.D. thesis in progress, York University (in 1981).
Freire, Paulo, *The Pedagogy of the Oppressed.* New York: Seabury Press, 1970.
Friedman, Milton, *Capitalism and Freedom.* Chicago: Phoenix Books, 1962.
Fullerton, Howard N. and James J. Byrne, "Length of working life for men
and women, 1970,"*Monthly Labor Review*, 99: 31–5, February 1976.

Gabin, Nancy, "Women workers and the UAW in the post-World War II
period: 1945–1954." *Labor History*, 21: 5–30, 1979–1980.
Gale, Rubin, "The traffic in women: notes on the political economy of sex."
in Rayma Reiter, ed., *The Anthropology of Women.* Op. cit.

Gelber, Sylvia M., *Highly Qualified Manpower Policies and the Canadian Woman Graduate: What Price Discrimination*. Women's Bureau, 1969, 1970, 27–31.

Geoffroy, Renee and Paul Sainte-Marie, *Attitudes of Union Workers to Women in Industry*. Royal Commission on the Status of Women in Canada, No. 9. Ottawa: Queen's Printer, 1971.

Gintis, Herbert, "Education, technology and characteristics of worker productivity." *American Economic Review*, 61(2): 266–79, May 1971.

Giroux, Claudette, *The Role of Women in the Canadian Trade Union Movement*. August 1978. An unpublished paper, available at Carlton University Library, Ottawa.

Glenn, Evelyn N. and Roslyn L. Feldberg, "Degraded and deskilled: The proletarianization of clerical work." *Social Problems*, 25: 52–64, 1979.

Gordon, David M., *Theories of Poverty and Underemployment: Orthodox, Radical, and Dual Labor Market Perspectives*. Lexington, Mass.: D.C. Heath, 1972.

Gordon, Michael, ed., *The American Family in Social-Historical Perspective*. New York: St Martin's Press, 1973.

Gorham, Deborah, "The Canadian suffragist." In Gwen Matheson, ed., *Women in the Canadian Mosaic*. Op. cit.

Great Britain: Central Office of Information, *Women in Britain*. London: 1971.

————: Department of Employment, *Equal Opportunities for Men and Women: Government Proposals for Legislation*. London: HMSO, 1973.

————: ————, *Women and Work: A Review*. London: Her Majesty's Stationery Office, 1975.

Guettel, Charnis, *Marxism and Feminism*. Toronto: Canadian Women's Educational Press, 1974.

Gunderson, Morley, "Male-female wage differentials and the impact of equal pay legislation." *Review of Economics and Statistics*, 57: 1975.

Harrison, Bennett, *Education, Training and the Urban Ghetto*. Baltimore: Johns Hopkins University Press, 1972.

————, "Education and underemployment in the urban ghetto." *American Economic Review*, 62(5): 796–812, Dec. 1972.

————, "Ghetto economic development, a survey." *Journal of Economic Literature*, 12(1): 1–37, March 1974.

———— and Andrew Sum, "The theory of 'dual' or segmented labor markets." *Journal of Economic Issues*, 13(3): September 1979.

Hartman, Grace, "Women in the labour movement." *Civil Service Review*, xxvi: 38–43, 4 Dec. 1973.

————, "Women and Unions." In *Gwen Matheson, ed., Women in the Canadian Mosaic*. Op. cit.

Hartman, Heidi, "Capitalism, patriarchy and job segregation by sex." In Zillah R. Eisenstein, ed., *Capitalist Patriarchy: The Case for Socialist Feminism*. Op. cit.

Hennig, Margaret and Anne Jardin, *The Managerial Woman*. New York: Pocket Books, 1977.

Henry, Alice, *The Trade Union Women*. New York: D. Appleton and Company, 1915.

———, *Women in the Labor Movement*. New York: George H. Doran Company, 1923.

Hersom, N. and D. Smith, eds., *Women and the Canadian Labour Force*. Social Sciences and Humanities Research Council of Canada, 1982.

Hewitt, Margaret, *Wives and Mothers in Victorian Industry*, pp. 14 ff. London: Rockliff, 1958.

Hilferding, Rudolf, *Finance Capital: A Study of the Latest Phase of Capitalist Development*. London: Routledge and K. Paul, 1981.

Hill, Ann C., "Protective labor legislation for women." In Babcock *et al.*, *Sex Discrimination and the Law: Causes and Remedies*. Op. cit.

Hill, Christina Maria, "Women in the Canadian economy." In Robert Laxer, ed., *The Political Economy of Dependency*, pp. 84–106. Op. cit.

Hodgetts, J.E., W. McCloskey, R. Whitaker and V.S. Wilson, *The Biography of an Institution: The Civil Service Commission of Canada, 1908–1967*. Montreal: McGill-Queen's University Press, 1972.

Horkheimer, Max, "Authority and the family." In *Critical Theory*.

Howe, Louise Kapp, *Pink Collar Workers: Inside the World of Women's Work*. Toronto: Longman, 1977.

———, *Pink Collar Workers*. New York: Avon Books, 1977.

Hunt, Audrey, *Management Attitude and Practices towards Women at Work: Employment Policy Survey Carried out in 1973*. London: Her Majesty's Stationery Office, 1975.

Hunt, Judith, "Organizing women workers." *Studies for Trade Unionists*, 1: 1–25, 1975.

Hutchins, B.L., *Women in Modern Industry*, p. 16. London: G. Bell and Sons, 1915.

Hyman, Richard, *Industrial Relations: A Marxist Introduction*. London: Macmillan, 1975.

International Labour Office, *Women Workers in a Changing World*. Geneva, 1963.

———, *Women Workers in a Changing World*. Geneva, 1964.

———, *Equality of Opportunity and Treatment in Employment in the European Region: Problems and Policies*. Geneva, 1972.

———, *Report on the ILO/SIDA Asian Regional Seminar on Labour Inspection in Relation to the Employment of Women or Protection of Children*. Geneva, 1973.

———, *Equality of Opportunity and Treatment for Women Workers*. Geneva, 1975.

———, *Employment of Women with Family Responsibilities: Summary of Reports on Recommendation No. 123*. Geneva, 1978.

International Labour Organization, *Women's Jobs, Men's Jobs?* Geneva: CIRF Publications, 1971.

324   WOMEN, UNIONS AND THE LABOUR MARKET

Issues and Options: Equal Pay/Equal Opportunity. Toronto, Ontario: Ministry of Labour, 1978.

James, Selma, *Women, the Unions and Work and the Perspective of Winnipeg: Wages for the Housework Committee.* London: The Falling Wall Press, 1972.
Jamieson, Stuart M., *Times of Trouble: Labour Unrest and Industrial Conflict in Canada, 1900–66.* Ottawa: Information Canada, 1971.
Jenson, P., "Nurses and unionization." Ph.D. thesis in progress, Sociology, Univ. of Toronto.
Jocelyn, Olive J., *English Apprenticeship and Child Labour*, pp. 149–50. London: T. Fisher Unwin, 1912.
Johnson, Leo, "The political economy of Ontario women in the nineteenth century." In Amy Curthoys *et al.*, eds., *Women at Work*, pp. 13–31. Op. cit.
Judek, Stanislaw, *Women in the Public Service, Their Utilization and Employment.* Ottawa: Queen's Printer, 1968.

Kanter, Rosabeth Moss, "The impact of hierarchical structures on the work behavior of women and men." *Social Problems*, 23: 415–30, April 1976.
———, *Men and Women of the Corporation.* New York: Basic Books, 1977.
Karsh, Bernard, *Diary of a Strike.* Urbana, Illinois: University of Illinois Press, 1958.
Kealey, Gregory, *Toronto Workers Respond to Industrial Capitalism.* Toronto, 1977.
Kealey, Linda, *Women at Work, 1850–1930.* Toronto: Canadian Women's Educational Press, 1974.
Kennelly, James J., *Women and American Trade Unions.* St Albans, Vermont: Eden Press, Women's Publication Incorporated, 1978.
Kerr, Clark, "Labor markets: their character and consequences." *American Economic Review*, 278–91, May 1950.
———, "The Balkanization of labor markets." In E.W. Bakke *et al.*, eds., *Labor Mobility and Economic Opportunity*, pp. 92–110. Op. cit.
Kerwin, Patrick, "AFL-CIO Seminar on Women's Rights." *Canadian Labour*, xx: 23–4, June 1975.
Kessler-Harris, Alice, "Where are the organized women workers?" *Feminist Studies*, 3(2): 92–110, 1975.
———, "Stratifying by sex: understanding the history of working women." In Richard Edwards *et al.*, eds., *Labor Market Segmentation.* Op. cit.
King, Dorothy, "Women's organization: learning from yesterday." In Amy Curthoys *et al.*, eds., *Women at Work.* Op. cit.
Klein, Alice and Wayne Roberts, "Besieged innocence: The 'problem' and problems of working women—Toronto 1896–1914." In Linda Kealey, *Women at Work, 1850–1930.* Op. cit.
Kohen, Andrew I., *Women and the Economy: A Bibliography and a Review of*

the Literature on Sex Differentiation in the Labor Market. Ohio: Ohio State University, 1977.

Kornhauser, Ruth, "Some social determinants and consequences of union membership." *Labor History,* 2: 30–61, 1961.

Kruger, Arthur and Noah M. Meltz, eds., *The Canadian Labour Market: Readings in Manpower Economics.* Centre for Industrial Relations. Toronto: 1968.

Kuyek, Joan, *The Phone Book: Working at the Bell,* p. 77. Kitchener, 1979.

Labour Canada, *Labour Organization in Canada.* Ottawa: 1980.

————, *Women in Labour Force, Facts and Figures.* Ottawa: Information Canada, 1976–1981.

Landsbury, Coral, "The feminine frontier, women's suffrage and economic reality." *Meanjin Quarterly,* 3: 1972.

Langan, Joy, "Trade union women's committees." *Canadian Labour,* 21(3): September 1976.

Lavigne, Marie and Jennifer Stoddart, "Women's work in Montreal at the turn of the century." In Marylee Stephenson, ed., *Women in Canada.* Op. cit.

Laxer, Robert, ed., *(Canada) Ltd., The Political Economy of Dependency.* Toronto: McClelland and Stewart, 1973.

Lazonick, William, "The subjection of labour to capital: The rise of the capitalist system." *Review of Radical Political Economics,* 10: 1–31, 1978.

Leffingwell, William H., *Office Management, Principles and Practice.* Chicago: A.W. Shaw, 1925.

Lenin, V.I., *Imperialism—The Highest Stage of Capitalism.* Peking: Foreign Languages Press, 1965.

Leslie, Genevieve, "Domestic service in Canada 1880–1920." In Linda Kealey, *Women at Work 1850–1930.* Op. cit.

Lester, R.A. and J. Shister, eds., *Insights into Issues.* New York: Macmillan, 1948.

Levi, Maurice D., "Stimulating recruitment of female managers." *Professional Management Bulletin,* xxii(8): 10–18, February 1972.

Lewenhak, Sheila, *Women and Trade Unions.* Canada: Ernst Benn Ltd., 1977.

Lipton, Charles, *The Trade Union Movement in Canada.* Toronto: 1967.

Lockwood, David, *The Blackcoated Workers.* London: Allen and Unwin, 1966.

Logan, Harold, *History of Trade Union Organization in Canada.* Chicago, 1928.

Loveridge, R. and A. Mok, *Theories of Labor Market Segmentation.* Higham, Massachussetts: Martinus Nijhoff Publishing, 1979.

Lowe, Graham S., "Insurance union squelched." Ontario Report, 1: 15–18, 1975.

————, *The Canadian Union of Bank Employees: A Case Study.* Toronto: University of Toronto Press, 1978.

————, "The administrative revolution: the growth of clerical occupations and the development of the modern office in Canada, 1911–1931." Unpublished Ph.D. thesis, University of Toronto, 1979.

————, *Bank Unionization in Canada: A Preliminary Analysis.* Toronto: Centre for Industrial Relations, University of Toronto, 1980.

326 WOMEN, UNIONS AND THE LABOUR MARKET

Lowenstein, Rudolph M., ed., *Drives, Affects and Behavior.* New York: International Universities Press, 1953.

Lutes, Carol, "Room at the top—a view of women in management." *Optimism,* 11(1): 49–53, 1971.

MacDonald, Martha, "The labour force of labour market segmentation analysis: the unanswered questions." In N. Hersom *et al.,* eds., *Women and the Canadian Labour Force,* pp. 165–208. Op. cit.

MacLeod, Catherine, "Women in production, the Toronto dressmakers' strike of 1931." In Janice Acton *et al.,* eds., *Women at Work, Ontario 1850–1930.* Op. cit.

MacMurchy, Marjorie, *The Canadian Girl at Work.* Government of Ontario, Ministry of Education, 1919.

Madden, Janice Fanning, *The Economics of Sex Discrimination.* Lexington, Mass.: Lexington Books and D.C. Heath & Co., 1973.

Manitoba, Department of Labour, Women's Bureau. *Mothers in the Labour Force: Their Child Care Arrangements.* Winnipeg: 1974.

———, *A Study of Part Time Employment.* Winnipeg: 1976.

Marchak, Patricia M., "Women workers and white collar unions." *Canadian Review of Sociology and Anthropology.* 10(2): 134–47, 1973.

———, "The Canadian labour force: jobs for women." In Marylee Stephenson, ed., *Women in Canada.* Op. cit.

———, "Women, work and unions in Canada." *International Journal of Sociology,* 4: 39–61, Winter 1975/76.

———, ed., *The Working Sexes.* Symposium papers on the effects of sex on women at work. Oct. 15–16, 1976, at the UBC Vancouver: Institute of Industrial Relations, University of British Columbia, 1977.

Marglin, Stephen, "What do bosses do? The origins and functions of hierarchy in capitalist production." *Review of Radical Political Economics,* 6(2), Summer, 1974.

Marsden, Lorna R., "Unemployment among Canadian women: some sociological problems raised by its increase." In Patricia Marchak, ed., *The Working Sexes.* Op. cit.

Marx, Karl, *Capital: A Critique of Political Economy,* volumes 1–3. F. Engels, ed. Moscow: Progress Publishers, 1967.

———, and Friedrich Engels, *Selected Works.* Moscow: Progress Publishers, 1968.

Mass, Michael A., "Sex discrimination based on pregnancy: the post-Gilbert environment." *Employee Relations Law Journal,* 4: 161–72, 1978.

Matheson, Gwen, ed., *Women in the Canadian Mosaic.* Toronto: Peter Martin Associates Limited, 1976.

Mattila, Peter J., "Youth labor markets, enrollments and minimum wages." In Barbara D. Dennis, ed., *Industrial Relations Research Association, Proceedings of the Fifty-third Annual Meeting.* Op. cit.

Maupin, Joyce, *Working Women and Their Organizations.* Berkeley: Union Wage Educational Committee, 1974.

Mayfair, Personnel Ltd., *Women in Leadership* (seminar announcement). Edmonton: 1976.

Mayo, Marjorie, ed., *Women in the Community*. London: Routledge and Kegan Paul (no date).

McArthur, John, "Why aren't there more women managers?" *Canadian Business*, x1vii: 34, 36, Dec. 1974.

McFarland, Joan, "Women and unions: help or hindrance." *Atlantic*, 4(2): Spring 1979.

McGill University, Industrial Relations Centre, *Women and Work: Papers Presented at the 23rd Annual Conference, April 3–4, 1974 in Montreal*. Montreal: McGill University, Industrial Relations Centre, 1974.

McIveen, Neil and Harvey Sims, *The Flow Components of Unemployment in Canada*. Special Labour Force Studies, Series A, No. 11, Statistics Canada, 1978.

McLaughlin, W. Earle, "Women in business: policies of three Canadian corporations." *Canadian Business Review*, 1: 8–11, Summer 1975.

McNally, Fiona, *Women for Hire: A Study of the Female Office Worker*. London: Macmillan, 1979.

Meissner, Martin, "Women and inequality: at work, at home." *One Generation*, xi(2): 59–71, 1976.

———, "Sexual division of labour and inequalities; labour and leisure." In Marylee Stephenson, ed., *Women in Canada*. Op. cit.

Meltz, Noah M., *Manpower in Canada, 1931–1961*. Ottawa: Queen's Printer, 1969.

Meyer, Mitchell, *Women and Employee Benefits*. New York: Conference Board, 1978.

Middleton, Chris, "Sexual inequality and stratification theory." In F. Parkin, ed., *The Social Analysis of Class Structure*. Op. cit.

Mill, John Stuart, *Principles of Political Economy*, volume 1. Revised ed. The World's Great Classics. New York: The Colonial press, (1848), 1900.

Mills, C. Wright, *White Collar: The American Middle Classes*. New York: Oxford University Press, 1956.

Mincer, J. and S. Polachek, "Family investments in human capital: earnings of women." *Journal of Political Economy*, 82(2), Part II: S76–S108, March/April 1974.

Mitchell, Juliet, *Women's Estate*. New York: Pantheon Books, 1971.

Moore, Jay and Frank Lewsky, "Positive action for integrating women into management." *Canadian Personnel and Industrial Relations Journal*, xxii: 15–21, March 1975.

Nelson, Ann and Barbara Wertheimer, *Into the Main Stream*. Ithaca, New York: New York State School for Industrial and Labor Relations, 1977.

Novarra, Virginia, *Women's Work, Men's Work*. London: Marion Boyars, 1980.

O'Neill, William, ed., *The Woman Movement: Feminism in the United States and England*. Chicago: Quadrangle Books, 1969.

————, *Everyone Was Brave*. Chicago; Quadrangle Books, 1969.

Ontario, *Report of the Ontario Commission on Unemployment*. Toronto: 1969.

Oren, Laura, "The welfare of women in labouring families: England 1860–1950." *Feminist Studies*, 1(3–4): 107–25, Winter-Spring 1973.

Organized Working Women, *Reports, Pamphlets and Papers*. Don Mills, Ontario: 1976–1979.

Orly, Ashenfelton and John H. Pencavel, "American trade union growth: 1900–1960." *Quarterly Journal of Economics*, lxxxiii: 434–48, August 1969.

Ortner, Sherry, "Is female to male as nature is to culture?" In M.S. Rosaldo, et al., *Women, Culture and Society*. Op. cit.

Ostry, Sylvia, "The occupational composition of the Canadian labour force." *1961 Census Monograph Programme*, Dominion Bureau of Statistics, Ottawa: Canada 1967.

———— and Mahmood A. Zaida, "Labour economics in Canada." In Harry D. Woods et al., *Labour Policy and Labour Economics in Canada*. Op. cit.

Parkin, Frank, ed., *The Social Analysis of Class Structure*. London: Tavistock, 1974.

————, *Marxism and Class Theory: A Bourgeois Critique*. London: Tavistock, 1979.

Parsons, Talcott, *Social Structure and Personality*. New York: Free Press, 1974.

———— and Robert F. Bales, *Family, Socialization and Interaction Process*. New York: Free Press, 1955.

Pask, Judith M., *Women and the Economy: A Selected Bibliography*. West Lafayette, Indiana: Krannert Graduate School of Management, Purdue University, 1977.

Pearson, Mary, *International Decade for Women, 1976–1985: What it Means to Canadian Women*. Ottawa: Canadian Advisory Council on the Status of Women, 1977.

————, *The Second Time Around*. Ottawa: Canadian Advisory Council on the Status of Women, 1979.

Penner, Norman, *The Canadian Left*. Toronto: 1976.

Pentland, H.C., "The Canadian industrial relations system: some formative factors." *Labour/le Travailleur*, 4: 9–23, 1979.

Perlman, Mark, *Labor Union Theories in America*. Evanston, Illinios: Rows Peterson and Co., 1958.

Perlman, Selig, For Perlman's Theories on Trade Union Movement see Mark Perlman, *Labor Union Theories in America*. Op. cit.

Phelps, E.S., "The statistical theory of racism and sexism." *American Economic Review*, 62(4): 659–61, 1972.

Pinchbeck, Ivy: *Women Workers in the Industrial Revolution, 1750–1850*. London: Frank Cass, 1930; reprinted 1969.

Piore, Michael J., *Internal Labor Markets and Manpower Analysis.* Lexington, Massachussetts: D.C. Heath Co., 1971.
———, "On-the-job training in the dual labor market." In Arnold R. Weber *et al.,* eds., *Public-Private Manpower Policies,* pp. 101–32. Op. cit.
———, "Notes for a theory of labor market stratification." In R. Edwards *et al.,* eds., *Labor Market Segmentation,* pp. 125–50. Op. cit.
Pospisil, Vivian S., "Bluecollar women get organized." *Industry Week,* 23–8, 14 April 1975.
Prandy, Kenneth, *Professional Employees: A Study of Scientists and Engineers.* London: Faber and Faber, 1965.
Price, Enid M., *Changes in the Industrial Occupations of Women in the Environment of Montreal during the Period of the War, 1914–1918.* (Master of Arts thesis) McGill University, Faculty of Arts, Department of Economics and Political Science, May 1919.
Price, Robert, "Trade union recognition in the English clearing banks." Unpublished M.A. dissertation, University of Warwick, 1970.
Purcell, Kate, "Militancy and acquiescence amongst women workers." In Sandra Burman, ed., *Fit Work for Women.* Op. cit.

Ramkhalawansingh, Ceta, "Women during the Great War." In Amy Curthoys *et al.,* eds., *Women at Work,* pp. 261–307. Op. cit.
Rands, Jean, "Towards an organization of working women." In *Women Unite.* Toronto: Canadian Women's Educational Press, 1972.
Rathbone, Eleanor F., "The remuneration of women's services." *Economic Journal,* 27(1): 58, March 1917.
Reich, Carol and Helen Lafountaine, *Occupational Segregation and its Effects.* Edmonton: Women Associates Consulting Inc., 1979.
Reifers, Suzanne, *How to Hire and Supervise Women Legally.* New York: Executive Enterprises Publications, 1979.
Reiter, Rayma, ed., *The Anthropology of Women.* New York: Monthly Review Press, 1975.
Roberts, B.C., Ray Loveridge, John Gennard and J.V. Eason, *Reluctant Militants: A Study of Industrial Technicians.* London: Heinemann, 1972.
Roberts, Wayne, *Honest Womanhood.* Toronto: New Hogtown Press, 1976.
Robeson, Mary-Anne, "Are women workers and their issues represented in the trade unions: a practical study of Canadian airline employees' association." Unpublished paper. University of Toronto, 1979.
Robin, Martin, *Radical Politics and Canadian Labour, 1880–1930.* Ontario: Industrial Relations Centre, Queen's University, Kingston 1968.
Roderick, Roger D. and Andrew I. Kohen, *Years for Decision: A Longitudinal Study of the Educational and Labor Market Experience of Young Women.* Washington DC: US Dept. of Labor, 1976.
Rollen, Berit, *Equality on the Labor Market between Men and Women—A Task for the National Labor Market Board,* (Sweden). Wellesley, Mas-

sachussetts: Center for Research on Women, Wellesley College, 1978.

Rosaldo, Michelle S. and Louis Lamphered, *Women, Culture and Society.* Stanford University Press, 1975.

Rosenthal, Star, "Union maids, organized women workers in Vancouver 1900–1915." *BC Studies,* 41: Spring 1979.

Ross, A.M., ed., *Employment Policy and the Labor Market.* Berkeley: University of California Press.

Rostow, W.W., *The Stages of Economic Growth.* Cambridge University Press, 1967.

Royal Commission on the Status of Women Study No. 9, *To Determine Attitudes of Unionized Workers to the Employment of Women in the Province of Quebec.* Ottawa: 1970.

Rubin, Gale, "The traffic in women: notes on the political economy of sex." In Rayma Reiter, ed., *The Anthropology of Women.* Op. cit.

Ruggerie, Guiseppe C., "Hidden unemployment by age and sex in Canada 1957–1970." *Industrial Relations,* xxx: 181–9, 1975.

Ryan, Penny and Tim Rowse, "Women, arbitration and the family." In Amy Curthoys *et al.,* eds., *Women at Work.* Op. cit.

Ryten, Eva, "Our best educated women." *Canadian Business Review,* 2: 12–16, 1975.

Safilios-Rothschild, Constantina, *Women and Social Policy.* Englewood Cliffs: Prentice-Hall, 1974.

Sangster, Joan, "The 1907 Bell telephone strike: organizing women workers." *Journal of Canadian Labour Studies,* 3: 109–30, 1978.

———, "Women and unions in Canada: a review of historical research." In *Women and Trade Unions,* Resources in Feminist Research, 4(2): July 1981.

Saskatchewan: Office of the Coordinator, Status of Women, *Final Report, 1975.* Regina: 1975.

Sayles, L.R. and G. Strauss, *The Local Union.* Revised ed. New York: Harcourt, Brace and World, 1967.

Schonfield, David, *With Respect to Women Over 35: A Calgary Study.* Calgary: University of Calgary, 1976.

Scott, Jean, *The Conditions of Female Labour in Ontario.* Toronto: 1892.

Seccombe, Wally, "Domestic labour and the working class household." In Bonnie Fox, ed., *Hidden in the Household.* Op. cit.

Seidman, Joel, Jack London and Bernard Karsh, "Why workers join unions." *Annals of the American Academy of Political and Social Science,* 174: 75–84, 1951.

Sen, Joya, *Unemployment of Youth: The Importance of Education for Their Adjustment in the Canadian Labour Market.* Toronto: Ontario Institute for Studies in Education, 1982.

Sexual Harassment. Edmonton, Alberta: Department of Labour, 1979.

Shack, Sybil, *Saturday's Stepchildren: Canadian Women in Business.* Toronto:

Guidance Centre, Faculty of Education, University of Toronto, 1977.

Shaeffer, Ruth Gilbert and Helen Axel, *Improving Job Opportunities for Women: A Chart Book Focusing on the progress in Business*. New York: Conference Board, 1978.

Shaeffer, Ruth Gilbert and Edith F. Lynton, *Corporate Experiences in Improving Women's Job Opportunities*. New York: The Conference Board, 1979.

Shister, Joseph, "The logic of union growth." *Journal of Political Economy*, 61: 413–33, 1953.

"The Shmuta strikes", in Evelyn Dumas, *The Bitter Thirties in Quebec*, pp. 43–69. Op. cit.

Silverman, David, "Clerical ideologies: a research note." *British Journal of Sociology*, 19: 326–33, 1968.

Smelser, Neil, *Social Change and the Industrial Revolution*, ch. 9–11. Chicago: University of Chicago Press, 1959.

Smith, Adam, *The Wealth of Nations*. New York: P.F. Collier, 1909.

Soldon, Nobert, *Women in British Trade Unions, 1874–1976*. London: Gill and Macmillan, 1970.

SORWUC, *An Account to Settle*. Vancouver: Press Gang Publishers, 1979.

Statistics Canada, *Corporations and Labour Unions Returns Act* (CALURA), Report for 1976, Parts 1 and 2, 1979.

Stephenson, Marylee, ed., *Women in Canada*. Don Mills, Toronto: General Publishing Co. Ltd., second ed., 1977.

Stevenson, Mary. *Determinates of Low Wages for Woman Workers*. Ann Arbor, Michigan: University Microfilms, 1974.

Stinson, Jane, *Women in Trade Unions*. Unpublished paper. Ottawa: Carlton University.

Stromberg, Ann H. and Shirley Harkness, eds., *Women Working, Theories and Facts in Perspective*. Palo Alto: Mayfield.

Strong Boag, Veronica, "Canadian working women in the 1920's." In Janice Acton *et al.*, eds.,*Women at Work, Ontario 1850–1930*. Op. cit.

Summers, Ann, "Damned whores and god's police." In *The Colonization of Women in Australia*. Melbourne: Penguin 1975.

Sunpster, D., *The Role of Woman in the Economy*. i, 107, 1. Micro (RPG/73/16). Ottawa: Department of Manpower and Immigration, 1973.

Sutton, John R., "Some determinants of women's trade union membership." *Pacific Sociological Review*, 23: 377–91, 1980.

Sweezy, Paul and Paul Baran, *Monopoly Capital: An Essay on the American Economic and Social Order*. New York: Monthly Review Press, 1966.

Swidinsky, R., "Trade union growth in Canada: 1911–1970." *Relations Industrielles*, xxix(3): 435, 1974.

Tannenbaum, Frank. For Tannenbaum's Theories on Trade Union Movement see Mark Perlman, *Labor Union Theories in America*. Op. cit.

Taylor, George W. and Frank C. Pierson, eds., *New Concepts in Wage Discrimination*. New York: McGraw Hill, 1957.

Thompson, E.P., *The Making of the English Working Class*. New York: Vintage Books, 1963.

Thurow, Lester C., "The determinants of the occupational distribution of Negroes." In *The Education and Training of Racial Minorities: Proceedings of a Conference*. Madison: Center for Studies in Vocational Education, University of Wisconsin, 1968.

———, *Poverty and Discrimination*.

———, "Education and economic inequality." *The Public Interest*, 28: 66–81, Summer 1972.

———, *Generating Inequality*.

——— and Robert E.B. Lucas, *The American Distribution of Income: A Structural Problem*. Joint Economic Committee Print, 92nd Congress, 2nd session, 1972.

Tokariuk, Donna. *Employer Awareness Publicity Report: The Attitudes of Employers Towards Hiring Women in Non-traditional Roles*. Ottawa: Canadian Employment and Immigration Commission, 1980.

Tolson, Andrew, *The Limits of Masculinity*. London: Tavistock, 1977.

Townson, Monica, "Organized working women." *The Labour Gazette*, 349–53, 1975.

———, *Women in the Public Service: An Analysis of Employment Statistics 1972–1974*. Ottawa: Advisory Council on the Status of Women, 1975.

———, *The Structure of the Workplace in the 1980's: The Implications for Women*. Montreal: Canadian Association of Administrators of Labour Legislation, 1980.

Trofimenkoff, Susan Mann, "One hundred and two muffled voices: Canada's industrial women in 1880." *Atlantis*, 3(1): Autumn 1977.

——— and Alison Prentice, eds., *The Neglected Majority*. Toronto: McClelland and Stewart, 1977.

Urquhart, M.C. and K.A.H. Buckley, *Historical Statistics of Canada*. Toronto: Macmillan Company of Canada Ltd, 1965.

Vanek, Joan, *Keeping Busy: Time Spent in Housework, United States 1920–1970*. 1973.

Veblen, Thorsten, *Absentee Ownership and Business Enterprise in Recent Times*, pp. 305–6. New York: 1923.

Wages for House Work Committee, *In Defence of Family Allowance*. Toronto: 1976.

Webb, Sidney, "The alleged differences in the wages paid on women's wages." *Economic Journal*, 2(1): 172–6, March 1892.

Weber, Arnold R., Frank Cassell and Woodrow L. Ginsberg, eds., *Public-Private Manpower Policies*. Madison: Industrial Relations Research Association, University of Wisconsin, 1969.

Weeks, Wendy, *Part Time Work in Canada: A Study of Ideology and the Implications for Women.* Hamilton, Ontario: McMaster Univ. M.A. thesis (Sociology) x, 322, 1, 1977.

Weir, Angela and Elizabeth Wilson, "Women's labor, women's discontent." *Radical America,* Fall 1973.

Wells, Robert V., "Demographic change and the life cycle of American families." *Journal of Interdisciplinary History,* 2(2): 273–82, 1971.

Welter, Barbara, "The cult of true womanhood: 1820–1860." In Michael Gordon, ed., *The American Family in Social-Historical Perspective.* Op. cit.

Wertheimer, Barbara and Anne H. Nelson, *Trade Union Women: A Study of Their Participation in New York Locals.* New York: Praeger, 1975.

White, Julie, *Women and Work: A Resource Kit.* Ottawa: Women's Programme, Secretary of State, 1978.

———, *Women and Unions.* Prepared for the Canadian Advisory Council on the Status of Women. Ottawa: 1980.

Wilensky, Harold, "Women's work: economic growth, ideology, structure." *Industrial Relations,* 7: 235–48, 1968.

Williams, C. Brian, *Canadian Trade Union Philosophy: The Philosophy of English Speaking Trade Union Movement of Canada, 1935–1967.* Draft Study Prepared for Task Force on Labour Relations (Privy Council Office), 1969.

Williams, Jack, *Unions in Canada,* pp. 2–3. J.M. Dent and Sons, 1975.

Wolf, Wendy and Neil Fligstein, *Sex and Authority in the Workplace: Causes of Sexual Inequality.* Madison: University of Wisconsin, Madison, 1979.

Wolfson, Theresa, *The Woman Worker and the Trade Unions.* New York: International Publishers, 1926.

Women and the Workplace; The Implications of Occupational Segregation. Chicago: University of Chicago Press, 1976.

Women at Work 1850–1930. Toronto: Women's Press, 1974.

Women in Industry: Proceedings of a Conference Held 8–9 April 1976 at Stony Brook. New York: South Oaks Foundation, 1977.

Woods, Harry D. *et al., Labour Policy and Labour Economics in Canada.* 2nd ed. Macmillan of Canada, 1972.

Zachon, Vivian, "Negotiary equal pay." *Canadian Labour,* 21(3): September 1976.

Government Publications

Canada

Advisory Council on the Status of Women, *Fringe Benefits.* Ottawa: 1976.

———, *The Price of Maternity.* Ottawa: 1976.

————, *Sharing the Power*. Ottawa: 1978.

————, *Women in the Public Service: Barriers to Equal Opportunity*. Ottawa: 1979.

Decision Marketing Research, *Women in Canada*. 2nd ed. Ottawa: Office of the Coordinator, Status of Women, 1976.

Department of Employment and Immigration, *Women's Employment Policy*. Ottawa: 1977.

Department of Labour Library, *Status of Women: A Selected Bibliography—Books and Articles*, 4 parts. Ottawa: 1978.

————, *Status of Women—Canada and Provinces*. Ottawa: 1979.

Ministry Responsible for the Status of Women, *Status of Women in Canada*. Ottawa: Information Canada (not dated).

Office of Equal Opportunities for Women, *The Employment of Women in the Public Service of Canada: Mandate for Change*. Ottawa: Public Service Commission, 1973.

————, *It's Up To You*. Ottawa.

Office of the Coordinator, Status of Women, *Federal Services for Women*. Ottawa: Supply and Services Canada, 1977.

Ontario: Ministry of Education, *Social Reform: Trade Unionism, Women's Suffrage*. Toronto: (not dated).

Ontario: Women's Bureau, *The Ontario Women's Bureau: What, Why, How*. Toronto, 1975.

Opportunity for Choice: A Goal for Women in Canada. Ottawa: Statistics Canada in association with C.D. Howe Research Institute, 1976.

Public Service Commission, *Equal Opportunity for Women*. Ottawa: 1971.

————, *Equal Opportunities for Women*. Ottawa: 1972.

————, *Equal Opportunities for Women: Justice and Equity*. Ottawa: 1973.

————, *Women in the Public Service of Canada*. Ottawa: 1976.

————, *Equal Opportunities for Women in the Public Service of Canada*. Ottawa: Supply and Services, 1978.

Royal Commission on the Status of Women in Canada, *Report*. Ottawa: Information Canada, 1970.

————, *Cultural Tradition and Political History of Women in Canada*. Ottawa Information Canada, 1971.

————, *Women at Home: The Cost to the Canadian Economy of the Withdrawal from the Labour Force of a Major Proportion of the Female Population*. Ottawa: Information Canada, 1971.

Statistics Canada, *Canada's Female Labour Force*. Ottawa: Supply and Services Canada, 1980.

Status of Women, *We are ...* Ottawa: 1978.

————, *Towards Equality for Women*. Ottawa: Supply and Services, 1979.

————, *Status of Women in Canada*. Canada: Information Canada.

Women's Bureau, *Fields of Work for Women*. Ottawa: Department of Labour, 1964.

————, *International Instruments and Canadian Federal and Provincial Legislation Relating to the Status of Women in Employment*. Ottawa: 1972.

————, *The Law Relating to Working Women*. Ottawa: 1973.

———, *Legislation Relating to Working Women*. Ottawa: Labour Canada, 1979.

———, *Master List of Information: Women in Non-traditional Occupations.* Ottawa: 1980.

———, *Women in the Labour Force: Facts and Figures*. Ottawa: Information Canada, (annual) 1969–1981.

Canadian Union of Public Employees

Department of Labour Library, *Women in Labour Unions: A Selected Bibliography—Books and Articles*, (6) 1. (LIB 166). Ottawa: 1977.

Canadian Union of Public Employees, *The Status of Women in CUPE*. Special report approved by the CUPE National Convention, September 1971. Ottawa: 1971.

———, *The New Status of Women in CUPE: A Report on Past Progress and the Challenges Ahead*. Ottawa: 1975.

———, *There's So Much To be Done*. Ottawa.

Labour Canada, *Labour Organizations in Canada*. Ottawa: 1980.

Labour Canada, Women's Bureau, *Women in the Labour Force: Facts and Figures*. 1976.

Statistics Canada

Canadian Labour Congress, *Equality of Opportunity and Treatment for Women Workers*. Policy Statement approved by the 11th CC Constitutional Convention, 1976.

Corporations and Labour Unions Returns Act (CALURA) *1979 Report for 1977*. Part II—Labour Unions, Ottawa.

Corporations and Labour Unions Returns Act (CALURA), Part II Cat. No. 71–202.

United States of America

Coalition of Labor Union Women, *Founding Conference, March 22, 23 and 24, 1974, Chicago, Illinois*. New York: 1974.

———, *Constitutional Convention, December 6–7, 1975, Detroit, Michigan: Press Clippings*. New York: 1975.

Department of Labor, *The One World of Working Women*. Washington, DC: United States Government Printing Office, 1978.

The Senate: Committee on Labor and Human Resources, *The Coming Decade: American Women and Human Resources Policies and Programs,*

1979, 2 vols. Washington: United States Government Printing Office, 1979.

Women's Bureau, *Handbook on Women Workers, 1965*. Washington, DC: United States Government Printing Office, 1965.

——, *How You Can Help Reduce Barriers to the Employment of Mature Women*. Washington, DC: 1969.

INDEX

232, 233

White-Collar Organizing Committee, 27

Williams, Jack, 166, 175

Wollstoncraft, Mary, 85

women—changing role of, 19–21;
status of, 19–21; votes for, 169;
workers, turnover of, 172

Women at Work (Curthoys), 141, 150

Women at Work: Ontario 1850–1930
(Acton), 141

Women in the Labour Force (Labour
Canada Women's Bureau), 241,
244, 260

*Women in the Production of Munitions
in Canada (Ramkhalawansingh),*
156

Women in Unions (White), 6

Women's Protective and Provident
League (1874), 10

Women's War Conference (1918),
168

World War I, 133, 147, 149, 156, 160–
61, 163–4, 168, 177, 179, 186

World War II, 34, 56, 57, 186–2334

Wright, Arthur, 93